CHRISTIANITY

THE BIOGRAPHY

I've enjoyed *Christianity: The Biography* enormously! What an original idea. It presents the current scholarship in church history in a very engaging way. I hope this book is widely read . . . An absolutely outstanding volume!
Ian Randall, Senior Research Fellow, Spurgeon's College

Christians today have largely lost their historical memory, and it is no surprise that as a result many are struggling to agree on the right way ahead for the church. Ian Shaw's remarkable book, encompassing in one volume the entire chronological and geographical range of Christian history, will prove invaluable in helping Christians to recover their historical memory and hence to find wisdom for the future.
Brian Stanley, Professor of World Christianity, University of Edinburgh

Believers need to know the story of their own faith, and *Christianity: The Biography* is a great place to start. It covers fascinating figures, movements and trends across two millennia without ever getting bogged down or side-tracked. It is not only clear and accessible, but also inspiring and wise.
Timothy Larsen, McManis Professor of Christian Thought, Wheaton College

The more we learn about Christianity's global reach, the more urgent is the need to re-frame how we understand Christian history. This book gets it right. It offers fascinating accounts of Christianity entering the ancient civilizations of Persia, India and China and its transformation of Ethiopia, Egypt and the Sudan – even while it was reaching the wild tribes of the remote British Isles. We learn too about the rise of Islam, the modern missions movement and the rapid worldwide spread of Pentecostalism. In sum, this text is a lively treatment of a truly global faith.
Professor Joel Carpenter, Nagel Institute for the Study of World Christianity, Calvin College, Grand Rapids

So-called 'histories of the church' are often essentially histories only of the church in the West. It is a joy to meet one that recognizes that 'world Christianity' began in the early centuries, and that the story of the Christian faith is a six-continent one. It is a joy also to find it so helpful and well written.
Professor Andrew F. Walls, University of Edinburgh, Liverpool Hope University and Akrofi-Christaller Institute, Ghana

ivp

CHRISTIANITY
THE BIOGRAPHY

TWO THOUSAND YEARS OF THE GLOBAL CHURCH

IAN J. SHAW

To Mary Shaw (1930–2016), my mother, to whom I owe so much

INTER-VARSITY PRESS
36 Causton Street, London SW1P 4ST, England
Email: ivp@ivpbooks.com
Website: www.ivpbooks.com

First published 2016

British Library Cataloguing in Publication Data
A catalogue record for this book is available from the British Library.

ISBN: 978–1–78359–466–5
eBook ISBN: 978–1–78359–467–2

Set in Monotype Garamond 11/13pt
Typeset in Great Britain by CRB Associates, Potterhanworth, Lincolnshire

Inter-Varsity Press publishes Christian books that are true to the Bible and that communicate the gospel, develop discipleship and strengthen the church for its mission in the world.

IVP originated within the Inter-Varsity Fellowship, now the Universities and Colleges Christian Fellowship, a student movement connecting Christian Unions in universities and colleges throughout Great Britain, and a member movement of the International Fellowship of Evangelical Students. Website: www.uccf.org.uk. That historic association is maintained, and all senior IVP staff and committee members subscribe to the UCCF Basis of Faith.

CONTENTS

MAPS

ACKNOWLEDGMENTS

I wish to thank the many people who have contributed to the completion of this book. Especial thanks are due to Dr Graham Keith, Professor Brian Stanley, Dr Ian Randall and Dr Nick Needham for their insightful comments and valuable suggestions about the text. I am grateful to Dr John Jeacocke for his skilful work in proofreading and compiling the index. Dr Philip Duce and the IVP team have been constant in their patience and encouragement over a number of years while this book has been completed. I also wish to express appreciation to Langham Partnership for their encouragement to me to continue research and writing as part of my work in the support and training of Langham Scholars from the Majority World. The first pages of this book were written sitting at the desk of John Stott at The Hookses, his retreat in South Wales. I think that the founder of Langham Partnership would appreciate the global focus of *Christianity: The Biography*, although he would have completed it much more quickly than I did!

INTRODUCTION: OPENING UP A LIFE STORY

This book charts the 'biography' of Christianity from its birth and infancy among a handful of followers of Jesus Christ through its years of development into a global religious movement, spanning continents and cultures, transcending educational and social backgrounds, with over 2 billion adherents.

Christianity: The Biography offers an introductory orientation to the richness of the Christian tradition and its heritage around the world. This outline of the major phases, developments, movements and personalities in Christianity's life story over the two millennia is necessarily painted on a broad canvas. It is designed to open the subject up for more detailed study. As well as covering the well-trodden ground of the history of Christianity in the West, it has a special concern for the story from the non-Western world.

This task is far from easy, especially if ideas as well as events are to be considered. As one writer joked, 'Writing intellectual history is like trying to nail jelly to the wall.' Others are negative about the historical enterprise. Oscar Wilde and James Joyce are both credited with the observation 'History is a nightmare from which I am trying to awaken.' Having taught and written about the history of Christianity for over twenty years I am well aware of the presuppositions with which many approach the subject – 'Why, after all, do we need to know all this about a bunch of dead guys?' Some years ago a student sat in my office sharing how excited he was about his first day at theological college; then his face clouded and, evidently not aware who he was talking to, he added, 'But I'm not looking forward to studying church history.' That might be the reader's sentiment on starting this book. I am pleased to say that three years later, as he was about to graduate, he sat in the same chair and said church history had been his most enjoyable subject.

To many, history is just events. 'Stuff happens, period.' Attempts to construct a coherent narrative or discern meaning in those events have been considered as fruitless as trying to make sense of the tracks made by a drunken fly, its feet wet with ink, staggering across a piece of white paper. The theologian Rudolph Bultmann commented, 'The question of meaning in history has become meaningless.' Postmodern thinkers like the French philosopher Michel Foucault argued that history was capable only of brilliant redescriptions of the past, while warning against looking for any sense of development across the unfolding centuries or extrapolating any meaningful conclusions. Foucault emphasized the distance between the past and the present, asserting that statements can only be truly understood in the historical context in which they were written. His cautions have some value, but the danger is that history is left frozen in time with little connectedness to today.

That approach is also a very Western reading of history, which has become intolerant and suspicious of the old. Technology becomes outmoded within months. Supreme confidence is placed only in the new, which by definition has to be better. Rolling news channels beam 'current affairs' across the world without historical perspective or analysis; immediacy is what has impact. Tradition is deemed institutionalism and resistance to inevitable progress. However, in many non-Western cultures the division between the past and present, the living and the dead, is much less sharply demarcated. There is deep respect for the wisdom of old people and their traditions and forebears; these exist in close continuity with the present. Immediacy breeds myopic vision. When Lot and Abram separated in Genesis 13, Lot looked down and chose life with a limited horizon in the plain of the Jordan. The Lord instead told Abram, 'Lift up your eyes from where you are and look north and south, east and west.' *Christianity: The Biography* invites the reader to look up and take a bigger perspective.

The Roman writer Cicero argued that the person without any knowledge of events from before he or she was born would forever remain an infant. The loss of community memory in some parts of the Christian world is deeply concerning. Those who have cared for a loved one suffering from Alzheimer's disease will know how debilitating the loss of memory is. Alzheimer's sufferers often cannot remember where they are, where they have come from or even who they are. Their sense of 'lost-ness' is frightening. It is very important that Christians do not lose the faculty of memory but understand the story of which they are a part, the historical journey in which they participate. For Christians the biography of Christianity is the history of their family and an exploration of their heritage. It should be an exciting adventure of self-discovery.

The present and future of the church is closely connected to its past. Just before his execution in 1896 José Rizal, the leader of the independence movement in the Philippines, said, 'To foretell the destiny of a nation it is necessary to open the book that tells of her past.' Understanding and preparing for the future of the church requires opening the book of its past. The biography of Christianity has not been one of constant advance and progress. In times of growth Christians should not exult overmuch; in times of decline they should not despair.

Christians today should realize that they too are making history. The individual life of faith, the endeavours of their churches, the decisions of Christian leaders, denominations and organizations – all leave footprints on the sands of time. The task of the historian is to trace those out. As with any faithful biographer the problematic and less savoury parts of a life story should be included alongside those that encourage and excite. Some have cynically used the name of God for their own personal and political ends; others have stumbled into difficulties despite their best efforts. To look at such failures should not just provoke lament but also prompt the question 'How can Christians today avoid making such a mess of things again?' This book affirms the value of the all-too-easily rejected axiom that 'those who do not learn from the mistakes of the past are destined to repeat them'.

The command to remember is strong throughout Scripture. In Joshua 4 the Israelites were told to build a monument from stones that had been in the middle of the River Jordan to provoke the question from passers-by, 'What do these stones mean?' Then the history of the miraculous crossing of the Jordan would be retold. The words 'Do this in remembrance of me' are spoken every time Christians partake of the Lord's Supper together. Remembrance is designed to feed faith: 'We have heard with our ears, O God; our fathers have told us what you did in their days, in days long ago' (Ps. 44:1).

Yet time, and therefore history, is not static. It involves change, and Christians must keep up with it: Christians should not live in the past. Jesus taught that looking back once the hand has been put to the plough can make a person unfit for the kingdom of God. Resisting change and development, and clinging tenaciously to how things used to be, or how people think they used to be, is problematic. Biography implies growth, movement and development. Far from letting the past impede progress, Christians should humbly respect and build on its positive achievements and critically discern the not so good. Recalling the past should build capacity to live faithfully in the present and to be prepared for the future.

The study of the history of Christianity brings maturity by rooting understanding in the reality of what actually happened, as opposed to misconceptions of what might have happened or what people wish had happened. The Israelites displeased God when they looked back to the fish, cucumbers, melons, leeks, onions and garlic they had eaten in Egypt, forgetting the fact that they had also been enslaved (Num. 11:4–11). Authoritarian regimes have learned that those who control the past control the present and therefore they carefully oversee the writing and study of history. The Nazis of Hitler's Germany built their ideology on falsehoods about the past. The leaders of some new religious movements deny their adherents access to the movement's history, fearing it will provoke unwanted questioning and undermine confidence in its authority and teaching. The Christian historian should not fall into the trap of airbrushing away mistakes and ugly episodes. Biblical history refuses to do this. The errors and misdeeds of Noah, Abraham, Jacob, Moses, David, and the apostles in the New Testament, are all depicted in technicolour detail. As one nineteenth-century scholar wrote, 'It does not answer to call whitey-brown white.' The Christian church has often failed to live up to its calling, and many of the 'greats' of the past had significant flaws. Hagiography is historically dishonest. It also undermines the confidence of Christian believers. Instead they need to know that God can use ordinary people in extraordinary ways.

Christian believers who make Scripture the authoritative basis for belief and practice need to develop a biblically informed Christian philosophy of history. The Bible offers a rich pattern in Old and New Testaments, freely making use of historical narrative and biography. Christians believe that the God of the Bible is the God of history. He uses historical reference in describing himself as 'the God of Abraham, Isaac and Jacob'. The birth of the founder of Christianity is given a specific historical locus – when Augustus was emperor of Rome and Quirinius was governor of Syria (Luke 2:1–12). So too his death – 'he suffered under Pontius Pilate, was crucified, died and was buried'. The Bible presents 'salvation history' – salvation being accomplished through historical events.

In Christian thinking, history has two perspectives: a divine and a human. The human side is extremely complex and confused, filled with problems and grievous errors, as well as examples of faithfulness, courage, heroism, wisdom and loving commitment. The church has often taken two steps back for every one forward. In the detailed morass of events it can be difficult to discern exactly what is going on. The other side of history is the unfolding plan of God 'who works out everything in conformity with the purpose of his will' (Eph. 1:11). Because of this Christians believe history has a purpose and meaning, and it is going somewhere. God's work in and through history did not end with Acts 28: the Bible gives an outline template for events thereafter. The kingdom of God will spread: Jesus said, 'I will build my church, and the gates of Hades will not overcome it' (Matt. 16:18). The gospel will be 'preached in the whole world as a testimony to all nations' (Matt. 24:14). The Bible depicts the biography of Christianity ending on a day, known only to God, when 'a great multitude that no-one [can] count, from every nation, tribe, people and language' will stand before God (Rev. 7:9). Then, as Jesus Christ returns in glory, history as we know it will end and he will begin his eternal reign.

This book accepts the premise of Edward Plumptre's hymn 'Thy hand, O God, has guided thy flock from age to age'. As Christian believers have read, preached and interpreted the Bible, and sought to live out their faith, God has been at work in what has been called the longest ever lesson in practical theology. Yet, between the two great events of the ascension and the return of Christ, understanding from the human side the exact meaning and place of each event within the divine plan is difficult. As the psalmist put it, 'Your path led through the sea, your way through the mighty waters, though your footprints were not seen' (Ps. 77:19). The challenge for Christian historians is to faithfully read, understand and interpret events within the biography of Christianity with the evidence and tools at their disposal. This interpretative task is done through 'a glass darkly', and any interpretation of a specific historical event can never be final or infallible. Yet this process of discerning is part of Christian maturing, fully deploying the skills of critical reflection. It poses the ever deeper question of 'Why?', which opens up issues of causation and consequence. It is hoped that with the long perspective of time, and accumulated wisdom, further clarity and understanding can be gained.

From the earliest years Christians have sought to create historical records of events and offer interpretations of them. The book of Acts is presented in terms of an historical account of early Christianity. Numerous writers from Eusebius, to Bede, John Foxe, Philip Schaff and A. M. Renwick in his *Story of the Church* have sought to continue the story. Yet Justo González claimed that the person who attempts to tell the whole history of the church 'must either be ambitious to the point of hubris or naïve to the point of folly'. That the author of this book is guilty of either fault is simply because he was asked by IVP to make the attempt – probably no-one else was willing to attempt such a huge enterprise and cover 2,000 years of momentous events in so few words!

Rather than presenting a recitation of dates, names and key events, some loose structure has been given to the story of Christianity by using the biographical format, while recognizing it is a far from adequate tool. Christianity's infancy and early years were a time of significant growth, despite opposition, and proved highly formative in the development of ideas and patterns of behaviour. If the medieval period (c. 600–1500) is judged as a time of youth, it was one of promise but also uncertainty and conflict. Early adulthood sees patterns and identities firmly established or questioned, and the 'early modern' era (1500–1650) was dominated by the profound social, political and theological change of the Reformation. Full adulthood can be marked by consolidation but also by crisis and change, and the period from around 1650 to the twentieth century, usually referred to as the 'modern' period, saw all these characteristics. After mature adulthood comes old age and decline but also the vigorous growth of children and grandchildren. So, while the postmodern era has increasingly looked like a post-Christian era in the West, such decline has happened surrounded by rapidly growing non-Western churches, just as parents age surrounded by children or grandchildren.

Christianity: The Biography seeks to avoid the tendency to draw a distinction between matters of faith or theology, and history. Indeed, J. I. Packer called church history the glue that binds Christian theology together. Opening up Christianity's biography should deepen theological understanding and build faith, and inspire a longing to meet the One behind the story.

1. THE CRADLE

Lifeline

753 BC – traditional date for the foundation of Rome
587 BC – Jerusalem captured by Babylonians, start of exile
364 BC – Aristotle begins studies with Plato
323 BC – death of Alexander the Great
192–188 BC – war between Roman and Greek armies
44 BC – assassination of Julius Caesar
c. 6–4 BC – birth of Jesus Christ
AD 14 – death of Caesar Augustus

Every biography begins with a birth, but the exact date when Christianity was 'born' is open to debate. Does Christianity begin with the birth of its founder, Jesus Christ, in squalid and obscure surroundings in Bethlehem? Or was it when the first disciples were called and became followers of Jesus Christ? A case could be made for Pentecost, when the book of Acts records that the Holy Spirit came upon those present, transforming the disciples of Jesus from a fearful, uncertain group into an empowered body of messengers witnessing to the good news of Jesus Christ. Some have stressed the importance of seeing Christianity as a movement, seeing its beginning as the time when the followers of Jesus were first referred to as 'Christians' in Acts 11:26. Most historians of Christianity consider the end of the Jewish–Roman War in Palestine in AD 70, towards the close of the lives of most of the apostles, as a vital moment. This roughly marks the transition from the era of the apostles, which is towards the end of the New Testament period, and certainly represents a new phase in the development of Christianity.

All this illustrates the challenge of pinpointing the 'birth' or 'foundation' of Christianity to a specific moment. Jesus did not call his followers Christians and he did not start individual churches. Founded on a commitment by individuals to the person and teachings of Jesus Christ, what became known as Christianity emerged over a period. It was a movement of those who found salvation through faith in him and sought to follow his example and teachings.

Every birth takes place in a geographical, historical and social context which has a role in shaping subsequent development. The cradle of Christianity was the intersection of differing worlds, both geographically and culturally. The Roman province of Palestine, historically the land of Israel, where this birth took place, lies at the junction of three continents, Africa, Asia and Europe, and if anything pointed to Christianity becoming a global religion this did. In its early years Christianity belonged more to the Middle East, Africa and the Orient than the West. It was originated at the crossroads of a series of major trade routes along which flowed the materials by which cultures are forged and changed – people, goods and ideas. Through this narrow strip of land marched armies bent on conquest, some heading east, some heading west. In the centuries before Christianity emerged, those armies redrew the political map of Europe, the Middle East and North Africa several times.

Ancient Greece

Christianity also developed at an intersection in political and cultural history. Palestine had been fought over and conquered successively by Egyptians, Assyrians, Babylonians, Persians and Greeks. By 1400 BC a group of people speaking an early form of Greek were scattered across parts of what is now modern Greece and the Mediterranean. They built cities and palace fortresses like that at Mycenae. Their unity was not political but came through language and culture, such as the oral traditions of the Homeric legends which looked back to the great days of the Mycenaeans. Such culture became known as Hellenistic, after the term *hellas*, which embraced these scattered groups. The religious ceremonies such as those associated with the god Apollo at Delphi, or the games in honour of the god Zeus on Mount Olympus, gave a further sense of unity. The *hellenes* were convinced of the superiority of their culture: all others were *barbaroi*, from which the term 'barbarian' comes. Between 800 and 500 BC Greek society demonstrated more order, with settlements developing round the temples dedicated to Greek gods. A series of small city-states emerged, each surrounded by a rural hinterland. It was the work of Philip of Macedon, who ruled from 360 to 336 BC, to bring unity to Greece. Under the rule of his son Alexander, a Greek empire rapidly appeared through a series of speedy and brilliant military campaigns. He came to be known as Alexander the Great, ruling from 336 to 323 BC. He swept all before him – conquering Syria, Egypt, Assyria, Babylonia and Persia – dreaming of a real union between the areas he conquered. Alexander sought administrative and cultural unity among the people he conquered, promising greatness as a ruler to match his military greatness. His tutor had been Aristotle, and Alexander sought to spread Greek ideas and culture throughout his territories, seeking peace and prosperity through his policies. Seventy cities claim Alexander as their founder, the best known being Alexandria, which was named after him, with a world-renowned university and library. Principles of systematic and scientific town-planning emerged, with significant advances in architecture. Cities were rapidly colonized by Greek traders and artisans, creating a vast single market.

When Alexander met his demise in mysterious circumstances aged just thirty-two, his empire was divided up by his generals, who ruled as semi-divine monarchs over territories which stretched from the Adriatic to Afghanistan. Beset by bitter rivalry, before long these territories had divided into a series of smaller kingdoms.

The rise of Rome

The traditional date for the foundation of Rome is 753 BC, and until 509 BC it functioned as a city-state with a king. After the overthrow of the monarchy a republic was instituted with power in the hands of a senate controlled by the patrician social elite, who appointed consuls. The ordinary people, the plebeians, had only limited influence on their work. The emergence of an empire based on this city was slow, but as Rome grew in size and influence, war between the Romans and Greeks became inevitable. A series of wars in the 190s and 180s BC saw the Romans victorious and taking control of the Mediterranean area. The Roman Empire was eventually to stretch to Britain, the Rhine and the Danube in the north, along the North African coast and to the borders of Asia in the east – but its trade routes reached much further. Palestine belonged significantly to the eastern half of the Roman Empire.

The political structure of the Roman Republic underwent momentous revolution in which the old rule of oligarchy was transformed into personal

Caesar Augustus

autocracy. This change came through a long and intermittent civil war lasting seventy years. Eventually, after the assassination of the general and dictator Julius Caesar in 44 BC, Octavian manoeuvred his way into power through a series of battles and political stratagems. He ruled as Caesar Augustus from 27 BC onwards, the first of the Roman emperors. Although he died in AD 14, the Roman Empire was to long outlast him, surviving, albeit in changed form, for over a thousand years. Augustus brought peace and stability to territories stretching from the English Channel to Sudan, and after his death he was declared a god. Most of the subsequent emperors, combining astute governance with occasional terror tactics, were also assigned the status of god after their lifetimes. Peoples of widely differing cultural backgrounds were ruled together in one empire.

Jewish history

After the Greek and Roman empires, the third great political, social and religious influence on Palestine was of course Judaism. The emergence of the Jewish people from a group of wandering herders, through slavery and conquest, into a small nation with its own modest empire under the kingships of David and Solomon, is told in the pages of the Old Testament. So too is its subsequent decline into division and defeat, with many of its peoples dragged into exile as a result of conquests by Assyria, Babylon and Persia. The capture of Jerusalem by the Babylonians and the destruction of the temple in 587 BC was a terrible blow which Judaism nevertheless managed to survive, as it did an attempt in the second century BC by the Seleucid ruler Antiochus IV, who arrogantly called himself 'Epiphanes' (Manifestation), to Hellenize the cultural and religious life of the Jews. This produced an uprising and a series of wars from 167 to 164 BC. After much blood had been shed, the Jews, led by Judas Maccabeus, secured a short period of existence free from the rule of a foreign power, which lasted until Roman occupation around 63 BC. Palestine then fell within the political orbit of the ruthless superpower that had superseded the Greek one. Between 37 BC and 4 BC Judea was subjected to the repressive rule of King Herod, from Idumea (Edom), who served as a puppet king of the Romans. After his death the territories he had ruled were divided up among his sons, before direct rule was imposed, exercised through Roman officials such as Pontius Pilate. An independent nation-state was not to exist again in Israel until 1948.

Defeat and exile had left the Jewish peoples scattered across the Middle East and into North Africa and Europe. This meant that some 80% of all Jews lived in the 'diaspora' (dispersion) outside Palestine. The land remained much troubled politically when Jesus was born, and after his death there were major rebellions against Roman rule, in 66–70 and 132–5, attempting to recreate what Judas Maccabeus had done; both of these rebellions were brutally crushed.

Greek and Roman culture

Palestine at the end of the first century BC was not only at a geographical and political intersection; it was also at a cultural one. The march of successive armies across this small but significant land left deep imprints. From the Greeks came their language and a culture deeply shaped by its literature and philosophy. In religion, polytheism (belief in the existence of many gods, such as Zeus, Artemis and Apollo) was the order of the day. The pantheon of Greek gods was large and diverse. The worship of Aphrodite, the goddess of love, could on the one hand be a high-minded celebration of beauty and love, and on the other a degraded form of fertility worship expressed in immoral sexual activity. A team of a thousand female temple slaves served the sexual appetites of the devotees of Aphrodite in Corinth, casting a moral blight on the whole city, reflected in the letters of the apostle Paul to the church there. Religious life in the Greek world was complex – from rituals involving prostitution, to sacrifices to appease gods, or seeking guidance by reading the entrails of slaughtered animals. Dissatisfaction with the ancient public religions led to the emergence of new secret cults, mystery religions, which only the initiated could join.

But Greek culture also produced profound intellectual and philosophical achievements, creating tension with the crude and unsophisticated depictions of the religious life of the gods of Olympus. Scientific discovery advanced in the fields of anatomy, astronomy and mechanics. The foundations of mathematics were laid by philosophers such as Pythagoras (c. 570–c. 495 BC). A user-friendly script emerged with a twenty-two-letter alphabet based on sounds rather than pictorial symbols, making easier the development of writing forms in which ideas as well as the names of things with physical form could be communicated. The fourth and fifth centuries BC saw the height of Greek philosophy, especially with the work of Socrates (c. 470–399 BC), Plato (c. 429–348 BC) and Aristotle (384–322 BC). Moral philosophy set out notions of right living and high ideals in life.

Plato was Socrates' pupil, and his writings helped to shape European thinking on big issues in life such as immortality, pleasure and politics. Plato also debated the question of the existence of a supreme god, and if one existed, what that god would be like. He concluded that the supreme god would be a unity, incapable of being divided, without moods and passions (unlike the Greek gods), and unchangeable. He struggled with the idea of how such a god could create the current imperfect world and concluded that it was just a poor reflection of ideal Forms which were a truer and higher reality, and had been created by one lower than the Supreme Soul, namely the *demiourgos*. The task of the human soul is to reach beyond the present world to the Forms which lie beyond it.

Plato's abstract, speculative, idealistic philosophy stands in contrast to that of his pupil Aristotle who emphasized that reality was to be understood through a process of critical reasoning based on observed facts. Studying a concept or object did not come by speculating on what its ideal form might look like, but by systematic study and the collection of facts and information, and upon the basis of that research coming to conclusions. To Aristotle this approach held good for all areas of knowledge, from science to the humanities; indeed it influenced Western education for more than 2,000 years after his death. Importantly, there was also a growing sense of the need for a clear connection between religion and morality, and that there was a relation between present conduct and life after death.

Aristotle

Throughout the remaining vestiges of Alexander's empire the educated classes spoke Greek, listened to classical oratory and poetry, and saw the same classical plays. Schools, temples and cities were united by a common cultural identity.

Early Roman religion had focused on the elements of air, water, fire. Natural forces – storms, lightning, drought – were manifestations of divine personalities. Deities were seen to influence different aspects of life, and so a host of minor deities were reverenced in order to secure protection for various activities. About the nature of these gods there was little reflection or speculation. Religion was in good part instinctive and governed by fear. The Roman military victory over the Greeks did not mean their culture was expunged; rather it was embraced and assimilated. Aphrodite became Venus; Zeus became Jupiter.

Religious life took many forms. Some adopted extreme forms of religiosity, with a profound fear of the supernatural. There were a number of enthusiastic or 'ecstatic' religious expressions, such as the cult of Mithras, which reflected the struggle between light and dark, good and evil, with an initiation ceremony involving passing under the carcase of a newly slaughtered bull and being soaked in its blood. The religious life of most was little more than the formal, nominal adherence that was required in the empire and seen as part of civil duty. Like paying taxes it simply had to be done, whether you were enthusiastic about it or not. This ensured the protection of the person and the State. The Romans accepted a vast range of religions with the proviso that they did not threaten the values or ethos of the State.

Early Christians were liable, when the local authorities demanded it, to be asked to sacrifice to the local gods. Refusing to do this was considered antisocial and dangerous, giving offence to the deities and endangering the fabric of the empire. This caused significant difficulties for Christians who honoured Christ above all, although there was no empire-wide requirement to sacrifice to local deities before AD 250. The scepticism about ancient religions that had characterized Greek thinking also became apparent in Rome: religious life became open to philosophical criticism. This dissatisfaction may also have been a reason for the interest many began to show in the new religion that emerged in the first century – Christianity.

Judaism

The other major religious influence on the first-century Palestinian context in which Christianity emerged was Judaism. The Jewish community, and its understanding of the religious life, was also not uniform. Those who returned from exile to Palestine after 537 BC retained their monotheistic belief in the one God who had revealed the Torah through Moses. They rebuilt their temple and restored daily sacrifice, but monotheistic religious life in a country stripped of its political independence was never easy. The elite group of Sadducees ran the temple and developed a working relationship with the Roman authorities to allow the continuance of religious practice and a limited degree of autonomy. This was not to the liking of the Pharisees, who were deeply uncomfortable coexisting with their pagan Roman rulers. They committed themselves to hard work, shunning power or association with the ruling authorities. They protected themselves from contamination from the pagan world by developing a complex series of legal religious restrictions to prevent them transgressing the law of God, the minutiae of which were observed and enforced. Their interpretation of the Torah was becoming dominant in the New Testament era and was a source of conflict with the first Christians. The Pharisees' work in emphasizing prayer, and devotion to the oral and written Torah, played a vital role in helping Judaism to reformulate itself as a viable religious system in the aftermath of the destruction of the temple in AD 70.

Others, such as the Essenes, saw the approaches of other Jewish groups as corrupt, and chose instead to withdraw from the complexities of such mixed engagement. Some lived in small groups within towns; some withdrew to the desert to live alone or in small communities isolated from wider society, awaiting God's decisive intervention in the world to restore the temple and the true faith of Israel. The Dead Sea Scrolls, discovered in caves in 1947, are thought to have been produced by a community of Essenes at Qumran who lived lives of austere self-denial, sharing property together. For other radical groups, like the Zealots, the only solution was a military one, and a form of low-key but persistent guerrilla warfare was conducted against the occupying Romans by some of their supporters. At times Palestine teetered on the brink of an uprising: in 6 BC there was a revolt in Judea over the imposition of the census, and again in AD 40 when the emperor Caligula sought to erect a statue of himself in Jerusalem.

For the diaspora Jews scattered across the ancient world, often in seaports and trading centres, there was the challenge of how to live in a pagan world. Whenever possible they returned to Jerusalem for the major religious festivals of Passover and Shavuot (Pentecost), and sent funds for the support of the temple. They chose not to intermarry with the Gentiles and avoided the amusements of the day – the theatres, the circus, the baths – but as members of a recognized religion under the Romans they were allowed to maintain their own synagogues and be judged according to their own law. However, most became Greek-speaking and this encouraged the translation of the Old Testament into that language – the Septuagint. The Jewish community in Babylon, where many had been exiled in the sixth century BC, was to remain of significant size for over a thousand years. Some estimate the Jewish population of Egypt to have numbered 1 million by the time of Christ. The wealthy, educated and prosperous Jews of Alexandria, who spoke Greek rather than Hebrew, began to express their religious convictions in ways shaped by the Hellenistic culture in which they lived. The Alexandrian Jew Philo (c. 20 BC–c. AD 40) used allegorical methods to suggest that underneath the stories found in the Hebrew scriptures were to be found deeper layers of truth. This issue of making belief accessible to educated Greeks, and the degree to which Hellenistic thought-forms could be used, was one which was soon to confront the early church.

Nonetheless, the distinctive and clear religious and ethical code of the Jewish faith proved attractive to some, tired of the empty formality or excesses of pagan religion. Around Jewish synagogues in predominantly Gentile cities groups of converts attached themselves to Judaism, adopting Jewish customs. This opened up the possibility that the religion of the followers of Yahweh might become universal, of key significance to later Christian mission. These 'God-fearers' were attracted by its strong monotheism and ethical code. Some accepted baptism and, for men, circumcision, becoming Jewish proselytes. Others held back from such a radical departure from pagan society, but kept the Sabbath and the outline of the law, abstaining from idolatry, sexual immorality and murder.

To such people the message of the radical new expression of the Jewish faith expressed in Christianity proved extremely attractive, with its emphasis on the existence of one true, universal God, a strong counter to the rivalries, competitive claims of supremacy, and divisions of the other religious cults. This may help explain why the message of the apostles met with such a ready response in places such as Philippi (Acts 16), although such changes of religious allegiance attracted hostility from both Jewish sources and local civic and religious leaders.

These huge contrasts in religious and cultural life were reflected in wider society at the time when Christianity was born. It ranged from the heights of the philosophy of Plato and Aristotle to the petty tantrums of the Greek and Roman gods. Roman society could be both incredibly sophisticated and singularly distasteful – from the wonders of civil engineering feats like aqueducts, the road system, water supply and public bath houses, to a population that comprised more than 50% slaves (some subject to regular physical and sexual abuse), and the depths of barbaric popular entertainments which included the spectacle in the 'games' of humans slaughtering animals, and even each other, urged on by a baying crowd. Rome was an attractive place populated by a rather unattractive people.

The life of Christ

Parents want the environment in which children are born to be stable, healthy and growth-inducing. The cradle in which Christianity lay was both the best of times and the worst of times. When the apostle Paul wrote, 'When the time had fully come, God sent his Son' (Gal. 4:4), he had no doubt that the birth of Jesus of Nazareth came at just the right time in God's plan, but that did not mean, from the human perspective, everything was going to be easy. Indeed, as the following chapters will show, the new faith was going to face considerable difficulties. The apostles spoke of the scandal of the Cross, but the birth of Jesus Christ was little better. He was born in poverty in Palestine, a socially and politically turbulent client state of the Roman Empire. Jesus was born in socially and politically troubled times. News of his birth brought a few visitors, some local, some from afar, and then provoked a horrific, although localized, episode of infanticide at the hands of a possessively jealous local king fearing the emergence of a rival. The exact dating of the birth of Jesus Christ has proved problematic. Because of mistakes in the calculations made by Hippolytus in the third century, and Dionysius Exiguus in around AD 530, it is unlikely to have taken place in the year AD 1. Instead, a date closer to 6 or 4 BC is more likely – Herod the Great died in 3 or 4 BC. Yet questions about the exact date of the birth of Jesus which arise because of mistakes made by later writers should not cast doubt on the historical existence of Jesus. As well as the historical record of the New Testament, written soon after the events it records, both Roman and Jewish historians record the existence of Jesus. The Jewish historian Josephus, writing in the late first century AD, reports that Jesus was a 'wise man . . . who did remarkable deeds and was a teacher'. Christianity was soon noticed even by those from pagan backgrounds. The Roman historian Tacitus, writing in around AD 115, dismisses the faith of the early Christians as a 'deadly superstition' and 'evil', yet he reports the historical existence of Jesus, whom he refers to as Christus, who 'suffered the extreme penalty during the reign of Tiberius at the hand of one of our procurators, Pontius Pilate'.

We know little about the childhood of Jesus, but it seems likely that his adoptive father, Joseph, died before Jesus reached full adulthood. After a life of about thirty years, of which again little is recorded, Jesus began a short public career as a freelance rabbi. There were many other such teachers around in first-century Palestine, but none was to have the lasting impact of Jesus. His ministry is reported as taken up with itinerant preaching and teaching, and performing miracles including healing and exorcism. He attracted around him a small band of disciples, some heroically faithful, others much less so, and an assortment of adherents from a variety of classes. He reached a number from the social margins, including tax collectors, Samaritans and those suffering from debilitating diseases such as leprosy. The large number of women recorded as his followers in the New Testament was surprising for the times, and some of them were the first witnesses to his resurrection. During his short years of ministry Jesus trained his disciples and sent them out on ministry trips to teach, heal the sick and help the poor. Jesus left behind no handwritten diary, memoir or autobiography; indeed from what we can tell, nothing written in his own hand survives, which is unusual for the founder of one of the main world religions.

For accounts of his life and teachings, and the miracles he was reported as doing, the historian must turn to his followers, or disciples, who in the years after his death collected together oral and early written materials into Gospels and epistles. Because of their apostolic source, and the authority accorded them by the early church, these accounts and writings became the Christian scriptures, the New Testament. Despite the hopes of some, Jesus the Messiah did not lead a victorious military campaign against the enemies of Israel, but instead chose the path of suffering and ultimately death on a cross. The end of this remarkable life came in Jerusalem at Passover time after Jesus was charged as an agitator, blasphemer against the Jewish religion (after claiming publicly he could forgive sins) and false prophet. He suffered horrific execution by crucifixion, a death reserved for the worst criminal offenders under Roman law, although it was not sanctioned by Jewish law. It was a violent death that reflected the social and political tensions of the time, and set a pattern that was to be followed by many of his disciples. The New Testament suggests that Jesus was around thirty-three years old when he was crucified, which would be sometime between AD 27 and 29. At the time it appeared an ignominious and final end to his ministry. But on the third day after his crucifixion his followers reported that everything had radically, and dramatically, changed.

2. SMILES

Lifeline

c. 31–6 – conversion of Saul (Paul)
46 – first missionary journey of Paul
48 – Council of Jerusalem
62 – James the brother of Jesus put to death by Sanhedrin
c. 63–5 – martyrdom of Paul
66 – start of Jewish revolt against Romans
70 – destruction of Jerusalem by Romans

Newborns grow and develop at a remarkable speed, and the same is true of early Christianity. Young children thrive best, however, where they are welcomed and secure, but as has been seen, the environment into which Christianity was born was challenging in a number of social, political and religious ways.

The dramatic news that came out of a Jerusalem graveyard on the first Easter Sunday morning transformed the lives of not only the eyewitnesses, but also those with whom they shared their message. The followers of Jesus Christ reported that his grave was empty and that they had met with him risen from the dead. In some of his final recorded words Jesus had commissioned his disciples to be his 'apostles', or 'proclaimers', commanding them to go into the world to proclaim what he had taught them. They readily responded to this task after Pentecost, fifty days after the Passover feast, when they recorded having received the gift of the Holy Spirit, filling them with boldness and power for sharing their message (Acts 2). Pentecost galvanized a small and fearful body of followers of Jesus Christ into a movement that would eventually touch all nations. From such small beginnings Christianity would grow to become the largest faith community in the world.

Wherever the followers of Jesus travelled, their message was clear – that Jesus was the Messiah, promised in the Old Testament, and the Saviour of the world. The good news they proclaimed, the gospel, included a distinctive belief pattern, centring on his entry into the world as one born of a virgin, the unique authority of his teaching and the physical reality of his miracles. They were convinced that, as Saviour, Jesus Christ brought salvation through his death to those who repented of sin and believed. They lived out their faith by following him and his teachings, believing that Jesus had established a kingdom based on faith that was to stretch throughout the world and impact all nations. Most striking of all was the belief that Jesus was also Lord and God incarnate.

Life in the new Christian community was radical – with believers selling possessions to give to the poor and, at least for a period in the Jerusalem church (Acts 2), holding possessions in common. Those from Jewish and Gentile backgrounds, men and women, and even slave and free, all worshipped, witnessed and ate together in one another's homes. Their message radiated out from Palestine along the roads and trade routes of the ancient world, both to the east and the west.

It is interesting to measure the growth of children, and the same is true of the early church. The New Testament gives some insights into its rapid expansion. The initial work of the apostles among the Palestinian Jews was expanded to include the Greek-speaking Jews of the diaspora spread across the Roman Empire and beyond. Before long the field of Christian mission was understood to be universal and also to include polytheistic pagan Gentile regions. Within twenty years of the death of Jesus, the apostles were being accused of 'turning the world upside down' (Acts 17:6 NRSV).

Paul

A key figure in this universal mission was a strongly anti-Christian Jewish Pharisee from Asia Minor, named Saul. Sometime around AD 31–6 while on one of his terror raids against Christians in Damascus, he reported a vision of the ascended Lord Jesus Christ and was converted (Acts 9). Using his Roman name Paul, he was commissioned especially to take the message of Christ to the field least expected for a Pharisaic Jew, the Gentiles. We know little about what Paul looked like. A description of him in the apocryphal *Acts of Paul*, not written until around 160, is of a small man with a bald head, slightly hooked nose and bandy legs, but full of charm and grace with a face that at times looked like that of an angel. Whatever the validity of this very late portrait, we know that he was tough and courageous, undertaking epic missionary journeys which helped to lay the foundations of Christianity in the Roman Empire, enduring shipwreck, illness, merciless beatings at the hands of enraged mobs, and eventual arrest and martyrdom.

Soon after his conversion Paul undertook a work of mission in 'Arabia', probably in what is modern Jordan, and in Damascus. As he often found, his message stirred up strong opposition (2 Cor. 11:32). He then did mission work around his home city of Tarsus (in modern Turkey), before being invited to join in the leadership of the church at Antioch, an important commercial centre in Syria (now in Turkey), one of the first places to which Christian believers from Palestine had travelled (Acts 11:20). It became a remarkable church. Jewish and Gentile Christians gathered freely, enjoying fellowship meals together and raising money for poor believers. Here the name 'Christian' was first used for the disciples of Jesus Christ (Acts 11:26). From Antioch Paul was sent on the first of his missionary journeys in the eastern Mediterranean, among Jews and Gentiles in Syria and Asia Minor. While he was at Troas in Asia Minor (Turkey), Paul reported a vision of a man of Macedonia (in the Balkans) appealing to him: 'Come over to Macedonia and help us' (Acts 16:9). It was a call to become the apostle to Europe, and it took place about AD 50.

Some of Paul's ongoing missionary exploits took him to what is now modern Greece, Italy, Albania, Crete and Malta, and the churches he helped to found are recorded in the book of Acts and his letters. He was arrested around 57 in Jerusalem and sent to Rome for trial in 59. When he arrived, there was already a well-established church in the city. During his period of imprisonment he wrote a number of epistles, which became part of the New Testament. He may have been released around 61, but he was executed for his faith sometime around 63–5.

Peter

While Paul made many of the headlines, he was one of a number of apostles, evangelists and teachers who criss-crossed the ancient world engaged in the missionary task. Although the apostle Peter's particular emphasis was upon mission to the Jews, he was given a decisive revelation at Cornelius's house (Acts 10), with the instruction not to 'call anything impure that God has made clean'

(v. 15). From this Peter concluded that God 'accepts men from every nation who fear him and do what is right' (v. 35), although at times he appears to have struggled with the practical implications of this (Gal. 2). In his first epistle, Peter wrote to Gentile-background Christians in Asia Minor, although he may not have personally visited them. He is also linked with Rome. 1 Peter is addressed from 'Babylon' (1 Pet. 5:13), which might symbolize Rome, although it could literally refer to the city of that name in Mesopotamia. The account that Peter and Paul were executed during Nero's persecutions of the church and were buried in Rome is not found in written form until late in the second century AD, but the evidence to support this comes from an earlier date. The tradition that Peter was bishop of Rome for the twenty-five years leading up to his death appears much later. Had Peter been in the city when Paul wrote his prison epistles, it is likely he would have mentioned the fact.

Expansion in apostolic times

Other texts in the New Testament reflect the significant early geographical spread of the church. From Ephesus (in modern Turkey) the gospel radiated out to Laodicea, Hierapolis and Colosse (Col. 4:12–16; Col. 1:2). The letter to the Hebrews mentions other Christians in Italy (Heb. 13:24). Paul wrote to Titus who was working with a church in Crete (Titus 1:5). The book of Revelation includes letters written to churches in Smyrna, Philadelphia, Sardis, Thyatira, Pergamum and Laodicea, as well as Ephesus. Apollos arrived in Corinth from Alexandria, in Egypt, the great intellectual centre of diaspora Jews, and it is possible he had heard the Christian gospel there (Acts 18:24–28). In Acts 11:20 we read of believers in Cyrene, in modern Libya. Clement, the leader of the church in Rome in about 95, wrote that Paul 'reached the limits of the West', although we don't know if he ever made it to Spain, which was his hope (Rom. 15:24). If he didn't, others soon did.

Beyond the New Testament we move into the evidence of traditions, some of which may have come from early oral sources. These link various apostles to other locations. Some are recorded by the fourth-century church historian Eusebius, who links Mark with Egypt and especially helping to found churches in Alexandria; Matthew with Ethiopia (other traditions place him elsewhere); Bartholomew with 'Upper India' (other traditions say he was martyred in Armenia); and Andrew with 'Scythia', a somewhat obscure reference to a vast region in Eurasia that stretched east from the Black Sea across Ukraine, parts of southern Russia, Kazakhstan and Kyrgyzstan to southern Afghanistan. By tradition he was martyred in Achaia.

These fragmentary and sometimes conflicting accounts cannot be historically verified with any degree of certainty. Nonetheless, within the pages of the New Testament and before the death of most of the apostles, there is evidence that Christianity had already spread from one end of the Mediterranean to the other. There are other intriguing possibilities. In Acts 2:9 we read of people present at Pentecost from as far away as Parthia, Media and the Mesopotamian area – modern Iran and Iraq. Did they travel home after Pentecost to report what had happened? This is not known, but there are traditions linking the apostles and early Christianity with these and other areas. The witness of ordinary Christians, some traders and craftspeople, some refugees scattered by persecution, did even more to increase the likelihood that Christianity would 'go global', and fulfil the promise of Jesus that the gospel would reach 'the ends of the earth' (Acts 1:8).

The fall of Jerusalem

In 66 the revolt that had long been simmering in Palestine broke out. The rebels captured Jerusalem and massacred the elite Sadducees as a punishment for their collaboration with the Romans. According to later tradition, the Christian population fled. In 70 the Roman army crushed the Jewish rebels and razed Jerusalem to the ground. The temple was demolished and the residents of the city were scattered. These catastrophic events fundamentally changed the worldview of both Jewish and Christian communities. With no temple, there was no longer a functioning sacrificial system. The Jewish law could no longer operate as it had previously. For Jews, the world as they had known it for centuries was over.

A significant Christian community had continued to meet in proximity to the Jewish temple, headed by James, the brother of Jesus, until his execution in 62. The events of 66–70 forced Christianity out of Jerusalem and into becoming a movement for which no land was home. Before long there were more Christians in Antioch than there had been in Jerusalem. As they spread across the Roman Empire, Christians were required to live out their lives in a predominantly Gentile and therefore alien cultural context, raising profound questions about the food they should eat, where they should go and how their children should be educated.

These were issues that the Jewish diaspora had wrestled with, but, shaped by the Great Commission of Jesus, the response of the early Christians was to adopt an outward-looking approach. Nonetheless, the presence of large numbers of converts from non-Jewish backgrounds created tensions with Jewish-background Christians, some of whom had once been Pharisees. They found it hard to see how the Mosaic law could be ignored. The profound debate that followed (Acts 15) led to the momentous, but controversial, decision at a council of the church in Jerusalem, in about 48, that Gentile converts did not need to become Jews physically by undergoing circumcision, but abstinence from fornication and refraining from eating meat sacrificed to idols were sufficient practices to separate them from wider society. The Christian faith was thereafter not tied to Judaism, and the principle became established that a convert did not need to be completely uprooted from his or her own culture to faithfully receive and live out the gospel. Some found this difficult to accept, and the 'Judaizers' dogged Paul's steps throughout the rest of his ministry.

Expansion beyond the Roman Empire

Rome, capital of the empire, became of increased significance to the new faith after the destruction of Jerusalem and the scattering of its important church, but the biography of Christianity from its beginning is a missionary story and also one of a non-Western religion. The extent to which Christianity spread beyond the ancient Mediterranean world after the close of the New Testament era is hard to assess. For the next generation the evidence becomes sketchy, or absent entirely, in terms of definite historical sources as to life and witness in the early church. Nonetheless, in the next 300 years or so, Christianity, often in the face of hostility and persecution, spread throughout the empire and beyond, although it remained an unwelcome minority-religion in a pluralistic scene, and Christians were often seen as forming a sectarian breakaway from Judaism.

There is strong historical and archaeological evidence for the early existence of churches around the Mediterranean and in the heart of the Middle East. Edessa in Upper Mesopotamia (now in south-east Turkey) became a centre of Christianity by 150, and King Abgar (179–216) ruled for a short time as a Christian king before he was deposed by the Romans. When a bishop from Phrygia (Asia Minor) paid a visit to Rome in 190, he returned via Syria and Mesopotamia and found churches wherever he travelled, all sharing the same faith and celebrating the same Eucharistic meal. The Christian message also penetrated deep into the Caucasus and may have reached Armenia within a decade of the death of Christ.

Irenaeus (c. 130–202) of Lyon in what is modern France reported that Christianity had reached the Germans and that he had preached to Celts when they had visited his city, both peoples from beyond the borders of the Roman Empire. When Tatian left Rome in the late second century, he moved east:

some think he reached Mesopotamia, others Arbela in Adiabene, east of the River Tigris. In the second century Clement wrote of there being Christians in Ethiopia.

Bardaisan (c. 154–222) in Edessa reported that there were Christians as far east as modern Pakistan. How it reached there he does not tell, but one of the early Christian traditions links the apostle Thomas to both Pakistan and India. The connection between Thomas and India was long disregarded. The discovery of a well-established commercial route from the Red Sea ports to India, and Roman settlement and trading influence around Chennai, has made this theoretically possible, although far from proven. However, the frequency of Thomas traditions is noteworthy. The third-century apocryphal *Acts of Thomas* gives an account of how he, a carpenter like Jesus, travelled to India, where he eventually preached and performed miracles before he was martyred by an angry king near Chennai after his wife had been converted through Thomas's preaching. It is claimed that he was buried on St Thomas Mount, now under the flight path into Chennai airport. Other Indian oral traditions have him landing in 52 in south India and winning many converts, before being martyred in 72 for refusing to worship the goddess Kali. Indian churches still celebrate 3 July as the anniversary of his death. The ministry of Thomas in the south of India is considered more likely than that in the north, but a visit to Pakistan is also possible as other traditions claim.

It should be noted, however, that other writers such as Origen and Eusebius have Thomas working among the Parthians, Medes and Persians. References to 'India' could therefore just mean the East, where, Eusebius records, 'Thomas obtained his portion'. Another tradition has Pantaenus, from Alexandria's famous catechetical school, travelling to India around the year 190 at the invitation of Indian visitors. Eusebius, the early church historian, records that Pantaenus found that it was the apostle Bartholomew who had been there before him, and discovered a copy of Matthew's Gospel in use. Again this remains an intriguing possibility, but in the absence of further evidence we cannot say more.

No early Christian documents written in an Indian script exist. The rich array of oral traditions of apostolic journeys may have been developed in the early centuries to assert the longevity and authenticity of the Christian presence in India. Nonetheless, these traditions do confirm that Christianity reached India early, and it could have been by Christians influenced in some way by the ministry of Thomas. It is more likely that Christianity reached India through the travels of merchants from the Graeco-Roman world and other unnamed missionaries. Either way, conclusive historical proof is difficult, but certainly Christianity in India was no eighteenth-century transplant from Europe and is one of the oldest religions on the subcontinent.

These oral traditions about the apostles, and the subsequent appearance of reports of geographically widespread Christian profession from the third century onwards, help us to see how from the very earliest period Christianity was viewed as a global faith rather than simply belonging to the Mediterranean Graeco-Roman religious scene. Mission to those who had never heard the gospel message was the core of its identity. One reason for the historical and archaeological evidence relating to the very early Christian presence being so limited is because the church was at the time a largely 'underground', house-based movement.

The churches that developed in the first two centuries of Christianity had a sense of connectedness – historically to Christ and his apostles but also to other believers. They were conscious of being part of a global movement utterly different from anything that could be measured or comprehended by human standards. The writer of the late second-century Epistle to Diognetus describes Christians as not distinguished by 'land, nor language, nor customs':

> inhabiting Greek as well as barbarian cities, according to each person's lot . . . they display to us their wonderful and admittedly paradoxical way of life. They inhabit homelands, but as strangers . . . Every foreign land is their homeland, and every homeland a foreign land.

The size of the early Christian community

It has been suggested by historians that by 300 around one tenth of the population of the Roman world professed Christianity – somewhere between 5 and 7.5 million out of a total empire population of 60 million. That figure had leapt to nearly 34 million by 350 (56.5% of the population of the Roman world), but by then the social and political situation for Christianity had completely changed with the conversion of the emperor Constantine. The growth of Christianity from a gathering of 120 believers in around AD 30 (Acts 1:14–16) to around 6 million over its first 270 years is astonishing. How that growth took place is unclear. Sociologists have extrapolated figures from the growth of recent religious movements to propose that a steady growth rate of 3.42% per year, or 40% per decade, would achieve this figure. However, the evidence of the book of Acts suggests a different pattern.

Church growth certainly started with a bang. Acts 2 records that 3,000 people were 'added to their number' as a result of the events of Pentecost. Immediately after Pentecost the number of believers is reported to have increased rapidly to 5,000 men (Acts 4:4), and clearly there were also many more women and children. That spectacular upsurge in numbers seems to have been somewhat unusual, and generally the pace of growth of the church was more modest, with various peaks and troughs. In Acts 21:20, on his visit to Jerusalem, Paul was told that 'many thousands of Jews have believed', a figure that probably included converts living outside the city. If the evidence of Acts is typical, the pattern of church growth may have included periods of rapid expansion followed by times of consolidation or even decline. In periods of repression and persecution of Christianity, many Christians were martyred and others abandoned their profession of faith.

There is a series of local snapshots of how the church was progressing between the first and the third centuries. In 177 it was reported that there were 7,000 Christians in Rome, around 1% of the city's population. There are also suggestions that Christianity became a predominantly urban movement, although that may be because the evidence has been best preserved in cities and towns. In Egypt, based on the presence of Christian names occurring on papyri, around 10% of the population were Christians in 278, and 18% in 315. There are indications that the rate of growth of Christianity after 250 was increasing, which is surprising in the face of the significant persecutions still occurring.

Explanations for church growth

Indeed, this growth did not take place in the safe, settled, affirming environment considered ideal for children, as the next chapter will show. The question as to why, in the light of what were at times extreme difficulties, Christianity expanded so rapidly and so widely in the first centuries after the death of Jesus Christ is significant. Christians believed that the hand of God was behind the growth of the church and that conversion was a work of the Holy Spirit. However, they also recognized that God works through various means. In this particular historical context there is no evidence of a single missionary strategy or apostolic plan behind the growth of the early church.

The religions of the ancient world certainly did not know of mission in the way the apostle Paul practised it. In the Ancient Near East religious expansion tended to follow in the train of invading armies. Instead the early evangelists went armed only with their message of repentance and faith in Jesus the Messiah – and their impact was more extensive and lasting. They usually first visited the local synagogue, the focal point of the local Jewish community, whose members they sought to meet. The welcome afforded to visiting rabbis allowed them opportunity to proclaim the message of their Teacher. They went to a people longing for the Messiah, although this figure was often understood in political rather than salvific terms. The diaspora, which saw four out of every five Jews living outside Palestine, provided an extensive network of such communities. Most Jews were able to speak both Greek and Hebrew, allowing ease of communication to communities spread across a huge geographical region. The Old Testament was also available in Greek (the Septuagint), allowing ready access to it across the former Greek Empire. An initial welcome by the local Jewish community often turned to hostility when the nature of the Christians' message was understood.

At first Christianity sheltered under the umbrella of the Jewish tradition and the legal protection Jews had gained from the Roman authorities in part to buy peace in Palestine. This exempted Jews from certain formal religious practices required in the empire. Because of the growing opposition to elements of Christian teaching from the synagogue leaders, as reflected in the book of Acts, disagreement often turned into outright hostility. Some Christians were forced to relocate as opposition intensified. The final separation between Christianity and Judaism took place around 100, leaving Christians without the legal protection to practise their religion that the Jews enjoyed. With growing numbers responding to the gospel message of salvation by faith in Jesus Christ, Christianity emerged as a distinctive form of belief and practice within the pluralistic religious world of the Ancient Near East.

Each time the gospel crossed a political boundary, it often also crossed a cultural one. Yet Christians found that their message transcended these boundaries. It was accepted and believed by many, regardless of racial, cultural or political background. Yet in each new context, fresh questions were raised for Christian believers and preachers – what they should do in these particular circumstances, how they should think and act, and how should the gospel be expressed. The task of the theological interpretation and application of the unchanging gospel in changing contexts was under way.

As well as in synagogues, evangelists proclaimed their message in the streets, the marketplaces and other public buildings, but most of their work took place in private homes or other premises. The key medium of communication was verbal, sometimes through preaching, at other times by conversation and dialogue. Many Christians travelled, either for the express purpose of extending the reach of the Christian message or for their business and employment, and as they went they could not help telling their faith story; this has been evocatively described as 'gossiping the gospel'. Curious friends, family members and neighbours asked questions about the new beliefs of Christians, or heard a visiting preacher or discussion in a home meeting they had been invited to join. The evidence suggests that the early Christians practised what they preached, or gossiped. Their distinctive lifestyle, turning from the immoralities of the day, and their strong practical, social support for widows, orphans and the sick (including plague victims whom no-one else was willing to touch) proved powerfully attractive. Roman and Greek society was very religious, as the apostle Paul found in Athens, but many were tired of the inability of the Greek and Roman cults to answer the major issues of life, and unhappy with the immoral values of wider pagan society. The Christians' dedication to their belief system and ultimately to Christ was strong; they were willing to embrace the cost – whether separation from loved ones, exile, prison or death.

Some aspects of the environment created by the Roman Empire proved conducive to the spread of Christianity. Its political unity meant that early evangelists had no frontiers to cross. They shared a common currency, and the presence of the Roman military meant that travel was relatively safe. The Roman infrastructure, constructed for trade and military domination, with well-made roads and regular shipping routes, made speedy travel possible, even over long distances. However, safety and security in travel could not be guaranteed, as the apostle Paul found.

Many of those who embraced Christianity tended to come from the middle or lower orders of society. Some were craftspeople and traders; others were slaves. Hostile observers dismissed them as the dregs of society – slaves, children, women, the uneducated – but the backgrounds of the early Christians were surprisingly diverse. Some were highly educated, powerful and wealthy, but most were not. With around 50% of the population being slaves, the appeal of the Christian message – one of dignity, justice, spiritual freedom and equality before God – was evident to that portion of society. Becoming a Christian involved a significant social transition, and separation from certain aspects of wider society associated with the pagan cults. However, this was countered by the Christian idea of *koinonia*, community and fellowship, bringing together, especially at the Eucharistic meal, women and men, Jews and Greeks, slaves and free.

A legacy of previous Greek empires was that the common language of much of the Roman Empire was Greek, an expressive, emotional language capable of conveying religious concepts as well as precise descriptions of historical events. It was in this language that the New Testament was written, using a contemporary conversational form, allowing maximum access to it for many. It was also, importantly, not the language of the dominant imperial power, Rome. The Greeks had also left a lingering fascination with the big philosophical questions about life, love and death, which may have made a number within that context open to the core content of the Christian message.

Another key reason for Christianity's expansion was altogether more sobering and perplexing – the impact on others of the witness of Christians prepared to die for their faith. In later years some expansion of Christianity was associated with political expansion and military force, but this was certainly not the case when Christians were a persecuted, often despised, minority. In its early years, Christians showed a level of commitment to the Great Commission of Jesus Christ not often found in later centuries, creating a necessity to share their message through the tears and sufferings of refugees, exiles and prisoners, and the witness of martyrs.

3. FIRST STEPS

Lifeline
c. 96 – first epistle of Clement written
c. 80–100 – *Didache* written
c. 107 – Ignatius's letters written
c. 112 – Pliny's letter to the emperor Trajan
c. 150 – Justin Martyr's *Apology*
c. 197 – conversion of Tertullian
c. 235 – death of Hippolytus

Children grow all too quickly. Before long they are beginning to explore their world, crawling and then taking their first tottering steps. All this is part of forming their own identity and slowly building a capacity to eventually live independently. As it made its first forays into the world, Christianity was small, insignificant and dwarfed by other religions. For most of the first 300 years of its existence, being a Christian brought no social or political advantage. All who professed Christianity did so voluntarily and had to count the cost of taking up the cross and following Jesus (Luke 14:26–33) – what they believed and practised they needed to be prepared to die for. The prospect of paying the ultimate price meant that the religious convictions and moral values of those prepared to join this despised and persecuted band of followers of Jesus had to be well rooted.

Key early Christian beliefs

In a culture saturated with polytheism (the worship of many gods and goddesses), Christians had to be sure that their belief system was superior to that found elsewhere. Plato speculated about what a single true god would be like, but the clear monotheistic belief of Christianity, building on the Old Testament teaching of one almighty God, true Creator and Sustainer of the universe, cut across pagan religious understanding. Unlike the capricious, morally questionable and often juvenile behaviour of the pagan gods, the supreme God of the Christians was loving, compassionate, benevolent, holy and merciful. But Christians believed he was not a distant God: he had reached out to humanity by sending his Son to live on the earth in human form.

The early Christians exalted Jesus Christ as Saviour. In the traditional religions of the day, salvation was won by religious acts to gain the favour of the gods or to placate their anger. A range of options was available, including sacrifices (animal and sometimes human) and the performance of various cult practices such as fertility and sexual rituals. Magic and witchcraft were prevalent. The gods were seen to inhabit natural phenomena such as the seas, stars, mountains, streams and wells, the sun and the moon, and even powerful individuals like emperors. The Christian God instead transcended space and time. Salvation was a work of his grace, and the way to God was through repentance for sin, and faith in the work of Christ and his teaching. God did not treat his creatures as puppets to be played with. Human weakness was not a barrier to knowing God.

The crucifixion of Jesus Christ was a serious challenge to both Jewish and Gentile hearers. When the apostle Paul spoke about the resurrection to the philosophers of Athens they ridiculed him. Yet the message contained in the gospel, of salvation won through suffering, made it appealing to those who themselves faced suffering, social or financial deprivation, or even death. It was a source of hope and courage.

Christian life and worship

For many, the Christian lifestyle of devotion and self-denial was irrational and inexplicable. To others it was deeply impressive. Principles such as love for enemies, forgiveness for wrongdoers, refusal to kill; rejection of practices such as the abortion or abandonment of unwanted children and the prevailing sexual immorality; opposition to human or animal blood sports – all marked Christians out from pagan society. To most, the care of Christians for orphans, widows, the poor, the unemployed, asylum seekers and prisoners was highly unusual. Early Christianity was a revolutionary, countercultural force, transforming the lives of individuals and with the potential to transform societies.

Christian worship often had to be conducted in semi-secrecy to avoid the threat of persecution, so exact details as to its form and practice are limited. Early church writings, and sources from outside the faith community, give us some clues as to Christian life in the years after the New Testament had been written. A report written around 112 by the Roman governor Pliny to the emperor Trajan gives insights into some Christian practices in Bithynia (modern Turkey). Pliny had questioned and tortured some Christians, and learned that they met together 'on a fixed day' – which would be Sunday, or the Lord's (resurrection) Day. When they gathered they recited 'by turns a form of words to Christ as a god'. This repetition of a set prayer may have been the Lord's Prayer. Sunday was an ordinary working day in the community, so Christians needed to gather 'before daylight'. After the meeting they ate 'ordinary and harmless food' together. Pliny also found a very strong moral code among Christians, who promised on oath together 'not to commit theft or robbery or adultery, not to break their word, and not to deny a deposit when demanded'.

Another late first- to early second-century Christian writing was the *Didache*, a summary of apostolic teaching, including on the subjects of prayer and baptism. The Lord's Supper, or the Eucharist (meaning thanksgiving), was taken regularly and included sharing a cup of thanksgiving and breaking bread. The person partaking of this was to be well prepared: it should be taken only after 'first confessing your sins', to ensure that the sacrifice of praise and worship was not 'defiled'. Preaching was to be listened to with discerning, tested according to the scriptures and respected greatly: 'where the things of the Lord are spoken, there the Lord is present'. Catechizing believers was also practised.

Justin Martyr

Sunday worship remained central. Writing from Rome in around 150, Justin Martyr (c. 100–165) in his first *Apology* describes Christians from both town and countryside gathering to meet in one place, to 'bless the Maker of all things through his Son Jesus Christ and through the Holy Spirit'. Sunday is chosen, Justin explains to his pagan audience, because it was the first day of God's work of creation and also the day on which 'Jesus Christ our Saviour rose from the dead'. Central to the worship service was the reading of Scripture and then a sermon, as the preacher 'urges and invites us to the imitation of these noble things'. After prayer, the Eucharist was shared and a voluntary collection taken and used for the care of orphans and widows, those suffering from sickness, those in prison (for their faith), refugees and 'all those in need'. The apostolic worship pattern of prayer, Scripture reading, preaching, baptism, Eucharistic celebration and giving has remained the core of Christian worship.

The *Apostolic Tradition*, compiled sometime between the mid-second and the mid-fourth centuries, confirms this pattern – prayer, an offering, instruction in piety, and encouragement to good works that please God. In discussing the Lord's Supper, words of institution from the Gospels and 1 Corinthians 11 are used. It indicates that believers were not 'Sunday only' Christians, urging them to wake every morning, wash their hands 'and pray to God' before they touch any form of work. When there is no regular gathering, the individual believer is to 'take up a holy book and read in it sufficiently what seems to bring him profit'. Some services were also held on weekday mornings, where again preaching was central. As this instruction is received, each should reckon 'in his heart that it is God whom he hears in the instructor'. The work of the preacher enabled the hearers to receive things they would not otherwise think of, and to profit from things 'which the Holy Spirit will give you through the instructor'.

Christian life entailed personal devotion and being part of a learning and worshipping community. The *Apostolic Tradition* linked devotional exercises to everyday life: 'He who prays in the church will be able to pass by the wickedness of the day.' But there were also warnings: 'Let none of you be late in the church' – Christian behaviour has not changed across the centuries!

Singing was a feature of some early church services. Pliny noted Christians singing 'a hymn among themselves to the Christ, as to a god' early in the morning. Other accounts indicate that the reading of Scripture was interspersed with singing psalms or hymns. At the beginning of the third century Tertullian describes Christians singing hymns, either from the Scriptures or of their 'own invention'. Some were great affirmations of the faith, such as the 'Hymn of the Saviour Christ' recorded by Clement of Alexandria, who died around 215:

O King of the saints
O sovereign Word of the Most High Father
Prince of wisdom

Support of toiling men
Eternal Joy of the human family
O Jesus, Saviour.

By late in the fourth century, the emphasis was on singing material found in the Scriptures, especially the Psalms. This was not, it seems, accompanied by musical instrumentation, which was associated in the minds of early Christians with the dancing and carousing which took place at pagan weddings and festivals. Musical instruments had been part of Old Testament worship, but in the synagogue they were not used. In his *On the Benefit of Hymns*, written late in the fourth century, Niceta of Remesiana (in Serbia) argued that music helped the singer to remember the words of a psalm: 'whatever the Law, the Prophets and even the Gospels teach is contained as a remedy in the sweetness of these songs'. A balance was nonetheless to be maintained, as Augustine, also in the fourth century, highlighted. He feared that the emotional impact of singing could easily overwhelm the understanding and that it was sinful to find greater pleasure in such tunes or emotions than in the words. Nonetheless, the early church agreed that God was pleased with the vocal praises of his people, which should be focused on the worship of Christ as God.

How Christian worship was maintained in remoter parts of the empire is less clear. One indication comes from Dura Europos, on the border of Iraq and Syria, along the trade route from Mesopotamia to the West. Here a house dating from around 240 which had been converted into a church was unearthed, possibly the oldest church building ever found. The largest room of the house, the atrium, had been converted into a meeting room opening on to the courtyard, in the centre of which was a pool which appears to have been the baptistery. The atrium contained a raised area where a table had been set – the place for the celebration of the Eucharist – and a chair for the presiding minister. A part of a text of a Greek harmony of the Gospels, thought to be from the late second century, was also discovered. This evidence again suggests continuity from the apostolic times in worship and Christian lifestyle even among widely scattered Christian communities, maintaining the core elements of reading and preaching from the Bible, baptism and the Eucharist.

Throughout the first three centuries Christians mainly met in private houses, and as congregations increased in size it was usually in the larger homes of the richer members. Larger congregations meant that the practice of the fellowship (*agape*) meal associated with the Lord's Supper became more difficult to continue. Hired rooms were also used during this period, but any clearly identifiable church buildings were at considerable risk in times of ongoing persecution. After the persecutions under Valerian in 260, some confiscated property was returned to Christians and there is evidence of larger structures being built. The persecutions of the early fourth century saw many of these destroyed, but as the threat of persecution receded they were rebuilt in a more splendid and permanent style.

Baptism

The mode by which baptism was practised in the early church has occasioned much discussion. Christian writings from the early centuries show that those who were interested in embracing the Christian faith underwent a long period of preparatory instruction before formally joining the church. This acted as a form of 'invisible minefield' around the community, ensuring high standards of teaching and morality, and helping to root out potential informers or those joining for the wrong motives. Once established as serious in his or her intentions the enquirer was registered as a 'hearer' (auditor) or 'catechumen' (someone under instruction). Only after completion of this process was baptism considered.

According to the *Didache*, the baptism of Christian believers could only take place after a period of preparation, including up to two days of fasting beforehand. No guidance on the age of the person baptized is given, but those who underwent the practice needed to be old enough to understand its meaning and significance. The preference is for baptism to take place where there is running water (echoing the baptism of Jesus in the River Jordan), but where this is not possible, still water could be used (cold is preferred to hot!). Where there isn't enough water it can instead be poured three times upon the head 'in the name of the Father, the Son and Holy Spirit'. Justin Martyr simply reported that baptisms took place 'where there is water', although over time special baptisteries – small pools with steps down into them – were built inside churches. He similarly described a period of probation for a person who has been 'born again', in which he or she is taught how to believe and live, followed by a period of prayer and fasting before being baptized; he claims this as apostolic practice. For Christians, baptism is a matter of 'choice and knowledge'.

By the time of Hippolytus early in the third century, the preparation time could stretch up to three years with further instruction to follow. Baptisms were at Easter, preceded by several weeks of fasting. The beliefs and lifestyle of a candidate were closely examined – did he or she live a pious life, give to widows, visit the sick? The ceremony of baptism was clearly a high point in the Christian year. The sense of anticipation increased as Easter approached, with an all-night prayer vigil in a darkened room the day before the baptism. When in the water, candidates turned to the west to renounce Satan before turning to the east to announce Christ. Each candidate was asked questions as to whether he or she believed in God the Father, Christ Jesus the Son of God, and the Holy Spirit. The baptized person then came out of the water to the sound of singing and was led by torchlight into the lighted church to partake of Easter communion.

A question that has caused much debate and division through Christian history is whether infants were baptized in the early church. Some argue, based on the New Testament references to households being baptized (such as that of the Philippian jailer in Acts 16), that this must necessarily have included children or infants, although it is also possible that any children in those households were old enough to understand the meaning of baptism. The documents from between the first and early third centuries focus on the baptism of believers or converts to Christian faith. These were adults or children old enough to understand and respond to preparatory questions, and to fast and prepare themselves. The baptisteries found in early churches are of sufficient size for full immersion or pouring significant quantities of water on to adults. If babies or infants were being baptized we do not read of this, nor are there any instructions for how they or their parents should be prepared. This appears unusual if the practice was prevalent. However, the question remains: is absence of evidence in fact evidence of absence?

It is unclear when the practice of baptizing babies began. Tertullian, late in the second century, wrote strongly against this practice, but his need to do so suggests that by then it was happening. In the middle of the third century the bishop Cyprian (c. 200–58), writing from Carthage in North Africa, connects the baptism of infants with Old Testament circumcision, but indicates that infants did not need to wait for the eighth day and should be baptized on the second or third day after birth. This appears to be new thinking – in the second century circumcision was seen as a mark of the old covenant and Jewish identity from which Christians had separated. At a similar time Origen, writing from Alexandria, also mentions the practice of administering baptism 'even to little children', for which he claims a tradition stretching back to the apostles.

Whenever infant baptism began, it was by no means universal. Many Christian leaders of the period appear to have been brought up in Christian homes but for various reasons delayed their baptism until later in life. Ambrose of Milan was baptized at the age of thirty-four in 374; Basil the Great was baptized around the age of twenty-five in 355, although he criticized believers who were delaying their own baptism. Gregory (c. 330–c. 390), bishop of Nazianzus, wrote that it was permissible to baptize children at the age of three, when they were old enough to understand Christian instruction and answer questions put to baptismal candidates. However, when the emperor Constantine converted to

Christianity in the fourth century, he postponed his baptism until just before his death for fear of committing post-baptismal sin. This points to another set of issues raised by the theology of baptism in the third and fourth centuries.

Over time the baptism of the babies born to Christian parents appears to have become widespread. Augustine (354–430), writing as bishop of Hippo, argues strongly in favour of it, although his need to present a case suggests not all agreed. His theological writings on paedobaptism are the most extensive in the early church but appear nearly four centuries after the New Testament. By the eighth century, infant baptism as the means of initiation into the Christian church had become normative practice. In later Catholic missionary work, recruitment to Christian identity through the application of baptism to infants became significant, with an expectation that personal faith commitment would follow. The limited evidence from the early church means it is not possible to 'prove' infant baptism was the practice of the church from its beginnings, nor to state definitively that believer's baptism was the only form administered.[1]

Church leadership

Also controversial in the subsequent history of Christianity was the structure and form of early church leadership. In the book of Acts, Paul and Barnabas appointed elders in the churches they helped to establish, following the model in Jewish communities. In Paul's address to the leadership of the church in Ephesus in Acts 20 he refers to the same group, using what appear to be interchangeable terms: *episkopoi* (a term from a Gentile background translated as 'overseers', 'supervisors' or sometimes 'bishops') and *presbyteroi* ('elders' or 'presbyters' – a term from a Jewish background). The same words are used, again apparently interchangeably, in Paul's letters to Timothy and Titus. The role of the overseer or elder was one of spiritual care, direction and teaching for the local church. Deacons were also appointed to assist with the daily running of the church, distributing support to the poor and assisting with the Eucharist.

The special ministry of apostles and prophets appears to have slowly disappeared from regular church life in the aftermath of the New Testament era.

1. Dearly held beliefs have been maintained on each side of the debate about baptism, but for many Christians it is seen as a matter on which believers can differ without breaking fellowship. Almost all Christians are united on the necessity of some form of baptism.

The *Didache* suggests a plurality of church leaders in an egalitarian structure. Those with an itinerant prophetic ministry were still found in the church, although much attention is given to how to distinguish true from false prophets, suggesting that they could not be guaranteed as a source of reliable teaching. This element of unpredictability in the ministry of the itinerant preacher, and the increasingly settled nature of local churches, shifted the emphasis in teaching on to the leaders of the local church and their need to safeguard their flock against false doctrine.

The gradual emergence of a leading figure presiding over a local church is indicated by the pattern described by Ignatius from Antioch in 115. He describes a single leader who conducted baptisms, presided at the Eucharist and *agape* meal, and guided the church in maintaining true teaching. Ignatius asserted the role of the bishop strongly: 'You must follow the bishop as Jesus Christ [followed] the Father . . . Let no one do anything apart from the bishop that has to do with the Church.' This is quite different from the flexibility and openness to prophetic leading portrayed in the *Didache*, and other early second-century writings from Rome suggest a plurality of leaders running the churches at both Rome and Corinth. The Antioch model only became widespread in the middle of the second century. By the third century the monarchical view of leadership had prevailed and a hierarchical pattern was established, with bishops (*episkopoi*) holding the highest office, under whom a series of presbyters served in a group of churches – by 250 there were forty-six presbyters in Rome alone.

The role of deacon, derived from the word for servant, was initially one of offering practical service associated with the Christian congregation. This dimension appears to have been gradually lost, with deacons either assisting the local bishop or occupying the lowest rung on the ladder of ordained clergy, although some progressed from being deacons to becoming bishops. Over time the threefold clerical order of bishop, presbyter and deacon became established. Bishops became key figures in large cities, guarding Christian unity and preserving continuity with the teaching of the apostles. They maintained the Christian network, ensuring communication through letters and personal visits.

Church unity

The relative importance of the different bishops in the first three centuries of Christianity does not appear to have been a matter of great discussion, although it later became contentious. Larger churches enjoyed a mother–daughter relationship with those in the surrounding countryside. The term 'catholic', meaning whole or universal, was used from early in the second century to describe this sense of connectedness and unity in fellowship (*koinonia*) and love (*agape*) between different churches, be they small or large. Ignatius in his letter to the Smyrnans wrote, 'Where Jesus Christ is, there is the Catholic Church.' Christianity was from the outset a stateless faith with no earthly homeland. Its identity derived from common faith in its founder, Jesus Christ. Its future homeland was eternal, transcending the present earth in which Christians were pilgrims and non-resident refugees.

Unity did not always mean uniformity. On matters of church practice, such as the date on which Easter was to be celebrated, debates between local bishops could be bitter. As the issues became more controversial and potentially divisive, the need for an ultimate authority figure among the bishops was argued for. Faced by growing divisions and heresies in North Africa in the first part of the third century, Cyprian, the bishop of Carthage, argued that the bishop of Rome should have primacy of honour among the other bishops, although this did not stop him disagreeing with Bishop Stephen of Rome over some of his teachings. This contention of the primacy of Rome was supported by appeal to Matthew 16:18, where Jesus Christ announces to Peter, 'On this rock I will build my church . . .' This saying was now claimed to have conferred authority on Peter's supposed successor in Rome, although it could have been a reference to the great declaration of faith he had just made. The letters of Paul played a vital role in shaping Christian teaching, but it was the legacy of Peter that was appealed to in order to shape the order and governance of the church. Although a shrine was built on the supposed place of his burial in the 160s, it is uncertain whether Peter ever held the office of bishop of Rome. Nonetheless, the 'successor' of Peter in Rome was to rise to pre-eminent place in the Catholic Church.

Cyprian began to speak of both Christian sacraments and ministers using Old Testament sacrificial and priestly categories. He also believed that there was only one true church, the Catholic Church, and all should belong to it to be sure of their salvation. Its baptism and communion, he claimed, were alone the true ones: 'No one can have God for his Father who has not the Church for his mother.' In the face of disputes and heresies this appeared understandable at the time. Yet, as the church grew in size and diversity across the empire, and struggled with the question of whether those who had recanted their faith in the face of persecution should be readmitted with or without rebaptism, the maintenance of unity became ever more difficult. Local bishops, who came to mirror the roles played by local state officials, increasingly sought to impose their authority.

Personal faith and practice

Justin Martyr described his conversion in terms of an intellectual search through a range of philosophies, but this does not seem to have been the usual pathway to faith. Instead apologists were keen to emphasize the attractiveness of the life and witness of ordinary Christians to those outside the Christian community. Justin speaks of the constancy, patience and integrity of Christians, overcoming the 'violent and tyrannical disposition' they often faced. Non-Christians were won over by the 'extraordinary forbearance they have observed in their fellow travellers when defrauded'. Similarly Tertullian notes how outsiders commented of Christians, 'See how they love one another . . . see how they are ready even to die for one another.'

The need for high standards of moral conduct is stressed throughout the early Christian writings. The *Didache* speaks of the code of love for God, love for neighbour and keeping the Ten Commandments as the 'way of life'. Right doctrine and right conduct went together. Integrity in financial matters was essential in a world where bribery and corruption were rife. Regularly the question arose in the mind of their observers: 'Why do Christians live in this way?'

Christianity attracted those on the social margins, who often made up the largest part of congregations, although this is less surprising because they formed the largest proportions in society. One of the criticisms of Celsus, a pagan opponent of Christianity, was that Christianity was all too often found in the shop of the cobbler and the washerwoman. The writer of the Epistle to Diognetus captured the ironies of the Christian position: 'They love all men, and are persecuted by all . . . They are poor, and yet make many rich; they lack everything, and yet in everything they abound . . . They are abused, and they bless.'

Within the church, slaves were considered spiritually equal to those who were free, making Christianity an attractive option for them. Although Roman society gave women a greater legal status than did Judaism, the equality between women and men proclaimed at the heart of the gospel was of a different order. The significant role played by women in early Christianity is reflected in the pages of the New Testament. The biblical instructions to mutual submission in marriage, and consideration of the other partner, were socially transformative in the face of the patriarchal domination usually found in Roman families. Singleness is also presented as a positive lifestyle choice, and celibacy as a gift to be celebrated. In death Christians were equal, be they bishop or slave, and were buried in the same graveyards.

In a context in which medicine was non-existent or not effective, prayer for those who were sick was an important part of pastoral care and a form of witness to neighbours. Exorcism for those who were spiritually troubled was also significant. The mutual help and support found in early Christianity attracted outsiders. Tertullian explained how Christians gave to the church each month gifts 'of modest coin'. This was not spent on feasting and drinking, as in the pagan temples. Instead it went on the care of the poor and their burial after death, on orphaned children, slaves too old to work, and the families of believers banished to the mines or remote islands 'or shut up in prisons for nothing but their fidelity to the cause of God's Church'. In 251 a bishop in Rome reported that his church was supporting 1,500 'widows and persons in distress'. Not only were the orphans of church members supported, but also unwanted babies were rescued from rubbish dumps, where they had been left to die or be claimed by 'baby farmers' who brought them up to serve as prostitutes.

When plague struck Alexandria in the middle of the third century most of the populace fled, leaving the dead or dying in the street. Members of the Christian population chose to stay in the city to tend the sick and bury the dead. Such kindness cost some their lives but left a powerful impression on the rest of the population. When the fourth-century Roman emperor Julian tried to undermine Christianity, he found it difficult because of its strong system of social care and the high reputation Christians had gained for their generosity – something that paganism could not match. Social concern was an essential part of early Christian practice and closely accompanied the message of Jesus Christ as Saviour. This combination of deep faith commitment, high standards of personal morality and compassion, and the willingness of believers to witness to their beliefs is part of the story behind the rapid early growth of Christianity. Even more remarkable is that such expansion often took place in the midst of the severest opposition.

4. TEARS

Lifeline

c. 49–53 – Claudius expels Christians from Rome
64 – Christians persecuted after blamed by Nero for fire of Rome
c. 155–60 – martyrdom of Polycarp
177 – martyrdom of Blandina at Lyon
202 – Severus forbids conversions to Christianity
c. 203 – martyrdoms of Perpetua and Felicitas
249–51 – persecution under Decius
257 – persecution under Valerian
303–11 – the Great Persecution under Diocletian and Galerius

Tears are often never far away as little children grow up. They get hungry, have falls and bad dreams, or get frustrated. Usually such tears are short-lived – the child is pacified by the application of food, drink or tender loving care. They are part of growing up, but as far as possible distress and suffering should be kept to a minimum for healthy growth. Children do not thrive in a hostile, threatening environment. Yet, during the early part of the biography of Christianity, the first three centuries of its existence, Christianity was under severe threat. Christians had to live out their faith before their neighbours and remain law-abiding citizens, yet they were viewed at times with suspicion, alarm, revulsion and even hostility. At times it looked like Christianity might not survive, especially when official policy turned against the church and a terror campaign was launched to wipe it out completely. Yet, over these early centuries, it grew.

Violence was a regular feature of life in the Roman Empire, either at the hands of the authorities or through periodic mob unrest. The saying went that social order in uncertain times was only maintained by 'free bread and circuses'. The horrific barbarity of the popular entertainments included gladiatorial contests against animals or other humans, in which much blood was shed, usually resulting in the death of the opponent. In the victory celebrations of Trajan in 108, some 10,000 gladiators and 11,000 beasts were killed. The savagery of the times meant that it was almost inevitable that those who did not conform to social or religious norms would encounter, sooner or later, some sort of violent opposition.

Opposition from some Jews

For some first-century Jews the Christian message was profoundly disturbing. To the Sadducees, whose position of influence depended on negotiated power from the Romans, the ministry of Jesus Christ was disruptive of the status quo. For the Pharisees the Christian flexibility on matters of the law was too difficult to accept. The Essenes placed more emphasis on withdrawal from the world than the early Christians, and the rejection by Jesus of military revolt as a way of establishing his kingdom was not the solution the Zealots had in mind. As the book of Acts shows, for some Jews the message of Christianity was liberating and fulfilling, but for others Christians were blasphemers, following a false prophet. Itinerant Jewish preachers travelled in the wake of Christian apostles and evangelists, seeking to return converts to the fold of Judaism. The conversion of wealthy Jews or God-fearers meant the loss of income to synagogues. The refusal of Christians to participate in the revolts against Roman rule in Palestine in 66–70 and 132–4 was also unpopular with the Jewish community. From its formative years onwards, opposition from some Jews to the Christian message was strong. Jewish leaders handed Jesus over to the Roman authorities. His brother James, the leader of the Jerusalem church, was martyred at the hands of some in the Jewish community, as was his successor Simeon and then Stephen.

Early hostility

In around 49–53, during the reign of the emperor Claudius, Roman sources report Christians being expelled from Rome after rioting happened 'at the instigation of Chrestus', which may be a somewhat confused reference to communal tension between Jews and Christians. Acts 18:1–2 confirms these events. In the late second century Tertullian attributed ongoing upturns in persecution of Christians to Jewish influence. Early events sowed seeds of suspicion and hostility between the communities.

After the destruction of Jerusalem the Jewish community regrouped and by the end of the first century AD was growing in confidence, retaining its status as an officially recognized religion free from some of the civic religious duties of other citizens, such as the obligation to make sacrifices to Caesar or undertake military service. It was not easy for the Roman authorities to distinguish between Christians and the wider Jewish community, with Christianity seen as an offshoot Jewish sect benefiting from some protections. However, persecution pushed the communities apart, leaving Christianity in an increasingly exposed position and open to opposition from the Roman authorities.

The hostility from the leaders of the minority Jewish communities, with their homeland occupied by Roman forces, owed something to their struggle to maintain their own cultural and ethnic identity, surviving by state permission which could be withdrawn. Anything that potentially destabilized their community and threatened the measure of freedom they enjoyed was viewed with alarm. Christianity was believed to pose such a threat. However, this hostile response in turn saved Christianity from being exclusively associated with Judaism, pushing it into wider, and eventually global, interactions.

For most in the Roman and Greek world it was not hard to find reasons to mock or ridicule Christians. To many pagans Christianity was simply a joke. One of the earliest examples of such derision is a small piece of graffiti found etched on a wall in Rome, probably from some time in the second century. It depicts a boy looking at a figure hanging on a cross, but where a human head should be, the head of a donkey has instead been drawn. Underneath is the inscription 'Alexamenos worships his god', mocking the Christian worship of Christ, executed on a cross, a place of punishment and shame. Other ways in which Christianity was misunderstood and misrepresented are summed up in a work called *The True Word*, written about 150 by a pagan intellectual called Celsus. Here Christianity is depicted as a fraud, and Jesus as a fraudster, the son of a liaison between a Jewish prostitute and a Roman soldier. Celsus wrote mockingly that only fools and women and children would believe in a crucified carpenter from Palestine.

The association of much of public life with pagan ritual and sacrifice forced Christians into withdrawal from aspects of society. Wild tales circulated about what Christians did at their meetings, such as practising cannibalism (a misunderstanding of the Lord's Supper) or committing incest (a rumour based on the Christian love feasts). In times of persecution the necessity for Christian gatherings to be held in secret added to such rumours, which further alarmed the authorities, who feared that revolution or disorder was being planned in such meetings. The separation that the Christian moral and ethical lifestyle demanded created the charge that Christianity wrecked family life. If the daughter of a pagan family converted to Christianity and refused an arranged marriage to a pagan, this caused divisions in families. So too did the refusal of Christian wives to partake in pagan ceremonies with their husbands, or to abort or abandon unwanted babies. The message of spiritual equality within Christianity cut across class divisions and the social order, which some considered threatening. As Christianity was driven further underground, its meetings notified by secret symbols such as the fish, rumours spread all the more.

Such low-level misunderstanding and derision could sometimes erupt into popular mob violence against which the authorities had little to say. In Smyrna, in around 155, an afternoon of popular entertainment in the arena got out of hand. The blood of the crowd was up and they thirsted for more. Voices in the crowd called for the arrest of the elderly bishop Polycarp. He was a revered, godly man, over eighty years old, and early church sources said he had known the apostle John. He was dragged before the Roman proconsul, who asked him to deny his faith, swear by the genius of Caesar and curse Christ. This the old man refused to do: 'How then can I blaspheme my King who saved me?' Hearing of this, the rage of the crowd in the stadium burned against Polycarp and the cry went up that he should be killed. And so this famous man of God met his end, burned alive and stabbed, amid the cries of his oppressors. He held unshakeably to his Christian beliefs, victim to mob rule and a local official unwilling to intervene to prevent it.

Roman persecutions

The official Roman response to Christianity was not consistent over the first 300 years of its existence. In Acts 25, faced by Jewish hostility to his preaching, the apostle Paul was able to appeal as a Roman citizen for protection from the State, although he still ended up with a prolonged period of imprisonment. The New Testament teaches obedience to the constituted government, and the payment of taxes, with a sense that justice is generally to be expected. By the time Revelation was written, however, times have changed and Rome appears depicted in Revelation 13:1 as a beast with seven heads – seemingly the famous seven hills on which Rome stands.

Nero's persection of the Christians

The events of 64 reflected this changed scenario, when the emperor Nero blamed the Christians for the devastating fire that engulfed Rome. According to the Roman historian Tacitus, Nero 'punished with the utmost refinement of cruelty' the people 'commonly called Christians'. They were accused of 'hatred of the human race'. Some were clad in the hides of beasts and torn to pieces by dogs; others were crucified, and some victims set alight as human torches to illuminate the grounds of his palaces. Despite such horrific events, there was no continuous, wholesale onslaught on the church. Instead persecution came in a series of waves which were felt more strongly in some areas than others.

Further episodes of persecution followed under Vespasian, who ruled from 69 to 79, and Domitian (81–96). When Pliny, the newly appointed governor of the province of Bithynia, asked the emperor Trajan in around 112 what to do about the Christians in his region who were drawing people away from temple worship, the reply was ambivalent. Pliny had tortured two of their serving women but found them believing only what he described as an 'extravagant superstition', and against this Trajan did not advise a wholesale witch-hunt. Those brought before the courts were to be forced to recant, and if they did so they could be released. If they did not, they were guilty of refusing the order of the local governor and were, if necessary, executed.

There was no Roman law which officially forbade the practice of Christianity, but its alternative worldview and increased size and public presence in Asia Minor, North Africa, Italy and southern France were deemed a growing threat to the established social and religious order. From the time of Augustus until then, the official policy had been to respect local religious practice as long as it had some tradition associated with it, with Roman citizens worshipping local gods, and those in the provinces also joining local rites. Personal religion faced no restrictions, with no constraints on someone's personal belief system as long as Roman society was not disrupted, although such faith was dismissed as nonsensical by Romans. However, matters of public religion – *religio* – were about civic loyalty and obedience. All subjects had to offer some form of allegiance to the cults sponsored by the emperors. Without this, the gods might be offended and withdraw their protection from the State.

The ultimate issue for Christians was their conviction of the uniqueness of the Christian God, and their loyalty to Christ alone as their Lord and Saviour. In a pluralistic religious culture this inevitably created conflict. Since the time of Augustus it had been an offence to refuse to acknowledge the divinity of the emperor: it was a treasonable offence. The emperor Domitian wanted to be known as 'our lord and god'. Jews were exempt from this law, but when Christians began to be viewed as non-Jews they lost this exemption. What appeared a perfunctory civic duty – to honour Caesar above Christ, even offering only a pinch of incense as sacrifice to him – was to Christians impossible. Jesus had taught his followers to 'render unto Caesar what is Caesar's', but to swear by the *genius* of the emperor (his guardian spirit) was to deny the status of their Saviour as King of kings and Lord of lords. Yet such a refusal was accounted an act of disloyalty to the State. Honouring Jesus Christ as King, Sovereign, Lord and God was deemed the act of a rebel and a traitor, offering obedience to another ruler.

Other factors were at play. There seems to have been an increase in superstition, belief in magic and occult practice in the later third century, against which Christians resolutely stood. Dionysius of Alexandria reported that the persecutions exacted by Valerian were at the behest of his Egyptian astrologer. The overall nature of Roman cultural practice was also significant. School teachers were required to celebrate days dedicated to certain gods; for example, the schoolroom was to be decorated with flowers on the celebration of the feast of Flora. Some guilds and crafts were specifically dedicated to different gods and goddesses. These caused major problems for Christians with their unique commitment to Christ alone. Sometimes work was commissioned explicitly for the temples, and when a group of Christian craftsmen refused to carve an image of the god Aesculapius, they were killed.

The issue of whether Christians should serve in the army was also much debated. For those who chose or were forced to do so, the army was one of the most difficult places to be a Christian, with its insistence on the routine duty of sacrificing to different gods on certain days. For their rejection of the demands of the other gods, and adherence to only one God, Christians faced the surprising charge of being atheists.

By the middle of the second century the Roman Empire began to weaken, with constant pressures on its borders in the north, and in the third century especially in the east, towards what is modern Iran. Pressure on the borders was matched internally by third-century power struggles and civil war. With fears for the empire growing, attempts at measures of religious compliance and conformity intensified. In 202 the emperor Severus made becoming a Christian illegal. As taxes and inflation soared, the military enforced their rule on society with increased ruthlessness. Amid the uncertainty and chaos, there was evidence of increased interest in religion, including Mithraism imported from the East. Others were fascinated by the teachings of a prophet called Mani, from Parthia, who travelled as far as India and created a religion synthesizing elements of other religions he had encountered with Gnosticism and Christianity. By the fourth century the Manichaean cult had adherents in regions as far spread as Egypt and China. During the reign of Decius, with Christians beginning to be found in high places, the increasing weakness of the empire was blamed on those who had refused to offer sacrifice to the gods of Rome and had brought forth their displeasure. A scapegoat was needed. Tertullian bitterly satirized this blame culture: 'If the Tiber reaches the walls, if the Nile does not rise to the field . . . if there is famine, if there is plague, the cry is at once, "Christians to the lion"', adding ironically, 'What, all of them to one lion?'

During the 240s the millennium of the foundation of Rome was celebrated. After he seized power in 249, Decius enforced traditional religious practice by requiring that a representative of each family offer a sacrifice of petition and congratulations to the gods. Those who did so were provided with a certificate, but refusal would incur at least imprisonment and in some cases the death penalty. This was the fate of many Christians, including the bishops of Antioch, Rome and Jerusalem, in the first empire-wide persecution of Christians. Decius was vainly trying to preserve the dying Roman world and maintain the social and religious beliefs of the old families of the ruling elite. Although Decius died in battle in 251, his policy was continued intermittently for the next twenty years, notably in 257 under Valerian, with edicts passed to remove the hierarchy of the church and seize its property.

The ultimate sanction was obviously death, but Christians faced an appalling catalogue of other sanctions: imprisonment, whipping, torture, rape, fines, dismemberment of various limbs, cutting out the tongue, being fettered in chains that could dislocate the wrists, and confiscation of goods and property. This created thousands of orphans, widows, refugees, families with their breadwinner in prison, and people deprived of the means of employment. Places such as the Colosseum in Rome, and arenas across the empire, were stages on which, for many, the final battle for the Christian faith was played out. The practice of Christianity was widely disrupted. Places where Christians met were destroyed and precious copies of the Christian scriptures were burned; indeed, handing over copies of scriptures to the persecutors was viewed as a grievous sin.

Martyrologies

The accounts of those who determinedly kept their faith and bore witness in the midst of trial and persecution were recorded by their followers in what became known as martyrologies. The word 'martyr' means witness, and from the martyrdom of the senior Christian leader Polycarp, to the simple yet unshakeable witness of the slave girl Blandina, these accounts were written to strengthen, encourage and deepen the faith of those who might face the same fate. Under the duress of torture in Lyon (in modern France), Blandina simply repeated, 'I am a Christian.' The heroic endurance of this frail, uneducated girl amazed the witnesses: 'she the small, the weak, the despised, who had put on Christ . . . and in many rounds vanquished the adversary'. Such accounts suggested that, despite the physical agonies they endured, the martyrs experienced a deep sense of closeness to God. Some reported visions of Christ himself. Their sense of fearlessness in the face of death, and the reality of the heavenly reward the martyrs believed they would soon inherit, struck many witnesses.

This closeness to God of those called to give up their lives in death led to martyrdom being viewed as the highest calling, willingly embraced by many. Torturers seek to deconstruct the personality of their victims through threats, imprisonment and the infliction of pain. Some Christians trained themselves for prison and torture by ascetic practices such as voluntary fasting. Based on studies of torture victims, psychologists have identified altered states of consciousness whereby it becomes hard to feel further pain, but the willingness of Christians to embrace pain and death seems of a different order. When tortured in the 250s in Carthage, Cyprian reported that 'the body does not feel this at all when the mind is entirely absorbed in God'. With the meaning of pain thus reconfigured, the more it was inflicted, the closer it brought the sufferer to salvation.

When Ignatius, bishop of Antioch, was arrested and condemned to death as a Christian during the reign of Trajan (98–117), one of his greatest fears as he headed for execution in Rome was that well-meaning Christians might procure him a pardon. He wrote to his fellow believers, 'Suffer me to be the food of wild beasts, which are the means of making my way to God. God's wheat I am, and by the teeth of wild beasts I am to be ground that I may prove Christ's pure bread.' The well-known account of Origen (c. 185–254) in Egypt is another example. As his father was arrested and led away to martyrdom, the young Origen wished to rush out into the street to join him but was prevented by his mother, who took the precaution of hiding his clothes. As an older adult Origen was later to be brutally tortured for his faith, and he died several years later as a result of his injuries.

The prayers of those in prison facing martyrdom were seen to be very special, and as they came from those soon to pass into the presence of God, it was believed they would assuredly be heard. Fellow believers faithfully visited the prisoners in their condemned cells to make their sufferings more bearable, and treasured their words. After martyrdom their bodies were collected wherever possible for a Christian burial, and their remains began to be viewed as holding a special status. They were saints, standing on the threshold of heaven, to which they would assuredly go. From them came heroic testimonies of faith, but also a cult of veneration for the relics and remains.

Martyrologies also record how those who were enduring persecution and death bore witness to their faith. Many of them were women who gladly embraced the public ministry of martyrdom. How much could be heard by the baying crowds is not clear, but by sign and word the realities of their faith were presented. Tertullian believed that some were converted to Christian faith by the witness of the martyrs. Others were certainly made to stop and think by the willingness of the followers of Christ to die for their faith. Tertullian's famous saying was, 'The blood of the martyrs is seed for the Church.' In the accounts of the deaths of Perpetua and her slave girl Felicitas, which took place in Carthage, North Africa, in the early third century, by word and gesture they boldly stood before their persecutors, pointing out that as they were being judged by human authorities, their human persecutors would in turn be judged by God.

Behind the faithful testimonies lay tragic personal stories, as the record of Perpetua shows. Although she may only have been a Christian for a few years, after she was arrested for her faith she was visited by her elderly father, who was not a believer and pleaded with her to renounce her Christianity. He even tore out his beard and threw himself on the floor, begging her not to abandon him in his old age. Defying the conventions of society, she steadfastly refused his demands, asserting, 'I cannot call myself anything other than what I am – a Christian.' Thrown into a dungeon Perpetua is depicted as being frightened of the darkness but comforted by her baby whom she is still breastfeeding. The child is taken away and then eventually returned to her, but tragically now the child will no longer feed from her. Felicitas is also taken out to die at the hands of the gladiators straight after giving birth to a baby. In the face of misunderstanding, opposition and persecution, the desire of Christians to explain and defend their beliefs grew. A type of writing known as apologetics developed, aimed at a non-Christian audience and presenting Christians as obedient, law-abiding citizens, with a faith that was reasonable and no threat to the State.

The number who died for their faith is uncertain. Nero probably killed several hundred Christians, which, while not a vast number, was still immensely shocking to the small Christian community. The total, after then, is hard to calculate – seemingly several thousand during the first three centuries, maybe fewer if the records of the known martyrs are complete. Persecution was aimed mainly at prominent figures and bishops, and less at the rank and file.

Yet, for all the heroic efforts of some, it seems that others could not withstand the onslaught of persecution. Some fled. Some fell away from their Christian profession or temporarily renounced their faith in Christ rather than pay the price demanded. The losses under the short but vicious persecution of Decius seem to have been large. A serious difficulty was created for church leaders when those who recanted asked to be restored when the persecution was over. They debated whether true believers could ever renounce their beliefs, even temporarily, and was forgiveness possible for them? Could one who had become an apostate ever be trusted with Christian office again? Some argued that persecution was the way that the church was 'winnowed': those with genuine faith, the true grain, remained, while those with nominal or insincere faith were blown away like chaff. This purified and strengthened the church. Discussions over whether to take a hard line, or whether to readmit those who repented of their recantation, were at times bitter and caused some of the first major divisions in the early church, especially in North Africa.

The Great Persecution

Persecution came from all sides and took a variety of forms, but in the third century persecution of Christians became official policy. Then matters reached a head in the years 303 to 311. With Christianity approaching 10% of the population of the Roman Empire, the emperor Diocletian sought to restore Rome to its former glory, and this involved honouring the Roman gods. Diocletian sanctioned an attempt to eliminate Christianity from the empire, which was proclaimed ominously on 23 February at the festival of the god Terminus. The gospel had advanced significantly among the educated and upper classes, and there were Christians in the Roman Senate and the army. The church was certainly placed in very great danger.

It was a mini-holocaust, a brutal attempt at religious cleansing of society, and it lasted much longer than Decius's earlier attempt. It continued under Diocletian's successor Galerius. The persecution was empire-wide, although enforced with different degrees of severity. Churches were razed to the ground, Christian writings burned. Christians were tortured and horribly mutilated. Around half the martyrdoms known of in the early church took place in those eight years. Even if the termination of Christianity had been successful within the Roman Empire, it would not have resulted in Christianity being wiped out. The gospel message had already stepped over the shifting imperial boundaries in the east: there were strong Christian communities in Syria, near the Tigris and Euphrates rivers in what is now modern Iraq and Iran, around the Persian Gulf, and in the Central Asian regions of Turkmenistan and Uzbekistan. All were territories that were under the control of empires other than Rome and to which Greek- and Syriac-speaking Christian refugees from the Roman persecutions fled. Here, however, they were not immune from other persecuting rulers: it tragically remained the historic fate of many Middle Eastern Christians to face harassment and opposition for their dearly held beliefs.

Yet Christians of the time understood this was what Christ had promised. It was through many tribulations that the believer would enter the kingdom of God; the Cross of Christ was to be taken up gladly. As the Saviour had walked the path of suffering, so should his followers. Each symbol of suffering was seen to evoke the pattern of Christ. The wooden club with which the believer was beaten spoke of the Cross; chains were ornaments when worn for Christ's sake; to be robbed of clothing in prison was to be reminded of being clothed with Christ. The blows and torture endured were seen as aimed not at the Christian, but at Christ himself (Acts 9:5). To be martyred was to be crucified with Christ (Gal. 2:20). The apostle Peter had taught, 'Rejoice insofar as you share Christ's sufferings, that you may also rejoice and be glad when his glory is revealed' (1 Pet. 4:13 ESV). Harassment, discrimination, imprisonment, exile and martyrdom were viewed as a blessing and an honour. They remained a reality for many Christian believers through successive centuries.

In 311 the official policy of persecution was abandoned. It had cost the lives of many faithful and loyal members of society and had signally failed to restore the fortunes of Rome. Nor had it succeeded in wiping out Christianity – in places the opposite was true. The ageing emperor Galerius called a halt to the terrible events and is said to have asked for the prayers of the Christians. Within two years of this their situation within the empire had been completely transformed.

5. LEARNING TO WRITE

Lifeline
c. 130 – conversion of Justin Martyr
c. 140 – Marcion arrives in Rome
165 – martyrdom of Justin Martyr
c. 165 – beginnings of Montanism in Phrygia
177 – Irenaeus becomes bishop in Lyon
c. 200 – Muratorian canon
230–3 – Origen moves to Palestine
254 – death of Origen

As they interact with their family and friends children readily learn to speak, but writing takes a little longer. The ability to express complex ideas and concepts only develops gradually. Christianity spread initially by word of mouth. The disciples of Jesus Christ treasured and carefully learned his words and actions. Within a few decades of his death the written documents which make up the New Testament had been produced. Christians increasingly became known as a people of the 'Bible', from the Greek word *biblos*, meaning book.

Recording the teachings of Christ and his apostles in written form helped to guard the church against error and false teaching, an increasing problem as the church grew in size and geographical extent. Yet it is easy to overplay its early purity and simplicity. The church in the second and third centuries faced significant turmoil, beset by false teachings, accusations and persecution from without, and heresies from within.

Writings to explain, or ensure, the correct interpretation of the teachings of Christianity emerged. Right teaching and understanding became known as *orthodoxy*, whereas wrong doctrine was called *heterodoxy* or *heresy*. 'Apologetic' writings, using a word from the law courts referring to a defence of oneself and one's actions, were produced to articulate or defend the Christian faith with a wider audience in mind, especially those in the pagan community. Plato's 'Apology' was his version of the speech Socrates gave when he was on trial in 399 BC, defending his teaching and conduct. Christian apologists sought to defend Christianity as greater than the wisdom of the age, and rebut the false accusations against Christian teaching that were contributing to the bitter persecution they were facing. The forms adopted included an open letter to an enquirer and even an address to an emperor. Some of the early attempts have survived and include the writings of Tatian (c. 110–80), a convert from Assyria, and Theophilus (a bishop from Antioch who died c. 183–5), who stressed the superiority of Christian knowledge over that of Egyptian, Chaldean or Greek prophets and sages. Despite persecution, Christianity was not a ghetto faith but was outward-looking, seeking to engage from a biblical foundation with classical culture in culturally relevant and intellectually plausible ways. Simply quoting Bible verses was not enough.

Justin Martyr

Justin Martyr was born in Samaria around 100 and met his death by martyrdom in 165. He was well educated and studied the great philosophies of his day in an ever deepening search for truth. His quest illustrated to him their weaknesses: from Stoicism he learned about self-control and self-regulation, but nothing about God; Aristotelianism was too practical and systematizing. His Pythagorean teachers required him to be an expert in astronomy and geometry before he was permitted to explore the mysteries that the sciences illustrated. Platonism was more satisfying but still did not yield the answers he craved. Then he reports meeting near the seashore outside Ephesus an old man who explained how Jesus Christ fulfilled the message of the Hebrew prophets. Justin's search for the noblest and truest philosophy met its answer in Christianity.

Once converted, Justin set himself to defend Christian teaching against misrepresentation and ridicule. In his first *Apology*, written around 152, Justin complains about the injustices faced by a Christian – not persecuted for being thief, robber or criminal, but as one who 'has only confessed that he is called by the name of Christian'. It was a theme taken up by Athenagoras (c. 133–c. 190) who reported that Christians were being accused of 'atheism, Thystean feasts [cannibalism], and orgies'. Should these charges prove true, Athenagoras urged, 'proceed at once against our crimes; destroy us root and branch'. But if the charges were empty slanders, then Christians should be granted 'the same rights (we ask nothing more) as . . . those who persecute us'.

In his second *Apology* Justin drew on terms from Greek philosophy to demonstrate the truth of Christian teaching. He was prepared to see elements of Christian teaching in the writings of pagan philosophers from before the time of Christ, such as the concept of the supreme God, although these truths had been distorted by demons who diverted pagans from the truth. Followers of Jesus were therefore the true philosophers. Justin saw Jesus Christ as the incarnate appearance of the divine Logos spoken of by Greek philosophers, and controversially believed that writers who reflected the influence of the Logos on their works and 'who lived with reason' were Christians, even though they were thought to be atheists. In effect he suggested they were Christians before the time of Christ. Other apologists were less sure, believing that pagan philosophy turned seekers for the truth away from the true message found in Christianity.

Justin Martyr's *Dialogue with Trypho* is an open letter written around 150 to a learned Jew, in which he seeks to answer the significant questions that Jews might have about Christian teachings such as the death of Christ upon a cross. Justin's aim was to persuade Trypho to accept the teaching of 'the Christ of Almighty God'.

Irenaeus

Irenaeus (who died c. 200) was probably born in Smyrna and as a boy heard the great Polycarp preach. Through Polycarp he could trace a connection back to the apostle John. Irenaeus served in a missionary capacity as a presbyter in Lyon in Gaul (modern France) and saw many converts from different tribes, including those of Celtic background. After the death of Bishop Pothinus of Lyon in the persecutions of 177–8, Irenaeus was elected his successor.

One false teaching circulating was a form of Gnosticism, which Irenaeus challenged strongly. This set of New Age type beliefs, growing out of Greek and Eastern thought, portrayed a dualist struggle between equally matched cosmic forces of light and darkness, good and evil. Gnosticism took a negative attitude towards the physical world, especially the body, which was prone to disease and death. Rejecting the Old Testament account of creation, it presented the current, inferior world as the product of a lesser creator God (a *demiurge*) who was equated with the God of the Old Testament. His creative work was a mess and interrupted the supreme God's original scheme. Above the work of the demiurge was the first cause, the supreme God. Between this world and the Supreme Being, Gnostics spoke of a complex hierarchy of beings.

The difficulties Gnostics had with the physical world left them a problem with the incarnation of Christ. In their scheme the flesh and the spirit world can never be truly united and so he could not have flesh or suffer as humans did. Thinking of Christ's physical body as not fully human, and his death as not physical, was to cause significant problems for the church, feeding into a serious error known as Docetism (from the Greek verb *dokein*, 'to seem'). Gnostics believed that the route back to original perfection came through the possession of *gnosis*. This special knowledge of heavenly secrets about the world, the Saviour and salvation was possessed by the *gnostikos* – one having knowledge – and was the key to salvation.

Gnostic teaching appealed to Christians reared in a Hellenistic world. It proposed a very simple solution to the problem of suffering, evil and death in the world, blaming it on the work of a lesser god and placing it outside the sway of the supreme God. Irenaeus showed that easy solutions to profound theological mysteries are not always the right ones. Drawing on sources and traditions from as far afield as Syria, Asia Minor and Rome, he argued that Gnosticism was opposed to fundamental Christian teaching. The world was created by one God. The Son of God came in the flesh and died as Saviour: how could a sovereign, loving, supreme God, the Builder, the Founder, the Lord of all, accept the presence of a flawed demiurge as the Gnostics proposed? He spoke of the present God in full trinitarian form: 'For with him were always present the Word and the Wisdom, the Son and the Spirit, by whom, and in whom, freely and spontaneously, he made all things.' He stressed the continuities at the heart of Christian teaching between the Old Testament and the New Testament, and between the body and the spirit, countering any docetic tendencies.

Irenaeus stressed the doctrine of *recapitulation* which emphasized the symmetries between the Old and New Testaments. The Fall at the tree in Eden was righted by the tree at Calvary; Christ, fully God and fully man, the second Adam, retraced the steps of the first Adam, passing through each perfectly, putting right all the effects of the Fall. In all this, Christ fully taking on human flesh was essential. Irenaeus strongly challenged the claim made by the Gnostics to possess special mysteries that the mainstream church did not possess. Instead he appealed to the tradition of Christian teaching, which could be traced directly back to Christ through people such as Polycarp who knew the apostles, as key to interpreting the Bible. If other knowledge existed, it would have been entrusted by the apostles to the churches they founded, and faithfully passed on, but 'they neither taught nor knew anything like these heretics rave about'. Irenaeus was one of the first to speak of Old and New Testaments, clearly asserting the Old Testament as part of the Christian scriptures.

Irenaeus places biblical theology at the heart of the Christian task, answering complex theological challenges by building arguments from the teaching of Christ and his apostles, using logical argumentation. The 'apostolic tradition' of which he speaks was historic, as recorded in Scripture, but also living as interpreted by faithful witnesses in the line of the apostles, and passed on through catechizing, teaching the creeds and faithful preaching.

Tertullian

Quintus Septimius Florens Tertullianus (c. 160/70–215/20) was a brilliant African theologian, reared in a Christian home in Carthage (present-day Tunisia). The circumstances behind his Christian conversion are unclear, but he may have practised for a while as a legal advocate, gaining skills which seem to be reflected in his writings. As the first great theologian to write in Latin, Tertullian is particularly significant. He was at times something of an intellectual maverick. His work is witty, penetrating, sometimes acerbic, full of quotable sayings. In *On the Soul*, written against Gnosticism, Tertullian argues that the human soul comes to children from their parents rather than through an independent creative act, meaning it was touched by continuing human sin and in need of redemption. The word *Trinitas* is used by Tertullian in *Against Praxeas* to describe the eternal oneness of the Godhead in three persons – the Trinity. In this he challenged adoptionist views which presented Jesus Christ as somehow adopted by God as his Son. Tertullian also challenged modalist, or Sabellian, views (named after a third-century proponent of the idea) which presented God as somehow changing himself like an actor playing different parts, so that in different modes he appeared sometimes as Father, sometimes as Son and

Tertullian

sometimes as Holy Spirit, rather than God eternally being three persons at the same time.

Tertullian's *To the Martyrs* was a work of encouragement to the 'Christian athletes' detained in prison. In his *Apology*, written around 197, he deplores the legal and moral failure that persecution represents. He highlights the absurdity of pagans torturing Christians to confess their faith, something which they freely want to do anyway. Then when they confess their faith they are tortured to force them to deny the truth. The purpose of any legal system, Tertullian argues, is to find the truth, not get people to deny the truth. In approaching the claims of paganism Tertullian rejected the intellectual bridge-building of Justin and rhetorically asked, 'What has Athens to do with Jerusalem?' In his works *De Idolatria* and *De Spectaculis* Tertullian presents idolatry as spiritual adultery, giving one's heart in worship to something that is false, and self-murder because such error brings spiritual death. He lived in an entertainment culture, where the 'love of spectacle' was effectively another religion which was hard for Christians to avoid, but Tertullian condemned the games held in honour of the gods or the dead. The 'circus' had a temple dedicated to the sun in its centre, together with many pagan statues around the arena. Combat sports that involved inflicting blows on the opponent's face were to be seen by Christians as assaults on the very image of God, but this shedding of the blood of humans was seen by pagans as a way of appeasing the gods for the souls of the departed. The theatres of Tertullian's day were filled with immorality, obscenity and depictions of violence. His sentiment was clear – it is wrong to watch what it is wrong to do: 'We should have not connections with the things which we abjure, whether in deed or word, whether by looking on them or looking forward to them.'

Montanism

In around 206 Tertullian became interested in Montanism (or 'the New Prophecy'). He was drawn to it as a renewal movement in North Africa, with its emphasis on the presence and power of the Holy Spirit, and he became much more rigorous and ascetic, renouncing the possibility of remarriage after widowhood. Montanism had created some disturbance in the church in the years after 165 when a revivalist preacher from Phrygia in Asia Minor called Montanus, assisted by a number of fellow preachers, including the women Prisca and Maximilla, proclaimed an apocalyptic message of the imminent end of the world and the descent to the earth of the 'new Jerusalem' in Phrygia. Their work was accompanied by charismatic phenomena, including speaking in tongues and prophecy. Montanus called people to abandon home and family and prepare to meet Christ as Judge. In some ways it was a reaction to the way travelling teachers and prophets were being replaced by the settled pattern of local church leaders and bishops. Montanists condemned the Catholic churches for having lost the apostolic spirit and gone stale.

Montanism was a dynamic movement and it spread far. The leadership of the Catholic Church was deeply troubled and officially condemned it. Despite this, Montanism persisted in Phrygia until the sixth century, as well as attracting followers in North Africa. What Montanus taught was not overtly heretical, but he raised questions of emphasis and authority, and represented the desire, recurring through successive periods of Christian history, to return to an unstructured, egalitarian and spontaneous form of Christianity.

Origen

The second century was a high point in Greek and Roman culture, with new creativity in literature and pride in past achievements. Out of this came a vigorous intellectual assault on Christianity, which the Christian apologists sought to counter. One attack came from Celsus, a second-century pagan intellectual about whom we know very little. His work shows he was well informed on various Christian writings and biblical books. Celsus rejected the idea of the incarnation of God as 'shameful' – why would the supreme God come to earth? 'Was it in order to learn what was going on among men? . . . Does he not know everything?' He dismissed the miracles of Jesus as the work of a charlatan, preying on weak and gullible people. The resurrection was rejected as a hallucination. Celsus also claimed that Christianity was a threat to social harmony and order because it demanded a loyalty higher than that owed to the State.

The writings of Celsus indicate how the growth of Christianity was seen as a challenge to paganism, and are also a recognition that persecution alone could not stamp out this new religion, which needed to be rebutted on intellectual and philosophical grounds. Celsus was answered by another very able North African theologian, Origenes Adamantius (c. 185–254). In *Against Celsus* Origen systematically quotes his opponents' claims and charges, and builds cogent, simple answers to each one, using Scripture, to win the intellectual battle. He counters the charge that Jesus was a magician by stressing how Jesus taught doctrine as well as did miracles, and set out a way of moral life for his followers. What magician would ever do that? On the issue of Christians weakening the empire by their loyalty to Christ above emperor, Origen argues that more good was done for the State by the prayers of Christians than would ever be done if they took up arms, calling them 'an army of piety' through their 'intercessions to God'.

Origen had been born in Egypt to a devout Christian family. After his mother's prompt action prevented his martyrdom, he was able to study under the Christian scholar Clement (c. 155–c. 220) at the catechetical school in Alexandria – an early centre for apologetics and theological study. Origen proved an able researcher and a popular teacher, presenting the Christian faith in lively and attractive ways to inquisitive and intelligent non-Christians. Before long he succeeded Clement as head of the catechetical school.

Alexandria was a leading centre of higher education for Jews, Greeks and North Africans, and an extremely fertile and creative source for theological thought. During his career Origen wrote some 2,000 biblical, apologetic and theological works. He stressed the importance of studying the biblical text itself and wrote biblical commentaries. His *Hexapla* consisted of the Hebrew text and a transliteration of the Hebrew into Greek script, set alongside four other Greek translations including the Septuagint, presented in parallel form for reference and study. Origen was committed to bringing out the richness of the meaning of Scripture, but at times he betrayed the influence of his Alexandrian context and of Plato as he sought deeper allegorical levels of meaning beyond the literal when interpreting the Bible. This Alexandrian approach stood in contrast to the more literal readings favoured in Antioch.

On First Principles is the first Christian work of systematic theology, revealing Origen's tremendous range. But he was not entirely orthodox on issues such as the relationship between the Father and the Son within the Trinity, and suggested that the Holy Spirit was inferior to the Son. Origen was a controversial character. Zealous and determined in his faith, he lived an ascetic life as a Christian: some accounts suggest he took Matthew 19:12 literally and castrated himself to avoid any hint of scandal if he taught young women and men. Sometime between 230 and 233 Origen was ordained as a presbyter by the bishop of Caesarea. This created a breach with the formidable bishop of Alexandria, Demetrius, who had not sanctioned this. To the chagrin of Demetrius, Origen established a rival catechetical school in Caesarea, in Palestine. Origen was arrested during the bitter repression unleashed by Decius in 250–1, tortured and imprisoned. He died a few years after his release from the injuries he received.

Cyprian

Another North African, Cyprian of Carthage, had been a distinguished rhetorician in the city, with politically powerful friends, before his conversion around

245–6. Soon after his conversion Cyprian was made a presbyter and around 248–9 was elected bishop, although a number of local clergy were unhappy at this rapid promotion. During the fierce persecution of Decius, Cyprian slipped into hiding, maintaining leadership over his church through a series of letters to his flock before returning as the persecution eased. In the light of his own strategic retreat at the time of crisis, he surprisingly took a hard line on the question of readmitting to the church those who had lapsed from profession of the faith during the repression. A split in the church resulted when Cyprian later eased his stance, with the Novatian party maintaining the hard line on the readmission of the lapsed. After the emperor Valerian passed an edict in 257 demanding pagan sacrifice in the empire, Cyprian was tried, exiled and beheaded for his faith.

Creeds

The need to counter challenges to core Christian teachings (whether from pagans, Jews or Christian heretics) led to the development of short statements of faith that could be easily learned by believers and repeated publically. Known as creeds (from the Latin *credo*, 'I believe'), these helped to standardize expressions of belief, especially relating to heretical teaching on the way of salvation, the holy Trinity and the person of Christ. Early hymns also included affirmations of great Christian beliefs. At baptism new believers repeated carefully worded statements of Christian belief.

The canon of Scripture

Significant attention was also given to confirming the nature and extent of the Christian canon of Scripture. The Old Testament – the Law, the Prophets and historical books – was available in Hebrew and also in Greek translation (the Septuagint). In the years after the death of Jesus, the apostles passed on the teachings of Jesus verbally; in oral cultures the power of memory was very strong. Many eyewitnesses also served as a community memory-bank to ensure the accuracy of these accounts. Some of these oral accounts may have been written down in early collections of teachings, which were then used by the writers of the four Gospels, supplemented by their own records of events or those of others who were also eyewitnesses. New Testament scholars discern the traces of these traditions in parts of the Gospels. In John 16:12–15 Jesus had taught his disciples that there were further truths that the Holy Spirit would lead them into, ones they were not ready for at that time, indicating that the New Testament scriptures would not be confined solely to a record of his own words. Alongside the Gospels, writings and letters designed to be read in church gatherings were produced by the apostles, and these soon began to be regarded as Scripture. They helped to refute false claims about Jesus, and challenge false accounts of his life and teaching.

The canon of Scripture was established through a gradual process in the early church. The 'canon', which means a straight rule or standard, set out what was regarded as authoritative. In determining this, church leaders used key principles. One was the testimony of the generation of Christians who had known the apostles and what they had used, and quoted, as Scripture. In the late second century, Irenaeus of Lyon recorded what he had learned of the origination of the New Testament – suggesting that Matthew's Gospel was especially for the Hebrews, Mark's was a record of Peter's oral testimony, Luke was essentially Paul's gospel narrative, and John wrote his Gospel at Ephesus. Irenaeus also shows that most of what is now the canon of the New Testament was viewed as Scripture in his time. He refers to all the epistles except for Titus and Timothy, James, Jude, and those of Peter and John. To Irenaeus, the traceability of teachings and writings directly to the apostles was crucial.

There was a strong belief that the Holy Spirit had instigated the writing of the books and letters accepted in the canon. The self-attestation of Scripture itself was important. The New Testament writers affirmed the Old Testament as Christian Scripture, just as Peter affirms the letters of Paul as Scripture (2 Pet. 3:16). The principle of coherence was also important. Many writings that circulated in the post-apostolic period which were not in harmony with the witness of the apostles were discounted.

By the time the last of the apostles had died the books now accepted as the canon of Christian Scripture appear to have been committed to writing, which rendered them in a fixed form. These documents were then copied with a high degree of accuracy by scribes. The final authoritative canon slowly emerged through a process of extensive usage and debate. This was speeded up by false claims about Scripture, such as those of Marcion. The son of a bishop from Sinope, by the Black Sea, he arrived in Rome in around 140 and began promoting views that suggest some gnostic influence. Marcion believed that the Hebrew scriptures were objectionable and that the view of God contained in them was crude and offensive. Attempting to draw Christians away from their Jewish roots, Marcion rejected the Old Testament and reduced the New Testament largely to the writings of Luke and Paul. Anything that suggested continuity with the Old Testament was either removed entirely or had the offending portions expurgated.

Marcion's views became popular among those who wanted doctrine that was easier to accept in the Greek and Roman religious context. His teaching may have spread as far as France and even the eastern edge of modern Iran. His much-reduced canon challenged the church to state officially what Christian Scripture actually contained, and to counter the serious gnostic and Marcionite threat.

The Muratorian canon of around AD 200 gives a list of the writings being regularly used as Christian Scripture in Rome at the time, showing that Marcion's challenge had been resisted, although there is no mention of the letters of James, 2 and 3 John, 2 Peter and Hebrews. In 367, with the rigors of persecution over, a pastoral letter from Athanasius, bishop of Alexandria, includes a list of all the books now accepted as Scripture. This full canon was affirmed at the local church Council of Hippo in 393 and at the Council of Carthage in 397.

Some books and writings were also circulated as useful for the churches, but were not deemed part of the canon of Scripture. These included the *Didache*, and the *First and Second Letters* of Clement of Rome. Other pseudo-apostolic writings were rejected as not Scripture, such as the apocryphal *Acts of Peter* which contains an account of Peter being crucified upside down. Although the author of the *Gospel of Thomas* claims to be the apostle Thomas, most scholars date it to the second century AD. It contains some sayings similar to those in the canonical Gospels, but also speaks of secret teachings Jesus shared only with his closest associates, especially Thomas himself, suggesting its author was strongly influenced by Gnosticism. The Christian writer Eusebius (260–340) dismissed it as 'absurd and impious'. The *Gospel of the Infancy* records in fanciful fashion a series of somewhat trivial miracles performed by Jesus as a child, including making birds from clay and then bringing them to life so that they could fly away. This is in marked contrast to the judicious near-silence of the other Gospel writers on the early life of Jesus.

Modern writers have been drawn to ideas of a secret or forgotten Gospel which will one day come to light. John 21:25 notes that there were many things that Jesus said and did that were not recorded in Scripture. Nonetheless, the time and process over which the canon emerged, and the consistent reasons for excluding other writings, have led to widespread acceptance since at least the fourth century of the authenticity and authority of what is now the New Testament.

The fact that the Christian scriptures survived at all through times of bitter persecution and repression is remarkable. Some fragments of existing manuscripts may even be from the first century itself, and comparison with later texts suggest few mistakes were made by copyists. During the persecutions of the late third and early fourth centuries many scrolls were seized and burned:

the crime of handing over scriptures to persecutors was viewed as very serious. After the persecution of Christianity was ended by the emperor Constantine, he ordered the production of many copies of the Bible to replace those destroyed. These were often produced in *codex* (book) form, made from sheets of parchment or paper stitched together, rather than as scrolls. Early surviving examples of these include the fourth century's Codex Sinaiticus and Codex Vaticanus.

There were also early efforts to translate the Bible into other languages to make it as widely accessible as possible. Irenaeus reported hearing from Papias that Matthew had produced a version of his Gospel for use among the Hebrews 'in their own dialect' – possibly Aramaic or Syriac – although such a translation has never been found. The *Diatessaron*, a harmony of the four Gospels, was written in Syriac in around 170 by the Assyrian convert Tatian. By 300 several translations of the Bible into other languages existed, with portions of it in Latin, and in Syriac which included a paraphrase translation known as the Peshitta.

Reading, preaching and teaching the Bible was central to the life of the Christian community and the global transmission of its message. There was a determination to ensure that when Christian teachers and preachers spoke, they did so based on what they believed God had revealed through Scripture.

6. IT'S OFFICIAL

Lifeline
312 – Constantine defeats Maxentius
313 – Edict of Milan
324 – Constantine defeats Licinius
325 – Council of Nicaea
337 – death of Constantine
361–3 – Julian rules as emperor
381 – first Council of Constantinople
428 – Nestorius becomes Patriarch of Constantinople
431 – first Council of Ephesus
449 – second (Robber) Council of Ephesus
451 – Council of Chalcedon
529 – Justinian Code, revised in 534

Normally a child's birth is officially recognized within a few days. Further recognition comes when an identity card or a passport is issued. But this was not the case with Christianity itself. It was nearly 300 years before it was officially accepted as a legal religion within the Roman Empire, and there are significant debates about whether that was beneficial for Christianity or not.

A fundamental shift in the biography of Christianity took place when the most powerful person in the world adopted Christianity, impacting both state and church, including practice and doctrine. This had seemed impossible in the late third century, with the persecution of Christians at a peak, although the severity of the implementation of that policy reflected the growing threat that Christians in high places were considered to be. They were still no more than 5 million out of an empire-wide population of 60 million.

Constantine's conversion

For the sake of administrative efficiency Diocletian had divided the Roman Empire into the 'Tetrarchy', with senior and junior emperors in both the East and the West. Diocletian governed well, enhancing the imperial office, but after the abdications of Diocletian and Maximian the empire descended into a very messy civil war. After the death in 306 of Constantius I, one of the emperors in the West who had been unenthusiastic about the official persecution, his army proclaimed his son Constantine as his successor. Constantine had spent some ten years growing up in the imperial palace of Diocletian and looked every inch the emperor, tall, with a strong aquiline nose, a firm chin and a strong neck. After a series of military and political manoeuvres he marched on Rome to encounter his rival, Maxentius, and claim the position as sole ruler of the

Diocletian's Tetrarchy

Western Empire. Despite having a much smaller army, Constantine won a decisive military victory.

As he marched into Rome that day in 312, observers noticed that on the shields of Constantine's soldiers was an unusual logo – combining the Greek letters *X* (*chi*) and *P* (*rho*), the first two letters of Christ's name in Greek. Constantine had enjoyed a somewhat chequered religious journey to that point, showing at one time a strong allegiance to the cult of Apollo, the sun god. He later explained how sometime before the fateful battle with Maxentius (accounts slightly differ) he had seen a vision of 'a cross of light in the heavens, above the sun, and an inscription, *in hoc signo vinces* [in this sign you will conquer]'. His religious behaviour changed. He believed that the one God was on his side and had brought about victory against his pagan opponents. In terms of world history, let alone that of the Christian church, the events were of seismic proportions.

Whether this and his subsequent actions reflect a genuine conversion to Christianity or not is much debated by historians. Accounts of his religious profession make no mention of personal repentance, seeking forgiveness of sin, or an understanding of the work of Christ on the Cross as the core of salvation. He was baptized, but only in 337 during the days of his final illness, seemingly because of a view at the time that sin committed after baptism was difficult to forgive. In 315 Constantine ascribed his victory to 'the Deity', and only gradually do references to 'Christ' and 'our Saviour' begin to appear. But Roman emperors would not have been expected to share personal testimonies about their inner devotional feelings with the public, so judgments need to be made on the basis of carefully worded official pronouncements. Yet there seemed little political advantage in adopting Christianity, adhered to by less than 10% of the empire's population. Although Constantine's personal faith remains something of an enigma, clearly a decisive change in his attitudes and behaviour had occurred, and he showed his displeasure about pagan sacrifice.

Constantine

Constantine's religious policies

Change came gradually. Although the Chi-Rho symbol became a symbol of imperial Christianity, also appearing on small-change currency, coins bearing the images of pagan gods continued to circulate. The god Sol Invictus (the Unconquered Sun), popular among soldiers, remained on Roman coinage until 325. Constantine needed to ensure his army were not alienated: official pronouncements did not become notably Christian in tone but were carefully neutral. One of the most significant events came out of meetings in 313 with Licinius, the lead emperor of the eastern part of the Roman Empire. The resulting Edict of Milan gave freedom of worship to all people, allowing Christians to follow their religion 'without any annoyance or disquiet'. At a stroke official persecution against Christian believers was ended.

Within the Western Empire the position of the church changed. Property confiscated in the persecutions was returned, and funds were made available to replace copies of the scriptures destroyed and to reconstruct churches. Constantine's actions suggest he believed that the well-being of the empire was now dependent on the Christian God. Churches were built in Rome on the traditional sites of the tomb of Peter and the martyrdom of Paul, and of the nativity in Bethlehem. The large Church of the Holy Sepulchre was built in Jerusalem on the supposed site of the burial of Jesus. The 'Holy Land' gained a new attraction for Christians, increasingly viewed as a place for pilgrimage. These churches were very different from the converted houses or hired rooms of the previous centuries.

In 321 Sunday – important to Christians as the day of Christ's resurrection – was declared a public holiday, although the name 'Sun-day' was retained, referring to the sun god. Christian churches were offered tax reliefs, and Christian bishops became eligible for state funding. The word 'diocese' was taken from the administrative subdivisions Diocletian developed to run his empire. The homes of bishops became palaces, mirroring those of high state officials, the purple of their vestments matching that of the emperor. Before the century was out, Christianity was beginning to look like the religious arm of the State, and bishops were becoming channels of official communication. Many were drawn from the nobility, finding a route to power by means of ecclesiastical preference rather than through serving as municipal leaders. Constantine promoted Christians to positions of influence, shifting the power base from the noble senatorial ranks with their close connections with the pagan system, to the middle-rank 'equestrian class'.

Constantine's relationship with Licinius, the emperor in the East, cooled, apparently after reports emerged that the persecution of Christians was continuing. In 324 Licinius was defeated and killed and Constantine became ruler of both the eastern and western parts of the empire. After his victory the

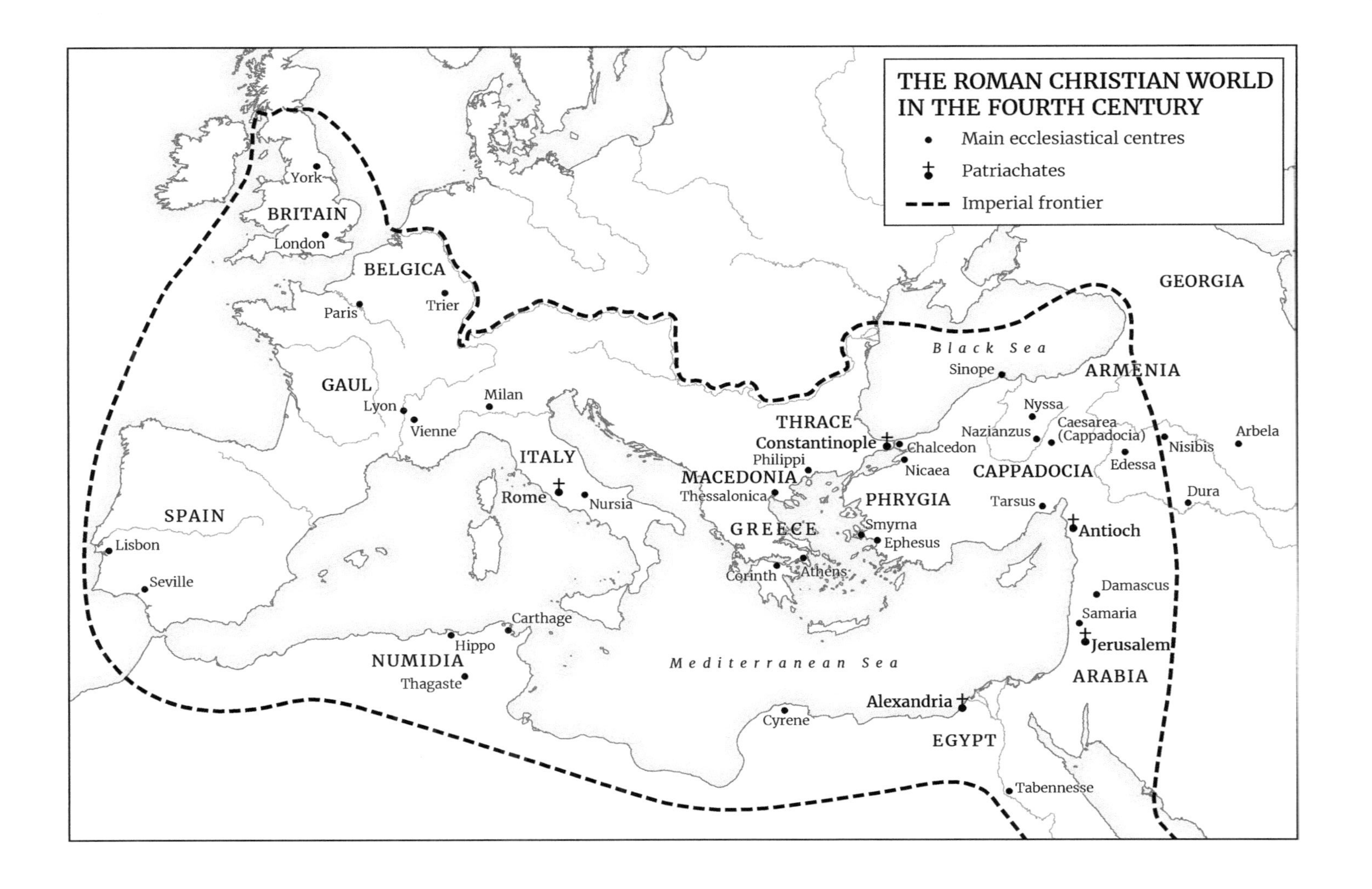
THE ROMAN CHRISTIAN WORLD
IN THE FOURTH CENTURY
Main ecclesiastical centres
Patriachates
Imperial frontier
BRITAIN
York
London
BELGICA
Paris
Trier
GAUL
Lyon
Vienne
Milan
SPAIN
Lisbon
Seville
ITALY
Rome
Nursia
Carthage
Hippo
NUMIDIA
Thagaste
THRACE
Constantinople
Chalcedon
Nicaea
Philippi
MACEDONIA
Thessalonica
GREECE
Corinth
Athens
PHRYGIA
Smyrna
Ephesus
Black Sea
Sinope
ARMENIA
Nyssa
Nazianzus
Caesarea (Cappadocia)
CAPPADOCIA
Nisibis
Arbela
Edessa
Dura
Tarsus
Antioch
GEORGIA
Damascus
Samaria
Jerusalem
ARABIA
Mediterranean Sea
Alexandria
Cyrene
EGYPT
Tabennesse

practice of pagan religion was not banned, but temples notorious for immorality were closed. Christianity's status changed from tolerated to favoured religion.

A bold decision was made to build a new capital, named after Constantine, at the heart of the united empire. The site he chose was Byzantium (from which the word 'Byzantine' derives) on the Bosphorus, at the junction between Asia and Europe. Here a 'new Rome' was built, free from the associations with pagan tradition and idolatry still found in old Rome. The new capital was called Constantinople, and it survived as a Christian city until 1453. At its heart was a church dedicated to the twelve apostles, in which Constantine was also to be buried as the 'thirteenth' apostle.

Donatism

Because of the previous role of Roman emperors in ensuring the maintenance of Roman religion, it was almost inevitable that Constantine would be drawn into church politics, in part to ensure security and survival in the empire. One issue he immediately encountered was a simmering controversy in North Africa over the consecration of Caecilian as bishop of Carthage in 311. It emerged that one bishop who took part in the consecration had been accused of handing over copies of the Scriptures during the persecutions. Although he was later cleared, some considered Caecilian's ordination invalid, and a rival bishop was consecrated who was then succeeded by Donatus, from whom the rival group took their name. The Donatists, fuelled by African nationalist feeling against the growing control of Rome, presented their case to various church authorities, including the Council of Arles in 314, but rulings went against them. Appeal was finally made to the emperor. Unfortunately for the Donatists, Constantine did not take their side and in 317 began a policy of coercing them back into the mainstream Catholic Church. Although unsuccessful, the policy continued until 321. Within a few years of the arrival of a Christian emperor and the proclamation of religious toleration, Constantine was using military power to enforce the views of one group of Christian believers against another. The Donatist split was never properly healed, leaving the North African church weakened in the face of the rise of Islam in the coming centuries.

The Arian controversy

After Constantine also became ruler of the East in 324, news reached him of an 'unprofitable question' being debated in the church at Alexandria. It was, in fact, far more substantial than that and represented a profound challenge to teaching on the nature of God. So alarmed was Constantine that in 325 he summoned the first ecumenical (general) council of the church at Nicaea, not far from his new imperial capital of Constantinople. Constantine paid for the bishops (numbering somewhere between 250 and 318) from the West and East of the empire to attend, with most coming from the East. He presided over the initial sessions, an extraordinary occurrence in terms of church–state relations. To Constantine, unity in the empire depended on unity in the church. Yet he did not resolve the issue himself by personal intervention as emperor, independent of the church, but worked through the bishops.

At the heart of the debate at the Council of Nicaea was the teaching of a brilliant preacher in Alexandria named Arius, who attracted large crowds including many working people. His views alarmed Alexander, the bishop of Alexandria, a profound thinker deeply concerned for orthodoxy. Arius drew on wider philosophical ideas to assert that as God is unknowable and indivisible it necessarily follows that, because Jesus Christ is both different from God the Father and can be known, he cannot be truly God. Arius argued that the Son, although different from the rest of creation, was 'begotten by the Father' in the sense that he had been created. There was a time before he had existed, a time when he 'was not'. He was only called 'God the Son' as an honour and favour, rather than as an expression of his true nature.

Arius was seeking to make the teaching of the Godhead more accessible to hearers schooled in Plato's thinking and thereby open doors to the wider pagan audience. He cited scriptures to defend his views, including John 14:28 and Acts 2:23, and much was made of Proverbs 8:22 (NRSV): 'the LORD created me', although Arius's opponents argued that the word 'created' was better translated 'possessed'. What Arius failed to do was to set these verses in the wider context of Scripture. His views were condemned at a synod of bishops in Egypt, but Arius had powerful friends. They rallied to his support and the issue became divisive. Pamphlets circulated, riots broke out, graffiti was scrawled on walls, and news eventually reached Constantine's ears. He was convinced that there should be one united church within the empire.

At the heart of the debates at Nicaea was whether Jesus Christ was of the *same* substance as the Father or whether he was only of *similar* substance: in Greek the words were *homoousios* or *homoiousios*. Although the only difference between the words was the Greek letter *iota*, the issue certainly made more than 'an iota of difference'. The maintenance of orthodox theology and the unity of the church hung on the presence, or otherwise, of that letter. The Council at Nicaea ruled against Arius, declaring Jesus Christ 'God of God,

Light from Light, True God from True God, begotten, not made, of one substance with the Father'. They rejected the view that 'there was [a time] when the Son of God was not' or that he is 'of another substance or essence' to God. To make clear exactly whom Christians were worshipping, they had to resort to using a word not found in the Bible in declaring Jesus *homoousios* with the Father.

Athanasius

Arius was condemned but, in 327, after an interview with Constantine in which he gave a rather bland statement of his beliefs, was restored by the emperor. Other bishops affirmed the Nicene formula without sincerely believing what had been asserted. One person who appreciated the danger of this was a young presbyter called Athanasius (c. 300–73), who seemingly attended only as secretary to Bishop Alexander. In 328, although less than thirty years of age, he succeeded Alexander as bishop, taking one of the most prestigious and influential positions in the church. To him fell the task of upholding the orthodox line set out at Nicaea when others around him began to weaken. He was tough and determined, and he needed to be. In his writings *On the Incarnation* and *Against the Arians* Athanasius reiterated in no uncertain terms what had been stated at Nicaea: 'the Son is other than the Father, but as God He is one and the same'. He argued that only if Jesus Christ was truly and fully of one substance with the Father could he truly reconcile humans to God: 'None other could create anew the likeness or image for men except the image of the Father.' Athanasius decisively asserted, 'How can one who is not God satisfy the demands of God?'

The opposition was severe. The situation appeared to be *Athanasius contra mundum* – Athanasius against the world. In the murky world of church politics, especially after Constantine's death, theological belief was mixed with political allegiances and powerful voices at court, and Athanasius was caught in the political fallout. Crowds took sides in the theological debates with the passion of modern-day soccer supporters.

Constantine's son, Constantius II, permitted the rise of Arian influence and encouraged a vague statement that the Son was merely 'like' the Father. Athanasius had the theological acumen to see the issue was one over which there could be no compromise. For this, he was beset by malicious allegations and was exiled on five occasions by different emperors. During times of exile he wrote the profound works that made him one of the greatest theologians in the history of the church.

The Cappadocian Fathers

Athanasius died in 373, and it was not until the emperor Theodosius called the Council of Constantinople in 381 that the issue was finally resolved and Arianism outlawed. Out of the creed of the 150 bishops assembled at Constantinople emerged what is now known as the Nicene Creed, which became part of the Eucharistic liturgy of both Eastern and Western churches, although it was not fully finalized and adopted until 451. The Council of Constantinople also reaffirmed the divinity of the Holy Spirit, 'the Giver of Life, who proceeds from the Father', and who is to be worshipped and glorified with the Father and the Son. In the debates leading up to this, the work of three bishops from Cappadocia, Gregory of Nyssa (330–c. 395), Basil of Caesarea (c. 329–79) and Gregory of Nazianzus (330–89), known as the Cappadocian Fathers, played a key role. They stressed that Father, Son and Holy Spirit were truly and fully God, and of the same *ousia* (substance), but also that they were distinct *hypostaseis* (persons). Although the Cappadocians identified three clearly distinguishable persons, Gregory of Nazianzus also spoke of *perichoresis*: each person in the Trinity interpenetrates the other, so that all three act together. Actions that begin with the Father proceed through the Son and are completed in the Holy Spirit. Again they drew on language from outside the Bible to explain these teachings, and the distinctions between the words used were very subtle.

As a force within the empire, Arianism was finished. Theodosius then worked towards asserting one 'Catholic' form of Christianity within the empire, backed by official sanction. Unorthodox Christian expressions were not to be permitted. However, the Arian party had been committed to mission, and in regions outside the empire its teaching continued to spread, including among the barbarian tribes of northern Europe such as the Goths and the Vandals.

Imperial Christianity

In the biography of Christianity few other changes were to be as momentous as those which took place as a result of Constantine's rule. Persecution ended and the church gained official permission to exist. Constantine ruled efficiently, but he was an emperor of his times, and some of his actions were highly questionable. His son Crispus, who ruled Gaul for a time, was executed after palace intrigue including allegations of gross immorality and possible political plotting. This was soon followed by the murder of his stepmother. Loyalty to Christ became mixed with loyalty to the emperor: the hierarchy of the church began to imitate that of the State, with the most influential bishops located in the most important imperial cities. Bishops were given powers to arbitrate in matters of legal dispute. Church leaders also appealed to the State to back up their judgments, by force if necessary. At times it looked like the emperor was above the authority of the church. Church leaders saw this as expedient rather than asserting that the true Head of the church was Christ.

Despite the severity of persecution in the second half of the third century, the church had thrived. Now the trials and temptations that beset the church were of a different order. Christians received preferential treatment, including the opportunity for influence, wealth and status. Large numbers now flocked to the churches, but nominal adherence became common. Religious art no longer depicted Christ as the Suffering Servant but instead as exalted King, sitting in an imperial court rather like that of Constantine. The Roman calendar was Christianized. Christmas, the birth of the Son, was fixed on 25 December, the midwinter Roman festival of Saturnalia, the rebirth of the sun. This was not without precedent: some earlier writers, such as Hippolytus, had favoured a December date, but there was no clear historical consensus on the issue.

Pagan religion was deeply embedded in Roman culture, including among the influential senatorial, aristocratic and upper-class families who influenced the administration. It was also strong in rural areas and in the army. Constantine sought to break up a system that had developed over centuries, but not by repression. He hoped that paganism, starved of official sanction, would gradually wither on the vine. Indeed, more force was used to put down divisions among Christians than to put down paganism.

Constantine's successors

After Constantine's death in 337, the rivalries between his sons descended into bloodshed and war. Constantine II was killed in battle with Constans, his brother. Constans then split the empire between himself and his brother Constantius II, before being assassinated during a revolt by his army officers. The revolt was put down by Constantius II, who ruled as sole emperor from 353 to 361. He pressed unity on the church but demonstrated some sympathies with Arianism.

After the sudden death of Constantius II, aged just forty-four, power fell to Constantine's nephew Julian, who had witnessed the dreadful strife among his 'Christian' family. Julian, whose father had been killed by Constantius II, was trained in the Christian tradition and even accepted a minor office in the church. In 355 he was given the responsibility of rule in Gaul; he was loved by his troops and shared their rations, adopting a simple and ascetic life. Although outwardly

Julian practised as a Christian, secretly he had a growing interest in pagan religion and philosophy. When he became emperor he openly adopted paganism. Pagan temples were reopened and pagan religion encouraged. Divisions among Christians were left unresolved – Julian the 'Apostate' hoped that Christianity would collapse through its own internal weakness. He dismissed Christianity as 'madness', arguing that 'one does not punish, but instruct, the insane'.

Julian also decided to rebuild the temple in Jerusalem to 'disprove' the prophecies of Jesus about its destruction. Although work started, something went disastrously wrong – it is unclear what. A devastating fire took place. Some said it was a lightning strike, others that it was sabotage by Christians, or by Jews offended at the actions of a pagan ruler on their sacred site. Whatever happened, work stopped and was never resumed.

Athanasius declared that Julian's reign, which began in 361, was only a cloud and would soon pass. By 363 it had. Julian was killed in battle against the Persians, and Jovian, the commander of the Imperial Guard, was proclaimed emperor by the troops. When he hesitated, declaring that he was a Christian and not a pagan like Julian, the generals cried, 'We are all Christians.' Such fickle shifting of allegiance suggested that neither paganism nor Christianity had a very secure basis of authority. Toleration and favour towards the church were again restored.

It fell to Theodosius, who ruled from 379 to 395, to call the Council of Constantinople in 381 and finally resolve the Arian issue. In 391 Christianity was made the sole permitted religion in the Roman Empire, except for Judaism. Becoming a Roman citizen involved acknowledging the Trinity, and failure to do so was deemed treason, carrying the death penalty. As a result of the Theodosian decrees (389–92) heretical sects were outlawed, non-Nicenes removed from church office, and pagan cults were banned from the empire. Officially the era of paganism was over, although its influence continued well into the sixth century.

Antioch and Alexandria

Controversy about matters doctrinal absorbed a good deal of time and energy in the fourth and fifth centuries. These were part of a process of clarifying and articulating Christian teaching in this context of residual paganism. The fourth-century debates had resolved the issue of the divinity of Christ and the Holy Trinity, and in the following century the relationship between the humanity and divinity of Jesus Christ was formally set out. Many were challenged by the question of how the real humanity of Jesus, born in a stable, walking the hills of Galilee, eating ordinary food, was to be understood alongside the reality that he was also God the Son. If the human Jesus wept, does God also weep?

Different aspects of this mystery began to be emphasized. In Alexandria the tendency was to stress the distinctiveness of the three persons of the Trinity – Father, Son and Holy Spirit. But, fearful of the divisions created by Arius and of being misunderstood as speaking of two gods, church leaders there were reluctant to speak much about the two natures of the Son, human and divine. Those who emphasized the one nature of the Son were criticized by their opponents as 'Monophysites'. Proponents of the Alexandrian view have preferred to use the term *miaphysite* for their approach rather than *monophysite*, which was used against them by their opponents when condemning them as heretics.[2] In Antioch, closer to the Jewish context, the oneness of the Godhead was asserted with monotheistic emphasis, but here church leaders felt more comfortable speaking of the two natures of the Son – divine and human.

One leader reared in the Antiochene school was Nestorius, an energetic reformer, who became Patriarch of Constantinople in 428. He had particular difficulties with the increasing use of the term *theotokos* for Mary, the mother of Jesus. It means 'God-bearer' but was often rendered 'mother of God'. Designed to protect the belief in Christ as Son of God against Arianism, there was a danger that veneration could be focused on Mary as well as Christ, as indeed began to happen. Nestorius preferred to speak of Mary as *Christotokos*, the bearer or birth-giver of Christ, or *anthropotokos*, bearer of the human nature of Christ. This avoided one difficulty but created another – Christ was both God and man, and both truths needed to be affirmed. Nestorius tried to get round the problem by stating that Mary bore only the human person Jesus and that the divine Son later united himself to the human Jesus. This created the suspicion that the divine Son only later adopted the human Jesus, rather than Jesus being both fully God and fully human from the moment of his conception.

The result was a major controversy, stirred up in good part by Cyril (c. 375–444), bishop of Alexandria. The arguments reflected a power struggle between the bishops of Alexandria, Jerusalem, Rome and Constantinople (affirmed as the 'new Rome' at the council held in the city in 381). In 431 a

---

2. Miaphysite teaching, from the Greek *mia* (single) and *physis* (nature), held that through the mystery of the incarnation of Christ both humanity and divinity were equally present within a single nature. This differed from the monophysite position they were accused of holding, which was the belief that Christ had only one nature which was divine, therefore effectively denying Christ's humanity.

church council was held at Ephesus, which affirmed that Jesus was both perfect God and perfect man, and that *theotokos* was acceptable language. Nestorius was banished. However, theologians from Alexandria wanted to gain full acceptance for their one-nature theology. In 449 they called a further council at Ephesus, making decisions before the bishops who supported the Antiochene emphasis on the two natures of Christ had arrived. This impetuous move alienated many bishops in the West of the Roman Empire – it is sometimes called the 'Robber Synod' – and aroused bitter controversy. In an attempt to hold the church in his empire together, the Eastern emperor Marcian was forced in 451 to step in and summon another council of the church.

Council of Chalcedon

Five hundred bishops attended the Council of Chalcedon, held near Constantinople under the watchful eye of the emperor and his troops. The creed which emerged was strongly influenced by Leo the Great, bishop of Rome from 440 to 461, especially his 'Tome', which summed up what others in the West of the church had taught. When it was read out at Chalcedon, the bishops are said to have declared, 'Peter has spoken thus through Leo; so taught the apostles.' The Chalcedonian Definition of the faith set out the boundaries of what was permissible to believe and what was not permissible. Four great truths were affirmed: Christ was fully God; Christ was fully man; Christ was one person; Christ existed in two natures. The teaching of the councils of Nicaea and Constantinople was confirmed. The Council of Chalcedon rejected the extreme monophysite view that the human and the divine were so fused into one nature that it was not possible to tell which was which, as when wine and water are mixed, with the divine tending to subsume the human (as the colour of wine overwhelms the colour of the water). The bishops also condemned the Nestorian view that the divine and human natures of Christ remained completely separate, as if they were oil and water in the same cup, as creating a double Sonship. Instead the bishops simply spoke of the Son as existing in two natures, divine and human:

> Our Lord Jesus Christ, one and the same Son, the same perfect in Godhead, the same perfect in manhood, truly God and truly man . . . of one substance with the Father as concerning the Godhead, the same of one substance with us as touching the manhood.

They stressed the eternal nature of the Son: 'begotten of the Father before the ages as touching the Godhead', but also the human birth of Jesus:

'in the last days for us and for our salvation, born from the Virgin Mary', of whom the term *theotokos* was used. False emphases were ruled out: 'Christ, Son, Lord, Only-begotten' was to be acknowledged in two natures, 'without confusion, without change, without division, without separation; the distinction of the two natures being in no way abolished by the union'.

What was thrashed out at Chalcedon became the widely accepted definition of the person of Christ, and remains so, among Roman Catholics, Anglicans and other mainline Protestants, and Greek, Slavic and Romanian Orthodox churches. Others saw the result as an imperially imposed version of Christianity, and the Nestorian position on the two natures of Christ continued to be strong in areas of Persia and Arabia. The East Syrian Church, where Nestorian thinking was often influential,[3] undertook missionary work in the East, in China and India. The miaphysite view continued to have a strong influence in Egypt, Syria and Armenia. Coptic Christians planted churches along the Nile, into what is now Sudan, and later forged a strong connection with the church in Ethiopia. Personality and politics, mixed with bitter attitudes in theological discussion, meant the disunited church was quickly swamped in some areas when Islam emerged and expanded in the seventh and eighth centuries.

The decline of Rome

Despite the apparently dominant position of Christendom in the Roman Empire, it was stunned in 410 when Rome was sacked by the forces of Alaric the Visigoth. It never recovered. In 476 the last Western Roman emperor was removed, leaving the Eastern Empire as the bastion of Christianity and Christendom. The gap created by weakening political power in the West was somewhat filled by the growing power and assertiveness of the bishop of Rome.

The efforts of the Eastern emperor Justinian (c. 482–565) to recreate a united Roman empire through a series of expensive military campaigns was only partly successful, and some gains made in the West were lost soon after his death. Justinian incorporated basic Christian doctrine and practice into Roman civil law. The Justinian Code (529, revised in 534) established the principle that Christian rulers were responsible for the establishment and maintenance of true religion and the church, based on the model of the kings of Israel in the Old Testament. The shift from the years before 312 when Christianity was a

3. In older literature these churches are often referred to as Nestorian churches, but not all East Syrian churches appear to have followed all aspects of Nestorian doctrine.

marginalized, despised minority was profound. Now 'Christendom' united church and state, with a Christian legal framework and worldview. To be Roman was to be a Christian. To some this was essential to ensuring the survival of Christianity for future centuries; to others it sowed the seeds of its decay, and eventual collapse, in Europe many centuries later.

However, Christianity had long since stepped over the boundaries of the Roman Empire and was already demonstrating its potential to be a global faith.

7. MOVING ON AND OUT

Lifeline
c. 300 – baptism of King Tiridates III of Armenia
c. 300 – David of al-Basra moves to India as an evangelist
c. 306 – birth of Syrian theologian Ephrem
c. 320s–360 – Ezana rules Aksum, Ethiopia
c. 330 – church built at Mcxeta, Georgia
386 – conversion of Augustine
407 – death of Chrysostom
430 – death of Augustine
578 – Mar Sergius (East Syrian missionary) in Lint'ao, central China
635 – Alopen in China

Before long, children begin to explore 'the big wide world'. Sometimes they return to their parents stronger and wiser; at other times they find themselves lost amid unfamiliar people and surroundings. Christianity had survived in a hostile environment within the Roman Empire during its first three centuries, before sheltering under the protective cloak of friendly emperors and administrators. How it would fare outside the immediate Graeco-Roman world was uncertain.

With its cradle in the Middle East, Christianity was strategically situated for expansion both west and east. It was a missionary faith from the start, both through the planned efforts of early Christian leaders and also in a more spontaneous, unplanned fashion, as Christians travelled to trade, or as people migrated, especially along the trade routes that fanned out to the east of Antioch and south of Alexandria. The Christian churches and communities that emerged were small and kept few records, but sought to remain connected with the leadership in the early Christian heartlands. Only when they became of sufficient size to attract the attention of the church administrators does a clear picture of their activities begin to emerge. Christianity was no respecter of national boundaries and could also transcend differences of language, culture and political structure.

Within 500 years of the death of Christ there were Christians living across much of Asia, including Armenia, Georgia, Azerbaijan, Syria, Iraq, Iran, Central Asia, the Persian Gulf, Afghanistan, Pakistan, India and China. These small Christian communities generally lacked political power and influence. They faced the same situation as those within the Roman Empire before the Edict of Milan in 313, without state subsidy, facing hatred, persecution and even death as ever-present realities. This afforded less time and space for participation in the sophisticated theological debates, spiced by political rivalries, which were possible under the protection of Constantine and his successors. Some centres of theological teaching developed in Edessa and southern Turkey, but generally it was reading and studying the Bible, the liturgy, the Christian family and lifestyle that were the glue that held Christianity together.

As core theological issues were settled at Nicaea, Constantinople and Chalcedon, those who deviated from orthodoxy retreated to the margins of, or even outside, the empire. The teachings of Marcion were influential in northern Mesopotamia into the fourth century. Away from the increasingly monocultural Christian Graeco-Roman world, Christians needed to learn how to interact with very different religious traditions. These included the Manichaeans, who drew on elements of Christian and Jewish teaching but were viewed by mainstream Christians as heretical. They also interfaced with Zoroastrians, Buddhists, Confucians and a host of local religious traditions.

By the late fourth century the Christian population of Antioch was reckoned to be 100,000. It was one of the five great patriarchates, along with Constantinople, Jerusalem, Alexandria and Rome. In their battles with the Persians on the eastern border of the Roman Empire, Antioch became the temporary residence of Roman emperors. It was a focal point for the emperor Julian's attempt to revive paganism, which remained strong in the city.

John 'Chrysostom'

John 'Chrysostom' (the golden-mouthed), one of the greatest preachers in the history of Christianity, was born in Antioch around 349. He studied philosophy

John 'Chrysostom'

and rhetoric before choosing the religious life, and was baptized at the age of nineteen. He was attracted to asceticism and lived for a while as a hermit in a cave, where he spent much time learning the Old and New Testaments, before he was made a deacon in 381 and a priest in 386. He was assigned preaching responsibilities in the cathedral of Antioch. His consecutive expositions of biblical books addressed the needs of all – the wealthy, artisans, soldiers, men, women, slaves and even children. His detailed exegesis focused on the literal meaning of the biblical text and opposed allegorizing tendencies. His aim was moral and spiritual reformation in a city where the faith of many Christians had become nominal. He was deeply respected for his personal holiness, and his pastoral care was extensive. His writings and homilies were widely used by the Syriac church, including 'On the Priesthood' in which he sets out the responsibilities of the Christian minister.

In 398, seemingly against his wishes, he was promoted to become Patriarch of Constantinople. Here he continued his work of preaching, reform, and promoting extensive social care for the poor and the sick. His plain speaking and willingness to address issues directly, even if they involved the imperial family, inevitably led to controversy, banishment and harsh treatment. He died in 407 on the way to his final exile near the Black Sea.

Edessa and Arbela

By 150 Edessa (modern Urfa in eastern Turkey) was a leading Christian centre. Here the Christian version of Aramaic known as Syriac was developed. Some early accounts claim that the apostle Thomas brought the gospel to Edessa, although other traditions suggest Thaddeus. The *Acts of Thomas*, written in Syriac sometime before 226, contains an account of the mission of Thomas, including ministry and martyrdom in India. It claims his relics were returned to Edessa by Christian merchants. There are significant questions about the accuracy of the text, but it does highlight early Christian connections between Syria and what is now Iran, Iraq, Pakistan, Afghanistan and India. Other traditions claim Edessa as the first Christian state after the conversion of one of its kings in the second century, but this is much disputed. The theologian who helped to shape the Syrian church was Ephrem (c. 306–73), born in Nisibis, Turkey. When that city was captured by the Persians he fled to Edessa, where he spent his life preaching and writing. He wrote exegetical commentaries on Genesis, Exodus, Acts, the Pauline epistles and the Diatessaron (a harmony of the Gospels), together with apologetic works against Marcion, the Manichaeans and Julian the Apostate. Ephrem's works were circulated widely and translated into Armenian, Georgian, Latin, Old Slavonic, Greek, Arabic, Chinese, Coptic and Ethiopic. He composed many hymns and poems (450 of which have survived) and helped to shape the liturgy. Ephrem is one of the few Christian theologians who is honoured by all branches of the Christian church.

The *Chronicle of Arbela* suggests a Christian presence from about 100 within the city of Arbela (Irbil in modern Iraq) in the state of Adiabene, which lay between the Persian and Roman borders. Here a large number of Jews converted to Christianity. According to tradition, the area was evangelized by Addai in the first century, and the first bishop was Pkidha in around 104. Arbela became a centre for Eastern Syriac Christianity, and the seat of a metropolitan of the Assyrian Church of the East. In the second century Adiabene was incorporated into the Parthian Empire, then into the Sassanid Persian Empire, which flourished from the third to the seventh century, stretching from the borders of Syria and Jordan to modern-day Pakistan. The growth of this church was marred by persecution and a steady stream of martyrs, including two bishops of Arbela, John in 343 and Abraham in 344. Christianity again flourished in Adiabene in the fifth century, with large numbers of churches and monasteries built.

Persia

As the Persian Empire spread during the third century, towns containing significant Christian populations were gradually overrun. Although there were already Christian communities within its bounds, the thousands of Christians from Greek- and Syriac-speaking villages deported into Persia brought with them their faith and church structures, and attracted a number of Persians to Christianity. They had to live out their faith in the context of constant cross-border warfare and amid non-orthodox Christian groups who had settled outside the borders of the Roman Empire. Asceticism proved attractive, especially among women, who devoted themselves to social ministries and prayer, although this left a shortage of Christian women for marriage.

By the fourth century there was a strong Christian presence in Persia, although it was divided by three languages: Greek, Syriac and Persian. As conversions increased, so did accusations of Christians being disloyal to the Persian kings and religion. They were called to either pay large fines, abandon Christianity or face martyrdom. There are indications that many thousands were martyred in Persia at a time when persecutions in the Roman Empire were ending. With that empire publicly identified as a Christian empire, being a Christian in the Persian Empire attracted suspicions of collusion with the enemy. This fuelled efforts to declare the Persian church independent of Constantinople.

The inclinations of the Persian church towards asceticism were reflected in the works of Aphraates (Aphrahat in Syriac) who wrote twenty-three treatises between 325 and 345. In the fifth and sixth centuries the theological school at Nisibis became an important intellectual centre for the churches of Asia, as theological and ecclesiastical separation from the Byzantine churches brought more secure times for Christians. The school at Nisibis was eventually split over whether to adopt the Chalcedonian Creed on the person of Christ, which had never been accepted by the East Syrian Church.

Persian Christians had strong connections with other Christian groups in Caucasia. Mar Aba I (d. 552), a convert from Zoroastrianism, then the national religion of Persia, was trained in theology at Edessa and taught at Nisibis before he was elected head of the East Syrian Church (540–52). When the Persian government exiled him to Azerbaijan he worked to lead the church from there. Azerbaijan was at the time part of Caucasian Albania, whose ruler, King Urnayr, had officially adopted Christianity as the state religion in the fourth century. Caucasian Albania remained a Christian state until the eighth century.

There is evidence of a Christian presence among Arabic-speaking people from the second century onwards, fostered by commercial relationships with Syriac and Coptic merchants. By the fifth century numerous Arabic Christian centres had developed around the Persian Gulf and Red Sea coasts. Christian mission was undertaken in the kingdom of Himyar in Arabia during the fourth century. Although it attained its political freedom in 378, Christians in Himyar faced intense persecution early in the sixth century because of their associations with Ethiopia. Between 523 and 525 Ethiopian forces were encouraged by Justin I, the Byzantine emperor, to mount an expedition to rescue these Christians, but with limited success. Southern Arabia fell under Persian control until the Islamic conquests.

Armenia

Various traditions attribute the evangelization of Armenia in the first century to Addai, also linked to mission in Arbela and Edessa. Others suggest the apostles Bartholomew or Thaddeus (for whom Addai might be another name). Exactly when significant Christian communities developed is uncertain, but at the end of the second century Tertullian was writing of Christian villages in Armenia. The early liturgies and the Bible versions used indicate that the influence of travelling Christian traders and their families from Syria played an important role. Armenia also found itself caught in the conflict between the Roman and Persian empires.

Armenia preceded Rome in becoming the first officially Christian state when King Tiridates III converted to Christianity. The traditional account of his conversion presents him as a one-time persecutor of Christians, but after suffering acute mental illness he turned for help to a local Christian leader Gregory, whom he had previously tortured and thrown in a dungeon. Gregory's prayers brought a remarkable healing, and the king and his family were baptized in around 300. After he was appointed a bishop Gregory oversaw Tiridates III's policy of state support for Christianity. Armenian identity became closely associated with Christianity. A complete Bible translation into Armenian was completed within a few decades. Gregory's son, Aristakes, succeeded him as king and represented Armenia at the Council of Nicaea in 325.

However, in the mid-fourth century Armenian princes martyred a number of church leaders after they demanded social justice and challenged moral lapses in the royal family. Armenia was also caught in the power play between the Roman and Persian empires, with Christians persecuted because they were seen as covert supporters of the Romans. The fifth century saw a restoration of the Armenian king and freedom of religion. In an attempt to restrict the damaging influence of external powers over Armenia, a separate alphabet, church hierarchy and structure was introduced.

Many Syriac, Greek and Arabic Christian writings were translated into Armenian, ensuring some works were preserved which would otherwise have been lost, together with a significant amount of original theological writing. The theological identity of the church was also linked to the attempt to form a national identity for the church. In 506 representatives of churches from the Caucasus, including Georgia, gathered to decide whether they would adhere to the decisions of the Council of Chalcedon (451). Partly as a way of affirming its independence from the political–religious sphere of the Roman–Byzantine world, and of reducing the Persian hostility associated with that, the Armenian Church rejected the Chalcedonian understanding of Christ in favour of a miaphysite expression. It was the only church of those who gathered to maintain this position long-term, with the others reverting to the Chalcedonian position. From the fourth century onwards, the Armenian Church helped to unite Armenians against foreign pressure and influence.

Georgia

Georgia also became strongly Christian in the fourth century. In the account of the origins of Christianity in Georgia given by Rufinus at the end of that century, the key figure was a Christian slave woman, Nino, from Cappadocia, who was reputed to possess healing gifts. These were brought to the attention of Queen Nana, and through Nino's prayers the queen was reportedly healed. Nino also helped to save the king, Mirian, when on a hunting expedition. As a result both were converted, and at Nino's instruction a church was built at Mcxeta in about 330 and Byzantine priests were sent for, to teach the Georgian church. By the fifth century a Georgian Bible had been produced. The independence of Georgia as a church and state was asserted by King Vaghtan Gorgaslan (446–510), leading to the rejection of the Chalcedonian Definition of the faith for a short period after the church council held in Armenia in 506. It was accepted near the end of the sixth century.

India

There are few written sources which record the progress of Christianity further east in the early centuries. Alongside the much-questioned traditions about apostolic missionary visits, there is evidence of the presence of Christian communities in both north and south India in the second century. Christian theologians from Alexandria travelled to India to study during the second and third centuries. At the Council of Nicaea John of Persia represented Persian and Indian churches, and Persian Syriac documents indicate regular contacts between churches in India and Persia, fostered by the regular trade between the regions. David, bishop of al-Basra (c. 300) in Persia, was reported to have given up his episcopate in order to travel to India to work as an evangelist.

In the fourth century Christian communities in India appear more strongly in the historical record, and the churches in Kerala were placed under the authority of a bishop located in the Persian Gulf. The Thomas Christians, with roots traceable to the fourth or fifth centuries AD, were able to forge a respectable place in Indian society. Syrian influences are seen in their tendency towards dyophysite (Nestorian) views, and Indian scholars also made their way to the centre of theological learning in Edessa. Here Daniel the Indian helped prepare a new translation of the Epistle to the Romans from Greek into Syriac (c. 425). By the late fifth century there may also have been a Christian community in Sri Lanka, although its origins are uncertain.

As with other parts of the Middle East, the Caucasus and Asia, it was the well-trodden trade routes into China and Tibet, which ran through northern Iran and Afghanistan from the Persian and Roman empires, that served as arteries along which the Christian message spread. Jewish communities were found in many cities along these routes, including Ecbatana (Hamedan in Iran), the burial site of the biblical Queen Esther. There seems to have been a Christian presence here as early as the second century and in other parts of Central Asia, including Kushan. By the end of the fifth century, missionaries had established churches in Bactria, between the Hindu Kush and the Oxus River, now in Afghanistan, and Tajikistan. Bishops from the East Syrian Church were also established in Herat (Afghanistan), at Merv on the ancient silk road in Turkmenistan and at Samarkand in Uzbekistan.

China

The Syrian gnostic writer Bardaisan (154–222) claimed that there were Christians in China as early as 180. Around 578 an East Syrian missionary, Mar Sergius, was living in Lint'ao in Gansu province, central China. By 635 another, Alopen (Aluoben), had reached China with a mandate to organize the Christians and to represent them before the emperor. Permission was given to start the first monasteries, including one in the imperial capital Xi'an, during the reign of the emperor T'ai-Tsung (627–49). A black limestone 'stele' almost 10 feet tall dated 781, and covering the period back to 635, is inscribed with the names of Syriac and Chinese Christian leaders in China. It includes statements of the Christian faith in Chinese and a list of Chinese Christian texts. Early Chinese Christian documents have also been excavated in western China: East Syrian Christianity had reached the Chinese imperial court, with attempts to make it understandable in a Taoist and Buddhist context. There are suggestions of a Christian presence in Japan in the period after it reached China. So too in Mongolia after 1007 when the Mongol ruler, the khan of the Keraits, accepted Christianity, followed by many of his people.

Although the collapse of the Tang dynasty in 907 closed the trade routes which had been the lifeline of the Chinese church, Christianity was certainly neither a seventeenth-century nor a nineteenth-century Western import into

China. Gospel transmission was more often from person to person than by missionary endeavour, crossing boundaries of culture and language, although this transfer brought with it a greater degree of theological variety than found in the Latin-speaking West. The dreadful persecution some Christians faced as enemies of the State made churches anxious to assert their doctrinal and ecclesiological independence of the Byzantine church, making miaphysite and East Syrian versions of Christianity more prevalent in the East.

Egypt

From its earliest days Christianity spread rapidly among the Greek-speaking population of Egypt, but also among the non-Greek-speaking Copts. Although rejected at the Council of Chalcedon, the influence of Cyril of Alexandria's teaching remained strong. Here the locally revered Bishop Dioscorus I was deposed in 451 for asserting the 'one nature' of Christ. Imperial Christian leaders oscillated between attempting to win back the Miaphysites by concessions and using brutal tactics to assert Chalcedonian orthodoxy. Non-Chalcedonian miaphysite teaching was strengthened by using the native Egyptian language of Coptic alongside Greek for the liturgy. The translation of Greek texts into Coptic, and significant engagement with Egyptian culture and local religious traditions between the third and sixth centuries, shaped a distinctive and deeply rooted form of Christianity. By the sixth century, non-Chalcedonian churches were dominant in Egypt. The Coptic Orthodox Church developed widespread connections with the churches in Syria, Iran and Iraq, as well as pushing southwards to Nubia and Ethiopia, and on to the Arabian Peninsula.

Nubia, Sudan and Ethiopia

Trade routes running south of Egypt along the Nile into Nubia and northern Sudan furthered the expansion of Christianity in that direction. Around 373 Athanasius of Alexandria consecrated Marcus as bishop of Philae in this region. By the middle of the sixth century Christianity was the official religion of the Nubian kingdoms.

It is possible that Christianity began in Ethiopia with the return of the official converted through the witness of Philip (Acts 8:26–40), but the first formal accounts are from the fourth century. These are traditionally associated with the work of two brothers, Frumentius and Aedesius, from Tyre, who were shipwrecked on the Ethiopian coast. Frumentius is credited with converting

Ezana the ruler (c. 320s–360) of the northern Ethiopian state of Aksum. They became officials in the Ethiopian government, and according to tradition Frumentius made his way to Alexandria where he was ordained bishop of Ethiopia by Athanasius. Fourth-century coins minted with crosses on them confirm the presence of Christianity in Ethiopia. Ezana left a fourth-century inscription announcing his adoption of the Christian trinitarian God and rejecting his previous status as a son of the Ethiopian war god. However, the Ethiopian Church followed the Copts in rejecting the Chalcedonian Definition of the faith. This was furthered by the missionary work of refugees – the legendary 'Nine Saints' from Mesopotamia and Palestine where Miaphysites were facing persecution – who worked in Egypt and Ethiopia in the late fifth century. By the sixth century much of Ethiopia was Christian, but links with the Semitic world led the Ethiopian Church to honour the Jewish Sabbath, practise circumcision (male and female) and follow some Jewish dietary laws.

Augustine

The churches along the north coast of Africa, where there was widespread Roman settlement, had close connections with Italy and Spain. From this region came Augustine (354–430), an African theological and ecclesiastical colossus. He ministered at a time of deteriorating political and social conditions in the Roman Empire, with rising taxes and inflation, and a growing military threat from the Persians in the east and the Germanic tribes in the north.

Augustine

Augustine was brought up in Thagaste (in modern Algeria). His mother, Monica, was a Christian; his father, Patricius, a pagan, who appears late in life to have converted to Christianity. Monica was not well educated but had a single-minded determination, marked by many tears and prayers, that Augustine would choose the Christian path. Augustine undertook higher-level study in Carthage (in modern Tunisia), abandoning himself to the social, sensual and intellectual opportunities of student life, before studying pagan philosophy and literature in Rome. Along the way he took to himself a mistress, whose name is not recorded, with whom he lived for fifteen years and by whom he had a son, Adeodatus.

During his twenties Augustine began a search for spiritual reality. His *Confessions* (397) explain how he explored pagan philosophy, then Gnosticism and Manichaeism. He eventually moved to Milan, where he encountered the powerful preaching of Ambrose (c. 339–97). In him Augustine found the first serious Christian intellect he could respect, especially for his conviction that the Christian Scripture was the source of true wisdom. In 385, as his religious search deepened, so did consciousness of sin. Social convention dictated that because his mistress was from a lower class they could not marry, so he put her aside, sadly, for 'I loved her dearly'. Adeodatus stayed with him. He embraced the celibate life, battling to understand the issue of sin and how that related to sexuality, which he equated with lust.

In the midst of a growing spiritual crisis, in 386 Augustine was walking in a garden in Milan when he reported hearing the voice of a nearby child calling, 'Take it and read.' Taking this as a word from God, he went inside, opened the Bible and read Romans 13:14: 'Rather, clothe yourselves with the Lord Jesus Christ, and do not think about how to gratify the desires of the sinful nature.' With this came his conversion and the answer to his mother's prayers. He was baptized by Ambrose at Easter-time 387.

Augustine believed God had given him intellectual abilities for a purpose. He debated intensely with his cultured friends on the new Christian ideas he had adopted, becoming the centre of a vibrant Christian intellectual community. But, much as he desired it, the retired life of a Christian scholar was not to be for him. When he visited North Africa in 391 he was importuned by the struggling Christian community in Hippo (now Annaba in Algeria) to accept the priesthood and become assistant bishop. He was appointed bishop five years later.

North Africa still had a significant pagan presence and was beset by regional political complexities. The Donatist issue had never been fully resolved and had created what was effectively a parallel nonconformist church. The Donatists accepted Catholic doctrine but not its claim to absolute authority over church affairs. They took a strict 'puritan' line on morality and associating with unbelievers, convinced there should be no compromise with the world. Augustine, instead, compared the church to the parable of the wheat and the tares, arguing that separation between believers and unbelievers should be left to God at the end of time. Through writings and debates Augustine attempted reconciliation, but the majority of the Donatists did not return to the fold. In 405 some Donatists were associated with a local revolt, and an imperial edict branded

Donatism heretical and illegal. Augustine supported the harsh repressive efforts to restore the separatists to the church, questionably applying the biblical text 'Compel them to come in' (Luke 14:23 KJV) to justify this.

Augustine was convinced that only the sacraments administered by the Catholic Church were effective and that schism was the worst of sins. Attempting to impose uniformity only created more division. Out of this episode came Augustine's teachings on the 'Just War', which was legitimate if declared by the proper authorities, waged to defend proper rights, and conducted by means proportionate to the threat and exercised with mercy. It was a sad episode, with brutal behaviour on both sides. The outcome was the gradual crushing of Donatism, which was in some ways an indigenized and independent African expression of Christianity. The conflict served only to weaken Christianity in North Africa.

Augustine's theological contribution was enormous. In *The City of God* (413–26), written in the aftermath of the sack of the 'eternal city', Rome, he sets out his understanding of the role of the church on the earth. *On the Trinity* offers a classic orthodox statement of trinitarian doctrine. His understanding of the way of salvation and the God of grace is set out during the Pelagian controversy, which began after the British monk Pelagius began an influential ministry in Rome. Pelagius taught that sin was not something inherited from one's parents; rather it came from outside, learned by exposure to bad example and society at large. Indeed humans had absolute free will to choose to sin or not, meaning there was no excuse for sin. Perfection was therefore possible in this life. When this teaching reached North Africa, Augustine rigorously rebutted it, arguing that Pelagius's emphasis on the freedom of the will left no room for the grace of God. Because of Adam's fall, all were guilty and none deserved salvation. Self-control was no answer – free will was marred, and without the help of God none could choose the way of God. Salvation was only possible by the grace of God; otherwise all would be lost because of the stain of original sin. Augustine also spoke of predestination, God's established plan to save and keep those he chose in eternity as his children.

Augustine's significance cannot be overplayed. Not only did his theological ideas lie at the heart of many of the debates of medieval theologians, but also in some ways the Reformation was a debate between Augustine's teaching on grace and the institutional legacy of his teaching on the church. He was brilliant, controversial and complex. Augustine held firm to his convictions as the world around him crumbled. Berbers in North Africa began to assert their identity, and then Vandal tribes crossed from Spain into North Africa. Augustine died in 430 with the city of Hippo under siege and crowded with refugees. The ancient world was collapsing. The fertile lands of North Africa would before long revert to desert, and the Christian presence drift away into the sands. The strong point of Western Christianity remained asceticism, which was growing in extent and significance, and owed some debt to Augustine's own practice.

The faint outlines of a global church could now be discerned. Christianity had grown, and faltered, in the Western Roman Empire, but now it stretched far beyond the Eastern Roman Empire. Here the Arab church, the Christians of Syria, Iraq and Iran, and further east, were called to live as minorities under successive waves of persecution. Across the emerging global church, almost all were in theological agreement about trinitarian theology and the deity of Christ. They agreed that humanity and divinity were united in the incarnate Christ, but not on how this had taken place. Christian leaders from Iran, Iraq, Armenia or Ethiopia had not been invited to contribute to the debates at Nicaea and Chalcedon, and the solutions agreed focused on promoting unity within the Roman Empire rather than finding a global ecumenical solution. So fierce was the resultant rivalry over such complex mysteries that some Syriac and Coptic Christians welcomed Islamic rule as preferable to the harsh opposition of Christians with whom they disagreed. Western Christianity was beginning to look different from that expressed in many parts of Asia and Africa.

8. REFLECTING INWARDLY AND REACHING OUT

Lifeline
c. 251 – birth of Anthony
c. 314 – conversion of Pachomius
370 – Basil of Caesarea ordained a bishop
412 – Symeon Stylites becomes a solitary monk
c. 415 – John Cassian founds monastery near Marseilles
c. 440 – Patrick begins mission in Ireland
496 – baptism of Clovis, king of the Franks
c. 529 – Benedict of Nursia founds monastery at Monte Cassino
563 – Columba settles on Iona
597 – Augustine arrives in Kent
634 – Aidan arrives at Lindisfarne, Northumbria
664 – Synod of Whitby

As they grow, children become increasingly aware not only of their surroundings but also of themselves. They begin to look inwards, and reflect on their own identity and how that relates to the wider world. During the period known as 'late antiquity' (c. 250–750), Christianity survived terrible persecution, consolidated, fell under threat and then expanded again; there was a growing emphasis on the need to bring discipline to the inward life and to keep firm control of the body. This became a strong feature of religious understanding and practice, and a powerful dimension of spiritual warfare. But looking inwards also strengthened the capacity of the church to maintain the faith and provided a base from which to engage in outreach.

Asceticism

Asceticism had numerous strands. To some it was the 'silent revolution', a quiet but sustained protest – often lay-led, especially after 312 – against an official imperial Christianity that was becoming centralized and bureaucratic, and losing the freedom, spontaneity and lay leadership of the past. Others were frustrated at the way lax lifestyles and nominal adherence were increasingly tolerated in church life. Although asceticism predates Constantine's rise, the ascetic movement was in some way a renewal movement from within the church. It combined a 'charismatic' emphasis on direct engagement with the Holy Spirit – spiritual warfare with demons – with a 'puritan' devotional quest for holiness and purity. The ascetic stressed self-denial, especially of the appetites of the body for food, wealth and possessions, worldly career and ambition, and sexual expression in marriage and family life. In his work *On Virginity* Gregory of Nyssa (330–95) described the intent of asceticism as to weaken 'bodily desire' and build a high wall of separation between the self and the senses, so that the Christian could 'inquire into the true object of desire', which was the ultimate reason 'we have received from our Maker our power of desiring'. Crucifying the self in this way made the Christian worthy to see God.

The world into which Christianity was born was familiar with the ascetic lifestyle, which was viewed as a mark of seriousness by some pagan philosophers. Within Judaism the Essenes and the Qumran community showed an ascetic tendency towards separation from the world. Some Christians began to believe such behaviour was an important part of devotion to Christ, believing denial of the body was a means of spiritual gain. There were scriptural patterns to follow. John the Baptist had lived an ascetic life. Jesus Christ himself lived in poverty and simplicity, never marrying, never owning a home, devoting his life to teaching and service to others. Jesus told the rich young ruler to 'go, sell your possessions and give to the poor, and you will have treasure in heaven' (Matt. 19:21). He spoke of those who renounced marriage for the kingdom of heaven (Matt. 19:11–12). Fasting and prayer were important New Testament disciplines. The apostle Paul wrote of the calling to singleness for some (1 Cor. 7) and of beating his body (whether physically or metaphorically) in 1 Corinthians 9:27.

The first evidence of widespread ascetic practice appears to have come in the aftermath of the persecutions under Decius in 250, and then in the Great

Persecution at the end of the third century. The martyrs were viewed with deep veneration as expressing the highest form of Christianity possible. After the persecutions were over, and 'red martyrdom' was no longer called for, 'white martyrdom' or 'living martyrdom' became an alternative. It became widely practised in Egypt, Palestine, Syria and Asia Minor. The holy men and women who chose this practice were believed to have a special connection with the divine and to be closest to God. They were deeply venerated in life, as were their relics after death. In the Middle East a retreat into the desert was fairly easy; indeed it had been necessary sometimes during the persecutions. In Egypt a rigorous form of Christianity had been practised in the third century by leaders such as Origen, who drank no wine, slept on the floor, went barefoot and may have castrated himself to ensure his sexual purity.

Anthony

The Egyptian ascetic Anthony (c. 251–356) is often portrayed as the first monk, but he appears to have been following the example of others. When he was a young man, around the year 270, his parents died, leaving him with the care of his younger sister. In church he heard a sermon on Matthew 19:21 and was troubled by his very comfortable economic state. He decided he needed to do what Jesus had told the young man to do to be 'perfect'. He sold his estates, encouraged by the text 'Do not be anxious about tomorrow' (Matt. 6:34 ESV). Leaving his sister in the care of a small community of Christian women, he set out on a new lifestyle of self-denial, prayer, meditation and pastoral work, learning from the example of others.

Then Anthony retreated deep into the desert wilderness, where he lived in a cave in the rocks, wearing simple animal-skin clothing (with the hair on the inside to help him renounce the flesh) and adopting a simple diet mainly of bread and water. His aim was not solely retreat. Anthony believed he was going into battle, not only with the flesh but also against the powers of evil (the desert was often perceived as the abode of demons), engaging in spiritual warfare for the sake of the community. For twenty years he lived alone like this on a remote mountain in the desert, and many travelled to seek his spiritual counsel. The *Life of Anthony*, attributed to Athanasius, is an idealized portrait of the holy life, written in the heightened hagiographical *panegyric* style. It tells of remarkable devotion and sacrifice, to which are added extraordinary accounts of spiritual battles, wrestling with demons, visions and miraculous occurrences. The work became a bestseller and did much to legitimate asceticism.

At a strategic moment in 311, Anthony reappeared from the wilderness to tend those suffering from persecution who had been imprisoned or forced to work in the mines, and to offer himself for the ultimate sacrifice in the Great Persecution raging at the time. That was not called for then, but he reappeared in 337–8 to stand by Athanasius in his heroic resistance to the Arians. Rather than weakening him, the ascetic life appears to have energized him – when he died he was apparently over a hundred years old.

Many others began to imitate the example of Anthony and retreat from society to the solitary state. They saw this as the place to find the truly 'spiritual' life, rather than in the organized churches. By 390 it was estimated that there were 2,000 monks living in the desert around Alexandria alone. Those who dwelt in the wilderness became known as the Desert Fathers, the holy men who, of all people, were closest to God. Stripping away the trappings of the daily life, they equipped themselves for spiritual warfare. The prayers of the ascetics were especially valued, with people from neighbouring villages travelling out to ask monks to pray for them, and to seek their advice and direction. They were considered the experts on the spiritual life, blessed by God. Their words were collected together as the 'Sayings of the Desert Fathers'.

Another famous ascetic was Symeon Stylites (c. 390–459). In 412 he left a monastery to become a solitary monk, living for a while chained to a mountain-side. He then spent thirty years living on a platform just 4 metres wide at the top of an 18-metre-high column. He devoted himself largely to prayer. This remarkable 'pillar of the community' attracted vast crowds, seeking his prayers and listening to him preach or offer words of wisdom. A number of tribespeople were converted, and burned their fetishes at the base of the column. Symeon even resolved community disputes. Living outside villages and towns, such figures became like 'patron saints' for the local community.

Anthony and the Desert Fathers represent the individual, 'eremitical' version of asceticism. Others who adopted the ascetic lifestyle chose to live in community rather than in isolation. The term 'monasticism', from the Greek word *monastes*, meaning a monk, originally referred to someone living a hermit-like lifestyle, in solitude, but came to refer to single, unmarried people, choosing to live separately from the secular world in a community as a full-time religious vocation. The vision of the monastic life was one of moral and spiritual holiness, with the conviction that separation from the wider world protected the individual from distraction and unnecessary temptation. Monks or nuns often took on a new name, representing their change of identity. Monastic life vows of poverty, celibacy and unquestioning obedience became part of entering the monastic vocation, especially in the West, whereas Eastern monasticism remained more unstructured.

Pachomius

In the long term the community, or 'cenobitic', form of asceticism was to become the most popular version. A key figure in this development was Pachomius (c. 292–c. 346), from Egypt, who founded a monastery at Tabennesse. He had been a soldier in the army when he was converted, in around 314, through the kindness of local Christians towards a group of raw recruits far from home. After he left the army he lived for a while with an older ascetic, before starting his monastic community on a bend in the River Nile with a small group of followers. His approach to the spiritual life proved extraordinarily popular. By the time of his death in 345 there were 1,300 in his community and 7,000 in other associated monasteries. Pachomius introduced an orderly religious life: monks lived in cells, which were grouped into houses, with a superior over each. They were to worship twice a day and spend other time in reading and learning Scripture (especially the Psalms), and in prayer. The community was to be self-sufficient, with monks engaged in a simple trade (such as mat making or weaving) to pay their way. The rules ensured that some of the excesses of individual asceticism were avoided.

Basil of Caesarea

By the late fourth century there were 490 monastic communities in Egypt. Leaders such as Athanasius worked hard to ensure these did not become isolated from the mainstream of church life. Basil of Caesarea (330–79), also known as Basil 'the Great', one of the Cappadocian Fathers, also sought to harness monasticism to the church, with a view to the service of society. His commitment to the Christian faith owed much to the influence of his mother and sister, and he was also deeply impressed by the lives of the monks he met. He was resolved to live a monastic life but accepted ordination as a deacon and then presbyter. Basil worked to combine church leadership with an ascetic lifestyle, and in 370 he was ordained a bishop. Basil set out a series of 'Rules' for the monks who lived in his area. They were to come out from their desert isolation and, rather than being fully preoccupied with their own souls, should live at the heart of the community which they were to serve. They were to worship regularly in the cathedral both day and night, with a monastic choir being established. Monks served society by running schools and hospitals. The worshipping, self-supporting fraternity of Pachomius had been transformed into a community of service, closely bound to the mainstream church, with the excesses and individuality of earlier expressions giving way to a more orderly and systematic life.

Jerome

Another monastic figure who did much to legitimate the ascetic life within the mainstream of the church, and connect it with learning, was Jerome (c. 347–c. 420). He was born at Stridon on the Adriatic, brought up in a Christian family and educated in Rome. He was baptized around the age of eighteen by Pope Liberius. He taught himself Hebrew and devoted himself to a life of scholarly study in some of the best libraries, and also to ascetic practice. In Antioch Jerome accepted ordination as a priest but only on the condition that he be allowed to continue to live as a monk. Eventually he left Rome to build a monastery in Bethlehem, near the site of the nativity, and also houses for three communities of women. He himself lived and worked in a large cave, and he opened a free school and also a hostel for pilgrims. His practice of the ascetic life was extremely rigorous, fasting until his bones protruded and wearing only sackcloth. With his growing learning he found himself increasingly asked to comment on doctrinal disputes. In the years after 382, Jerome was asked by Pope Damasus to produce a revised Latin translation of the New Testament, based on the Greek text. He also eventually translated most of the Old Testament using the Hebrew text rather than the Greek Septuagint previously used. Jerome's translation became known as the *versio vulgata*, the 'commonly used translation'. The Vulgate was pronounced the authoritative Bible version for the Roman Catholic Church in the sixteenth century by the Council of Trent. Jerome was buried in the Church of the Holy Nativity.

Jerome

Monasticism in the West

Monasticism was a very diverse phenomenon. On the one hand it allowed a freedom of expression and a role for the laity, demonstrating deep Christian devotion and commitment. But it also suggested the influence of Greek philosophy and Gnosticism, both of which were suspicious of the body, viewing it as a barrier to personal spiritual development. Early monasticism developed strongly in the eastern part of the Roman Empire, but a key figure in the transference of this model of spirituality and devotion to the West was John Cassian (c. 360–435). He was deeply impressed by the example of Pachomius in Egypt, where he learned of the monastic life, and also of other ascetics in Palestine. When he travelled to the south of France (c. 415) he founded near Marseilles two of the first monasteries in the West. He set out a series of rules to help the Gallic monks, mixing contemplation and activity.

Benedict of Nursia

John Cassian was to influence Benedict of Nursia (480–547), who in around 529 founded the famous monastery at Monte Cassino in Italy. Drawing on the rules of John Cassian and Basil of Caesarea he developed his own rule for his monks, which was extensively popularized in the late sixth century by Pope Gregory the Great. The Benedictine order, which stressed obedience without a moment's hesitation, service to other monks, contemplation, silence, and worship seven times a day, was to become one of the most significant of the following centuries. The monastery was to be a 'school to train men in the service of the Lord', and could be used by laypeople for retreats. This order of monasteries was reformed by Benedict of Aniane, who created a network of monasteries with standards and practices that were accessible and capable of attracting recruits more easily. Between 800 and 1000, Benedictine monasticism was to dominate the European landscape.

Also important in the development of Gallic monasticism was Martin of Tours, who after a period as a solitary hermit began a monastery at Ligugé in southern France. In 370 he was made bishop of Tours, seemingly against his will, but continued to live a life of poverty and simplicity. His work proved an inspiration for other monks, who undertook mission work through establishing monasteries which could serve as centres for outreach to scattered communities, including those on the Celtic fringes of Britain.

The spread of monasticism from the East in the fourth and fifth centuries represented a significant change in social, political and religious culture. By the fifth century monasticism was a major institution within Christianity. It attracted through its doors the full range of society, from the aristocratic elite, through the middle ranks, to eccentrics and poor uneducated people. Major church councils began to devote their attention to it, with monks playing a significant role in resolving church disputes. Although it had in some ways challenged official, imperial Christianity, it had been drawn into the mainstream of church life. This ability of the Catholic Church to embrace those who might otherwise have been on the fringes of church life was significant, and an achievement that had not been possible with Montanism or Donatism. Alongside Basil of Caesarea, it is slightly ironic that another key figure in achieving this was Augustine of Hippo, who had rejected the ascetic approach of Manichaeism. Both Basil and Augustine sought to channel the ascetic ideal to benefit the ordinary Christian in everyday life and help it to serve the church and its learning.

Monastics and mission

The missionary potential for monasticism soon became apparent. Much of the expansion of the church into the East came through establishing monastic communities, where monks could live and worship, find some protection and mutual support, and also engage in outreach into local societies. This also became a pattern in the Western part of the empire. The spread of Christianity from the fourth to sixth centuries was not just owing to the imposition of a top-down policy. Ambrose, bishop of Milan, was a formidable religious, social and political figure, who had previously been governor of the province in which Milan was set. But he was also a powerful and attractive preacher, as Augustine had found, as well as being a man of compassion. When he became bishop the first thing he did was to distribute his great wealth among the poor. Christianity was willingly embraced by large numbers across society, from the municipal and senatorial elites to many in the lower classes. Some did so simply because of the advantages Christian profession now brought, while others were drawn to its message and ethos.

Germans, Goths and Franks

Just as Christian communities evolved along the trade routes heading east into Asia and south into Africa, the same happened further west. At the start of the fourth century, the western regions of the Roman Empire were far less Christianized than those of the eastern, with perhaps only 2% of the population being Christians. They tended to be found in urban areas, with large swathes of rural Europe relatively untouched by the Christian gospel. The growing political division between the western and the eastern parts of the Roman Empire was also reflected in the church. As borders in the north of Europe along the Rhine and Danube became less secure, political power shifted towards Constantinople. The German tribes from the north which began to overrun Gaul, Italy and Spain were not all pagan, but many were unorthodox Christians, having been influenced by the teachings of Arian missionaries.

Christianity had spread into the Germanic world through the Goths, who arrived north of the Black Sea in the 230s. Christianity was first seen in Moldavia and eastern Romania after a group of Christians were abducted during a Gothic invasion of Cappadocia (Inner Anatolia) in 257. They were able to preserve their Christian faith and pass it on to their descendants, who settled in their Gothic environment. A formal Christian community was established with its own bishop, Theophilus, bishop of Gothia. He attended the Council of Nicaea in 325. The Christians in Gothia were largely Christian exiles rather than converts from the local community.

The conversion of the Franks to Christianity followed the conversion of Clovis. After he became king in 481, he successfully united the Frankish tribes. His kingdom began in what is now modern Belgium, and he extended it south and west to the Seine and the Loire, gaining ground from the Romans. Around 492 he married a Christian, Clotilda, and his conversion to Christianity from paganism followed sometime afterwards; an unexpected victory in battle may have contributed to this decision. He was baptized on Christmas Day 496. His decision to adopt Nicene orthodoxy was highly significant, for Catholics were in a minority in Gaul, owing to the work of the fourth-century missionary Ulfilas who had converted the pagan Goths to the Arian form of Christianity. The

Iona
Lindisfarne
Derry
Whithorn
Kells
York
Clonfert
St Albans
Llantwit Major
London
Canterbury
Dorchester
Aachen
Rhine
Danube
Seine
Paris
Orléans
Tours
Loire
Milan
Marseilles
Rome
Monte Cassino
CHRISTIANITY IN WESTERN EUROPE – FIFTH TO NINTH CENTURIES
0 km 400
0 miles 300

Visigoths and Vandals had also embraced Arian Christianity. Through decisive victories in battle against the Alemanni (496), the Burgundians (500) and the Visigoths (in 507), Clovis helped to establish a unified trinitarian and Catholic religion across what is now France and Germany. Gregory of Tours, who wrote his *History of the Franks* in the late sixth century, portrays Clovis as Gaul's Constantine. He became a powerful west European ally of the Byzantine emperor Anastasius I. The *Pactus Legis Salicae* (Law of the Salian Franks), a compilation of traditional laws, Roman written law, Christian ideals and royal edicts, probably comes from the time of Clovis. He worked closely with the Catholic bishops, summoning them to a church council at Orléans in 511, the probable year of his death. By then he controlled the northern and western parts of what had been Roman Gaul. He shaped a kingdom which formed the beginnings of France, with Paris as his capital.

Christianity in Britain and Ireland

By 150 Britain had been fully incorporated into the Roman Empire, although Roman influence did not reach much further north than central Scotland. The origins of Christianity in Roman Britain are obscure, especially as it had to function as a semi-secret religion until 313. The martyrdoms of Alban at Verulamium (now St Albans), and Julius and Jerome in the west of England, took place during the empire-wide persecutions of the third century. These deaths and other evidence suggest a Christian presence in some areas of Roman settlement in the third century, with more extensive evidence in major centres of settlement from the fourth century. A Romano-British cemetery from Dorchester in 350 suggests a quarter of that area's population was Christian. Christianity perhaps reached as far north as Carlisle, carried by merchants and soldiers stationed there in the border regions around Hadrian's Wall. However, after the Romans left Britain in the fifth century, invading pagan tribes from Europe destroyed much of what was left of the small Christian presence.

The sixth century was to see a mission of re-evangelizing Britain, especially from the Celtic fringes of western Britain and other parts of northern Europe, reaching areas that were beyond the previously settled Roman borders. Mission became important to the Western Church based in Rome as part of an attempt to reassert its spiritual leadership in the wake of the collapse of Roman political power and rule. Nicene Christianity was promoted, using Latin as the sacred language of liturgy and theological writing, and making use of the monastic movement.

Some monks fleeing barbarian advances in Gaul travelled to western Britain. One such may have been Illtyd (c. 425–505), who established a major Christian community at Llantwit Major in south Wales. Another important figure in the work of mission was Patrick, a native Briton possibly born somewhere near the Solway Firth in about 410. As a teenager he was kidnapped by Irish raiders and spent time in Ireland before he escaped back to Britain. However, Patrick had a vision calling him back to evangelize the tribes who had once kidnapped him, and he returned to Ireland in around 440. He was not the first missionary to Ireland, with the missionary-bishop Palladius having been sent by the bishop of Rome to work there for about ten years before Patrick arrived. Possibly other Christians were also already there, having sailed along the westerly trading routes from the Mediterranean, including Asia Minor, Syria and Egypt, where monasticism was strong. The Irish church developed a rich and flourishing intellectual life centred on the monasteries, at the same time as Christianity in much of the rest of Europe was struggling in the face of barbarian invasion. In the monasteries a strict asceticism was practised, with fervent prayer, deep devotion and dedication to mission. Brendan (c. 484–c. 577), who founded a monastery in Clonfert, Galway, sailed by coracle to Scotland, south-west England and Brittany. By legend he undertook an epic journey to the 'Isle of the Blessed', variously identified as the Canary Isles, the Azores and even America.

In mission to Scotland Ninian is an important, but less well-known, figure. His work was carried out sometime in the fifth or sixth century, based in the monastic settlement of Whithorn in Wigtownshire (a short sail from Ireland). Later accounts suggest he conducted an extensive work of mission across south-west Scotland. Ninian was seemingly influenced by the monastic tradition of Martin of Tours in Gaul, where he may have been trained or sent from. More widely known is Columba (521–97), a product of the Irish church, which was strongly monastic. Bishops were less significant than abbots and abbesses, and often connected with individual tribes. The Irish church became renowned for its devotion to Christian art. One example is the Book of Kells (c. 800), an illuminated manuscript of the New Testament. Education and a sense of connectedness with nature, which reflected the glory of God, were also important. The Irish church differed from the mainstream in Rome in a number of ways, and held only loosely to the authority of the bishop of Rome. The influence of the ascetic patterns of the Eastern Church seems quite strong, with parallels between the Christian art of the Celtic church, such as the high and decorated stone crosses and other religious symbols, and that found in Egypt and Armenia.

Columba was from a high-ranking noble family in the Gaelic Scots tribe, who lived in the north of Ireland. His involvement in tribal politics appears to have sparked a war in which many lives were lost. In 563 a deeply penitent

Columba vowed to leave Ireland and devote himself to a monastic life. He settled on the island of Iona, off the west coast of Scotland, a spot where his native Ireland was no longer visible. Here he started a monastic community, initially among Scots tribespeople who had migrated to the west coast of Scotland. Over time Iona became a missionary base for work among Picts, a tribe in mainland Scotland. His noble background helped him to negotiate access for his monks from the Pictish king. Their work helped firmly establish Christianity across Scotland, from the remote island of Eigg where Donnan worked (before he was murdered with fifty other monks by marauding Norse invaders in 617), to Glasgow where Mungo worked, and Paisley where Mirren worked. Iona also sent missionaries into the English kingdom of Northumbria at the request of its king, Oswald, who had spent a period of exile on Iona. When Aidan was sent from Iona to Northumbria in 634, he chose as his base the island of Lindisfarne, off the north-eastern coast. From here the Columban style of Christianity spread into the north of England.

Other missionaries from the Columban tradition, including Columbanus and Kilian, travelled into western Europe, planting monasteries with a strict penitential system and a devotion to art and learning. Columbanus, who was born around 540, travelled from Bangor in the north of Ireland to Gaul, and then Burgundy, where he sought to reach notable families. He established further monasteries in northern France, Switzerland and, in 616, at Bobbi in Italy. The Celtic model of Christianity was flexible, missionary-minded, highly mobile and transportable. Other monks from this area are thought to have reached Austria, Poland and Romania.

A Roman mission to the south of England was commissioned by Pope Gregory the Great, starting in 597, the year of Columba's death. There were already Christians in the region, but the arrival of Augustine (later of Canterbury) in Kent led to the baptism of King Ethelbert in 601 (his wife was already a Christian). A missionary base was established at Canterbury, which was later to become the principal see of the Church of England. With the support and encouragement of the royal family, many people in the south-east of England converted to Christianity, and mission across Anglo-Saxon England was undertaken. From here missionaries were sent into mainland Europe, such as Willibrord (658–739) who worked in areas under Frankish control, especially Frisia, and Boniface (680–754) who extended his work to the Germanic tribes.

In 664 the differences between the Irish and Columban expressions of Christianity, and those from the 'official' Roman mission to the rest of England, were resolved at the Synod of Whitby, with the Roman pattern of worship being accepted. In 667 Theodore of Tarsus was appointed the first Archbishop of Canterbury, ending the dynamic, missionary phase of the Christianization of England and replacing it with a more ordered, hierarchical church structure with settled parishes and parochial clergy.

Nonetheless, the role of the monasteries remained very significant. Not only were they a highly effective missionary tool, but they were also a vehicle whereby the traditions and teachings of the church could be preserved and articulated at a time when the western part of the Roman Empire was crumbling in the face of invasion by barbarian tribes. In socially and politically chaotic times, monasteries remained centres of learning and theological reflection. The first universities were modelled on the lifestyle and practice of the monasteries. Through extensive copying of the Bible and important Christian texts, vital resources for theological study and training were preserved. By the Middle Ages many monasteries had become the chief providers of education, and care for the sick and travellers. They were part of the fabric of medieval Europe, owning vast areas of land, developing high levels of skill in farming, and amassing great wealth. The ascetic life was also becoming the expected pattern for clergy and bishops, especially the commitment to celibacy.

9. DISAGREEMENTS AND RIVALRIES

Lifeline

590 – Gregory (the Great) becomes pope
622 – Muhammad flees to Medina
732 – Charles Martel defeats Arab forces at Poitiers
800 – coronation of Charlemagne as Holy Roman Emperor
1054 – Pope Leo IX and Patriarch of Constantinople excommunicate each other
1095 – First Crusade proclaimed
1291 – end of the Crusades

As children grow, sometimes they fall out or fight with siblings and their friends. Usually such incidents pass and relationships are quickly restored, but there are times when seeds of bitterness and division are sown that are deep and long-lasting. As Christianity moved from its early years into the so-called Dark Ages (c. 600–c. 1200), such tensions became a significant part of its experience. Yet the term 'Dark Ages' is misleading, for Christianity in this period was often filled with vitality, stretching from India, to northern and central Africa, and to the far north-west of Europe. This period brought enormous change, the most significant being the rise of Islam. Christianity was increasingly defined by the institutions which controlled it and by the development of a distinctive institutional hierarchy. Asceticism continued to be extremely significant in both East and West.

The rise of Rome

By the early fourth century Rome, the largest city of the empire and the seat of imperial power, was the only patriarchal centre in the west of the Roman Empire. Damasus, bishop of Rome from 366 to 384, referred to it as the 'apostolic see', connecting the office to the apostle Peter. In 451 the Council of Chalcedon gave Rome and Constantinople equal privileges, but considered the bishop of Rome the 'interpreter of the voice of Peter'. Under Leo I (bishop of Rome 440–61) appeals were made to Matthew 16:15–19 to legitimize the pope (from 'papa', meaning father) as the successor to Peter. Rome's political influence was seriously weakened by the fifth-century barbarian invasions, and the papacy increasingly filled a power vacuum. Gregory the Great, who became pope in 590, organized the defence of the city when it was besieged by the Lombards, and concluded peace without reference to the emperor. Gregory developed the Roman Catholic 'curia' (court), with an army of church lawyers and administrators.

The status and organization of the Roman church was further enhanced by Gregory VII (bishop of Rome 1073–85), who was determined to emphasize its universal rule above king or state. To Gregory, earthly rulers should not bestow office on clergy. He confronted Henry IV of Germany who had defied him over the right to appoint bishops. In a dramatic showdown Henry was forced to stand barefoot in the snow outside Canossa Castle, northern Italy, for three days as he pleaded with Gregory to lift the sentence of excommunication imposed on him. Gregory eventually allowed Henry inside and absolved him. Gregory's successors took the title not only of 'Vicar of Peter', but also 'Vicar of Christ', his representative on earth. Gregorian reforms included improving the moral and educational standards of the clergy, including stressing the importance of clerical celibacy. They ushered in an era of big government, or 'papal monarchy', which left little role for the laity and exerted close control over the everyday lives and thoughts of lay Christians.

Increasing numbers of pilgrims and petitioners made their way to Rome seeking resolution of ecclesiastical and personal issues. From the twelfth century a universal system of church (canon) law was set out in a systematic way, in which popes and bishops needed to be skilled. Gradually bishops took more power at the expense of the previously influential abbots and abbesses. Vast cathedrals came to dominate the heart of medieval cities such as Chartres, Rheims and Lincoln. Their towers and spires were designed to connect heaven with earth, soaring transepts lifting the eye and heart of the worshipper upwards to God, but also proclaiming the power and authority of the local bishop.

The claims of Rome appeared to be consolidated by the appearance in the eighth century of 'The Donation of Constantine'. This document claimed that when Constantine moved his imperial capital to Constantinople, the bishop of Rome was left pre-eminent in the church and that temporal authority in Western Europe was also placed in his 'safe' keeping. The exposure of this document as a forgery by Lorenzo Valla (1405–57) was one of the great scholarly discoveries of the Renaissance and did much to undermine confidence in the claims and prestige of the papacy before the Reformation. So too did attempts by later popes to resolve their disputes with earthly rulers by military means.

Charlemagne

Constantine's creation of a 'new Rome' in Constantinople added to the long-simmering conflict between the eastern and western parts of the Roman Empire, and significantly weakened Rome, as the barbarian invasions in the sixth and seventh centuries demonstrated. Eastern emperors proved reluctant to send assistance to the West. Popes instead played individual European kingdoms and the Byzantine emperors off against each other to secure alliances. After appeals for help from Byzantium proved futile, in 774 Pope Adrian I encouraged the king of the Franks, Charles (c. 747–814), to conquer the Lombard kingdom of northern Italy whose forces were threatening Rome. In turning to the man known by later admirers as Charlemagne, Adrian had chosen well. The conquest was successfully accomplished, and an alliance forged between the papacy and Frankish political power that had similarities with that between the Byzantine emperor and the Eastern Church. Charles' father had already granted the pope lands he had conquered in Italy, which became the Papal States.

The distinguished rule of Charlemagne lasted from 768 to 814. He was no mere 'barbarian'. He had a deep love of learning, was an astute military leader and, in contrast to other northern European rulers who had looted Rome, loved the city. His grandfather, Charles Martel, had famously halted the Muslim advance into France at Poitiers, and had appointed bishops and abbots at his own discretion. Charlemagne's father, Pepin (or Pippin) 'the Short', had legitimated his role by being

Charlemagne

crowned king by Boniface, the 'apostle' of Germany. Charlemagne built up a Frankish empire stretching from the Pyrenees to Germany, and from France to Switzerland. On Christmas Day 800, he was in St Peter's Church, Rome, to worship. As he knelt in prayer Pope Leo III placed a crown upon his head and crowned him 'Holy Roman Emperor', a new Constantine, although Charlemagne preferred to liken himself to Josiah in the Old Testament. It was an act of immense political and religious significance. Leo III boosted his authority by anointing an emperor and creating a rival axis of power to the Byzantine emperor. The growing East–West division deepened, especially after talks about marriage between Charlemagne and the Byzantine empress Irene came to nothing.

Charlemagne's statue on the bell tower of the great cathedral of Zurich, with the emperor wearing a golden crown, symbolizes the blessing of his rule by the church. But the relationship between a universal Christian monarchy ruling alongside a universal Christian spiritual head was complex and often difficult to manage. Charlemagne's achievements were many. He conquered the Saxons and forced their conversion to Christianity, and then pushed the Slavs out of Germany. He inspired an architectural revival, with great buildings, including cathedrals, modelled on patterns from the classical past. There was also a recovery of learning known as the 'Carolingian Renaissance', with a rediscovery of the great works of classical literature. What was effectively a revolution in information technology also took place. Scribes devised a regular written script, called Carolingian 'minuscule', on which modern typescript is based. It enabled easy reading, fast writing and accurate copying. Much great literature from the classical past was saved. As many as 50,000 books were copied in the monasteries of Europe in the ninth century.

The cream of European intellects were brought to Charlemagne's palace in Aachen, including the great scholar Alcuin (735–804) from York, who served as his close advisor. Under his guidance the Frankish church was reformed. Latin was promoted for secular and theological teaching, although preaching, when it occurred, was to be in the vernacular. The *Heliand* was produced as a ninth-century attempt to make the life of Christ accessible and understandable to the laity through the medium of Germanic legend.

It seems that Charlemagne was personally deeply devout and possessed of some humility. Alcuin produced a personal devotional manual for him. Charlemagne sought through church and society to ensure God's reign on earth. Laws regulated by the commandments of God were disseminated widely, and he oversaw the reform of church liturgy. In Charlemagne's eyes, learning was core to spiritual reformation. In this, clergy played a key role: they were to be kept from both business and the tavern, and instead encouraged to establish schools in their parishes. He also used the monks of the Benedictine order, admiring the simplicity of their rule and their commitment to mutual service and obedience. Although the empire Charlemagne had created did not remain intact long after his death in 814, the Holy Roman Emperor remained a crucial figure in the European church. By the thirteenth century the territory he ruled was known as the Holy Roman Empire. It lasted until ended by Napoleon in 1806.

The East–West Schism

Before the final schism came in the eleventh century, the deep and continuing division intensified between the church in the Latin-speaking West, and that in the East where Greek, and other languages from Syriac, were spoken. The relationship between church and state in the East was much closer than in the West, reflected in Caesaropapism, when the emperor sometimes acted as a chief bishop. As early as the seventh century, communion between churches in the East and the West had been broken off in a dispute over whether Christ had a single will, as some in the East argued. The bishop of Rome deposed the bishop of Constantinople, and in turn the Eastern emperor had the pope arrested and put in prison. The Sixth Ecumenical Council, held at Constantinople, resolved the issue in Rome's favour in 681.

Animosity intensified during the 'iconoclastic' controversy of the eighth and ninth centuries over the use of images, statues and icons in churches. Some argued that such practice broke the second commandment which forbade the use of graven images. It was also seen as a barrier to the conversion of Muslims, who rejected the idea of making images of God.

John of Damascus (c. 676–749), whose writings were much read by the later theologians Peter Lombard and Thomas Aquinas, wrote extensively on the nature of the orthodox Christian faith, the Trinity and the Christian moral life. He strongly endorsed asceticism. His most famous work was *Fount of Wisdom*. John of Damascus argued that icons were essential to the church because they demonstrated the two natures of the Son of God – human and divine – and made Christ more accessible. He claimed that he was not venerating the picture but the One portrayed, he who 'was the creator of matter, and who for my sake became matter'. This diverged from the views of earlier teachers such as Origen who in the third century rejected the use of religious images, arguing that Christians did not need man-made representations because they knew the spiritual realities. However, as paganism receded, the willingness of Christians to use images increased.

The fierce arguments came to a head after 726 when the Byzantine emperor Leo III (717–40) declared that icons were idols that should be destroyed – hence the term 'iconoclasm'. Under his successor thousands of religious images were destroyed, but the policy was not consistent. Iconoclasm was stopped by the Seventh Ecumenical Council in 787, resumed in 815, and then ended in 843 after intervention by the empress Theodora. The issue provoked widespread disturbances and added to the growing sense of alienation between Eastern and Western churches. The leaders of the Western Church believed the Eastern emperor was interfering too much in the affairs of the church, while also believing that saints and images were to be shown reverence but not worshipped. The growing threat of Islam, which pressed ever closer to Constantinople, heightened the feeling of Eastern Christians that the West should do more to help in their defence.

In 868 the Byzantine emperor dismissed Ignatius as Patriarch of Constantinople, replacing him with the more compliant Photius, who had to be quickly ordained in order to take up the office. Ignatius appealed to the pope for support, who demanded the resignation of Photius. When Photius rebuked the pope for some of his beliefs, he was excommunicated, and in return Photius excommunicated the pope. The resulting Photian schism from 863 to 867 saw East–West church relations broken.

In 1054 matters finally came to a head, ostensibly over the interpretation of the Nicene Creed, but it was the culmination of these long-growing tensions. Western theologians, including Tertullian, Ambrose and Augustine, had long argued for the view that the Holy Spirit proceeds from the Father 'and also from the Son' (*filioque*). It was asserted as a way of countering any residual Arianism. The statement was adopted by the Council of Toledo in 589. It passed into increasingly wide use, and Charlemagne enthusiastically promoted it. Theologians in the East took the view that the Holy Spirit proceeded only from the Father and were deeply upset at the addition of the *filioque* clause to the historic Nicene Creed. After prolonged negotiations came to nothing, in 1009 the pope communicated his acceptance of the *filioque* clause to Constantinople, and in 1014 the word was part of the creed used at the coronation of Henry II as Holy Roman Emperor.

In 1054 Michael Cerularius, the Patriarch of Constantinople, declared this Western view unorthodox, also highlighting other variations from Eastern practice as problematic, as well as the claims to papal supremacy. The close association between ritual and doctrine in the East meant that to interfere with ritual was to interfere with the very essence of the faith. The papal legate then served Pope Leo IX's bull of excommunication on Cerularius and his clergy as he was at worship in the great Hagia Sophia in Constantinople, even though

Leo had already died. An incensed Cerularius excommunicated the papal legate and the pope. Attempts at reconciliation in succeeding centuries were unsuccessful, and the mutual excommunications not revoked until 1965. The Orthodox Church thereafter refused to recognize any church council since 787 as ecumenical, and any pronouncements made by subsequent councils or by the pope have not been accepted. This deep fault line driven between churches in the West and East left the Eastern Church even more isolated, and vulnerable at a time of some danger.

The rise of Islam

From 600 to 1095 Christianity faced a very significant challenge from the rapid rise of a large and influential Arab empire with the new religion of Islam at its core. Muslims quickly conquered most of the Middle East, North Africa, Egypt and part of Spain. The Byzantine Empire was rocked, although there was a measure of recovery in the tenth and early eleventh centuries under the Macedonian dynasty.

Muhammad was born in Mecca, in Arabia, around the year 570. He was a man of deep feelings. He was troubled by the religious conflicts of his region and sought an alternative to the paganism that prevailed in Arabia amid the frequently warring nomadic tribes. Had early Christian mission effort in Arabia been sustained, the outcome of Muhammad's spiritual search might have been different. However, he had no access to a Bible in Arabic, and the references to biblical events and Christian teachings which he made appear to have been derived from occasional conversations with Jews or Christians, many of whom were from sects holding heretical views. These were reflected in the Qur'an, including the impression that the Holy Trinity consisted of Father, Mother and Son, and that someone else was crucified on the Cross in the place of Jesus. From the Jews and Christians he derived the idea of one true God, and made use of their name for him, *al-ilah* (the God), shortened to Allah, whose prophet he claimed to be. Other practices such as the Ramadan fast share parallels with the Christian Lent, and prostration in prayer and use of prayer mats was practised by some Christian communities.

Muhammad was determined to replace the polytheistic paganism of Arabia with the worship of Allah. A group of followers gathered around him, to whom he dictated his teachings, including revelations he said were made to him by the angel Gabriel. He presented Islam as the truth which had long been obscured by other religions. Muhammad's sayings were set out by his followers in what became known as the Qur'an ('that which is to be recited'), and this became the sacred text of Muslims. Opposition to his teaching led to the *hijra* (migration) in 622, from which the Muslim era is dated, as Muhammad fled from Mecca to Medina, where his fortunes turned. Nine years later he returned to Mecca in triumph, and he had won over all of Arabia by the time of his death in 632.

The teaching of Islam (meaning submission) came into contact with orthodox Christianity soon after its beginnings. Muhammad believed that Christians and Jews deserved respect and tolerance as 'People of the Book' because they held to monotheistic religion, although they had corrupted this and turned away from the true path. In the Qur'an God is presented as advising Muslims to engage in dialogue with them about his message: 'If you are in doubt about what we have sent down to you, ask those who were reading scripture before you' (Qur'an 10.94).

However, the aggressive expansion of Islam created an ideology of confrontation with non-Muslims which led to conflict. Some suras in the Qur'an develop the idea of holy war or *jihad* where Muslims are urged to fight for the cause of God. Those who fail to do so are castigated for their failure of religious duty. There are other passages speaking of preaching, persuasion and a non-violent approach to opponents of the new faith: for their faith in the one God and their good deeds Jews and Christians would have 'their rewards with the Lord'. This tension is summed up in the Qur'anic Sura 9.5:

> When the sacred months are past, kill the idolaters wherever you find them and seize them, besiege them and lie in wait for them in every place of ambush: but if they repent, pray regularly and give the alms tax, then let them go their way, for God is forgiving, merciful.

Within a hundred years of the prophet Muhammad's death in 632, Arab conquerors in the name of Islam had by a series of lightning strikes overrun vast areas once strongly Christian. Expansion came largely by military conquest rather than by proclamation of a creed or personal decisions to receive Islam. The weak and divided state of the Byzantine Empire meant that they encountered little opposition. Indeed Christian resistance to Islam proved far less determined than it had been in doctrinal disputes such as those over miaphysite views.

In 638 Jerusalem was captured, together with Syria. Three years later Byzantine troops retreated from Egypt, and Arab Islamic forces took control of North Africa. In 711 Muslim armies moved over the Straits of Gibraltar into Spain, and by 732 had crossed the Pyrenees and reached France, although here they were repelled at Poitiers. Without this battle, much of Western Europe might have fallen under Islamic control. Muslim invaders were held back from Constantinople in 678 after five years of attack. Much of Christianity was now effectively penned into Europe and Russia, its centre of gravity for the next thousand years. In 751 Muslim troops defeated Chinese forces in Kyrgyzstan and opened the door to the East. Further south, the church in Ethiopia survived, but largely because it was cut off from that in Europe and the Middle East, developing in consequence its own traditions and identity.

Christianity still existed in Muslim-majority areas, but it was increasingly a minority faith: within a century it was effectively eliminated in Arabia. In some parts Christians remained the majority of the population until the eleventh century, but in other large areas Christianity was slowly but effectively extinguished. Many Christian churches were turned into mosques or destroyed. A mosque was built on the site of the temple in Jerusalem. Christians sought to adapt life and faith to existence under Islamic rule, adopting the Arabic language for common use while retaining traditional languages for church purposes. In North Africa there were about forty bishops at the time of the Arab conquest in the late seventh century; by 1076 there were just two. The survival of the Copts in Egypt and the Maronites in Lebanon were exceptions. Copts lived in separate villages or urban centres, working as craftspeople, their writing and language skills needed by the rulers, although they were still subject to periodic episodes of Muslim violence. Some communities made agreements with the caliph which brought them protection, but also rendered them second-class citizens and required them largely to practise their religion in private, beset by extra taxes and constant discriminations. Between 847 and 861 Caliph al-Mutawakkil required Christians to wear distinctive yellow clothing.

John of Damascus maintained his work as a theologian in a monastery near Jerusalem under Islamic rule, even writing against its claims. Christian pilgrims continued to make their way to the Holy Land. Some Christians even served as physicians and astronomers in the courts of the caliphs. In the eighth and ninth centuries the Church of the East appeared to have stabilized its position. The remotest and most self-contained monasteries stood the greatest chance of survival, preserving their faith, together with many ancient documents. But, across the Arabic Muslim world, Christian evangelism was prohibited and Muslims converting to Christianity faced the death penalty. Christian apologetic against Islam was not strong. There were denunciations of Muhammad's morality, including his multiple marriages. There were some efforts to develop arguments by which to defend Christianity, such as those of John of Damascus in the eighth century and the Arab Christian theologian Ammar al-Basri in the ninth. Even if dialogue had been possible, the military might of Islamic rulers remained invincible. Christians debated the cause of this spectacular reversal, wondering if it was the use of icons which had brought such a fate upon them. Others believed it was unresolved theological debates.

The defeat of the Islamic armies at Poitiers led successive popes to consider the possibilities of pushing back Muslim power by military force, especially from the Holy Land. The decision to fight physically for the defence or even the expansion of Christianity had profound implications. The outcome was the Crusades, one of the most difficult and controversial episodes in the biography of Christianity, which lasted from 1095 to 1291. They left an indelible scar on the Middle East and on Christian–Muslim relations, and are fraught with political, ethical and theological challenges.

The Crusades

The years 1004 to 1013 saw major persecution of Christians, including the destruction in 1009 of the Church of the Holy Sepulchre in Jerusalem. The practice of pilgrimage to historic holy sites was becoming popular, affording spiritual or even physical benefit (including healing), it was believed. The replacement of the rule of the Arab Muslims in Palestine after 1071 by the less accommodating Seljuk Turks made access to traditional Christian sites increasingly difficult.

The Crusades were presented as a justified act of self-defence of Christianity against violent aggression. The term 'crusade' comes from the Latin word *crux*, the red cross placed on the flags or uniforms of the Crusaders. In response to Islam's doctrine of holy war Christians developed their own. At a time of economic recession in Europe, participants were lured by promises of land, tax and debt reliefs. Others sought fame or adventure. The Crusades also became associated with a revival of interest in religion and deepening piety, seen in the spectacular growth in church and cathedral building across Europe at the time, supported by the donations of the faithful.

There were possibly as many as twelve crusades, but there were four major ones. The First Crusade, between 1095 and 1099, was the most successful, catching the armies of the Islamic East by surprise, and was connected to the appeal of the Byzantine emperor for help in the struggle against the Muslim Turks who were advancing on Constantinople. Pope Urban II (c. 1042–99), who inspired the First Crusade, gathered support through sustained diplomatic activity and a successful propaganda campaign including accounts of atrocities committed against Christian pilgrims. Urban asserted that to die on crusade in a state of repentance and confession would ensure remission from penance and purgatory, with an immediate entry to heaven. Urban urged, 'Christ commands it', to stop Turks and Arabs from killing and capturing Christians.

A huge level of commitment was required to travel up to 2,000 miles, enduring illness, dirty water, scant provisions and the likelihood of death.

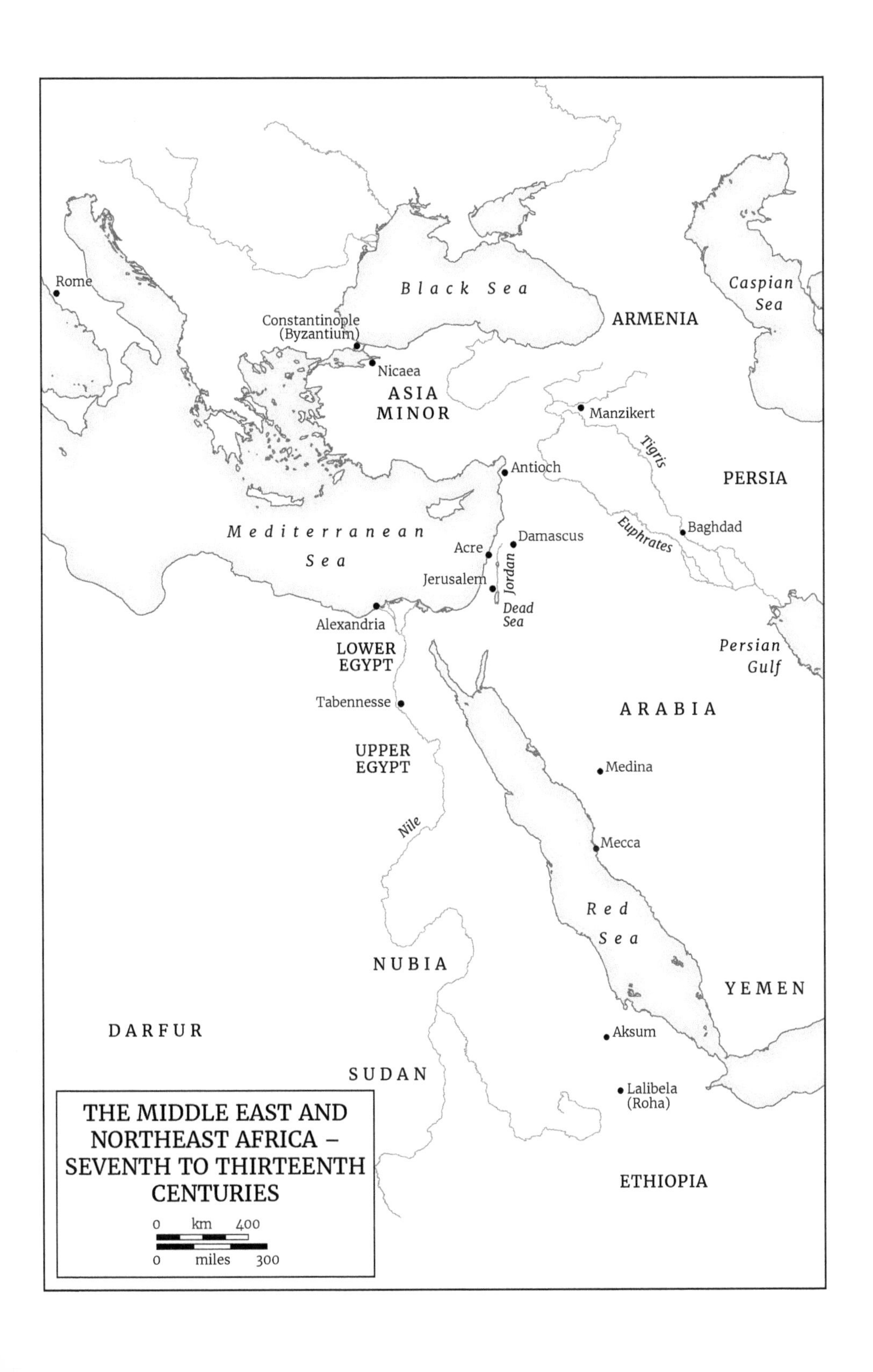
Rome
Black Sea
Caspian Sea
Constantinople (Byzantium)
ARMENIA
Nicaea
ASIA MINOR
Manzikert
Tigris
Antioch
PERSIA
Mediterranean Sea
Damascus
Euphrates
Baghdad
Acre
Jordan
Jerusalem
Dead Sea
Alexandria
LOWER EGYPT
Persian Gulf
Tabennesse
ARABIA
UPPER EGYPT
Medina
Nile
Mecca
Red Sea
NUBIA
YEMEN
DARFUR
Aksum
SUDAN
Lalibela (Roha)
ETHIOPIA
THE MIDDLE EAST AND NORTHEAST AFRICA – SEVENTH TO THIRTEENTH CENTURIES
0 km 400
0 miles 300

Thousands, from noblemen to humble peasants, rallied to the cause amid a sense of apocalyptic excitement. The First Crusade saw the recapture of the cities of Nicaea and Antioch, before in 1099 the capture of Jerusalem itself after a terrible siege. A dreadful slaughter of both Muslims and Jews followed, which awakened fury in the Islamic world. This was tragically the ethics of war at the time – those who surrendered were treated well, while those who chose to fight to the end accepted that their fate would be death in defeat. The establishment of a Western Christian kingdom in the eastern Mediterranean was not to last long, needing a constant supply of finance and soldiers from Western Europe. Therefore, from 1147 to 1149 a second crusade was undertaken, supported by the preaching of Bernard of Clairvaux (1090–1153), but this time the crusader armies were defeated near Damascus.

In 1187 Jerusalem fell back into Islamic hands after the victory of the armies of Saladin. This prompted the Third Crusade from 1188 to 1192, which involved Frederick Barbarossa (the Holy Roman Emperor), Philip II of France and Richard I (the 'Lion Heart') of England, with support from Pope Gregory VII. Although access for Christian pilgrims to Jerusalem was renegotiated, it was only a limited success. Long-term success in Palestine was dependent on co-operation with the Byzantine Empire, but hope of that was sundered by the Fourth Crusade from 1202 to 1204. This was launched to liberate Egypt, but the Crusaders ended up attacking Constantinople, robbing churches and monasteries in a failed endeavour to establish a Latin empire there. This episode only weakened the Byzantine Empire in the face of Islamic advance. It finally fell in 1453. One of the most tragic episodes was the 1212 Children's Crusade, which sought the liberation of Palestine by the 'pure in heart'. Many children died on the journey, while others were drowned, sold into slavery or slaughtered. Jerusalem temporarily returned to Christian rule between 1229 and 1244, but the last Christian forces were forced out of Palestine in 1291, effectively ending the Crusades.

The Crusades seriously affected families. Some Crusaders' wives followed their husbands, but many died. For most, there was a long and lonely wait for husbands or sons to come home, often after many years of silence. Some monks served as chaplains; others travelled in the rather forlorn hope that military conquest would open opportunities for mission among the Islamic communities. An unusual development was the emergence of crusader monastic orders, adhering to vows of poverty, chastity and obedience, alongside fighting for the Christian cause. The Knights Templar (founded in 1118), based at the site of the temple of Jerusalem, sought to protect Christians on pilgrimage to Jerusalem. The order of the Knights Hospitaller, started around 1099, was based at the Hospital in Jerusalem, initially caring for pilgrims and the sick in the Holy Land before becoming a military order. After the knights were forced out of Palestine they eventually settled on Malta, from the 1520s to 1798.

The Teutonic Knights were German monks who set up hospitals to care for pilgrims in the Holy Land after 1198. After the Crusades they undertook missionary work in the Baltic region, although conversion was often achieved at the point of a sword. They helped with the extension of Christianity into Lithuania in 1386. The crusading impulse was later used against those deemed heretics within Christian Europe, and in the thirteenth and fourteenth century rival popes declared 'crusades' against their political enemies. The military threat from Islam remained. In 1456 Belgrade needed to be defended against the Islamic armies of the Ottoman Turks, and as late as 1683 Vienna was besieged by Muslim forces.

The Crusades had some initial successes, but in the long term crusading failed to liberate the Holy Land and failed to secure Christians in the Middle East from military threat. It also drastically reduced the possibility of a sympathetic hearing for Christian missionaries in the Middle East. It was waged at a huge cost in lives, suffering and finance. Relationships with not only Muslims, but also Jews, were harmed, and between Eastern Orthodoxy and Western Catholicism. The indelible impression of Christianity as an imperialistic religion promoting itself by the sword was left among Muslims, while the image of Muslims persecuting Christians was also perpetuated. Within Europe the Catholic Church's sanctioning of military force against any apparently variant forms of Christianity formed a stark backdrop to the political and theological debates of the Reformation.

Yet the Crusades revalidated many Western European identities, such as aristocratic status, family values, service and reward. The theology of the Crusades presented salvation as more widely accessible to the laity and more certain. The expansion of Islam into Europe was halted, and the self-respect of Christianity restored, reflected in the soaring triumphalism of the Gothic cathedrals. The papacy consolidated its leadership role in Western Christianity. Contact with the East opened wider access to its science, mathematics and astronomy – the crusading period also saw the establishment of the first universities in Europe.

Islam was not invulnerable. In 1258 the Mongols conquered Baghdad, sparing the Christian population in the widespread massacre that followed. Attempts at further Christian mission into Central Asia followed, with a cathedral built at Olon Sume, in Inner Mongolia, established by Franciscans in the 1290s. The Franciscan diplomat William of Rubruck attempted to convert the Great Khan, Möngke, but conceded that he needed miracles of the type performed by Moses before Pharaoh to bring any prospect of success. Indeed, after 1256

Mongol rulers embraced Islam rather than Christianity. They then reduced the Christian presence in Central Asia to a tiny minority, struggling on the margins of existence.

10. DEEPENING THINKING CAPACITIES

Lifeline
1022 – Cathars condemned at Council of Orléans
1059 – Lateran Synod approves Augustinian monastic rule
1073 – Hildebrand becomes Pope Gregory VII
1084 – Carthusian order founded
1098 – Cistercian house founded at Citeaux
1208 – Albigensian crusade starts
1216 – Pope Honorius III sanctions Dominican order
1223 – Pope Honorius III sanctions Franciscan order
c. 1272 – Thomas Aquinas starts *Summa Theologica*

As a person grows in maturity he or she develops the capacity to think more clearly and profoundly, and apply those thoughts to life and practice. Such a maturing process takes place at different speeds in different people and contexts. To those steeped in the rich theological traditions of the East, the Western Church looked theologically undeveloped and lacking in sophistication. As the Christian centre of gravity shifted towards Europe in the medieval period, that changed. A wave of monastic renewal was coupled with a new emphasis on the need for formal theological training set within the newly emerging universities, influenced by the great centres of learning in the East.

The Eastern Church certainly continued to turn out theologians of the highest order, including Maximus the Confessor (c. 580–662), a major influence on spirituality in the Orthodox churches. Born in the eastern part of the empire, in the face of Persian invasion he moved to a Byzantine monastery near Carthage. Maximus wrote about doctrine, worship, Scripture and asceticism. He sought deeper levels of spiritual truth beneath the literal meaning of the text, and is famous for developing 100 maxims for living as a Christian. A key emphasis was Christ's incarnation, and the way a Christian can share God's nature by 'deification' – union with the divine. He spoke of the way the Uncreated reached down to the created, that he might draw them to himself, restore the image of God and destroy the fallen human condition. Christ brought not just religious knowledge but the power to live the virtuous life, and the key producer of deification is love. Maximus was a strong defender of the Chalcedonian understanding of the two natures of Christ, rejecting miaphysite views. When the Eastern emperor Heraclius and Patriarch Sergius of Constantinople sought a compromise to end the ongoing controversy, Maximus stood firm. It was impossible for the incarnate Christ to have anything other than a fully human nature and will. For this, Maximus was summoned to Constantinople, his tongue cut out to stop him speaking and his right hand cut off to stop him writing, before he was sent into exile where he died of his injuries.

Scholasticism

For churches east of Jerusalem, the Christian life was increasingly that of a persecuted minority. Contrastingly, in Europe Christianity moved into a monopoly position, although, not far beneath the surface, continuing patterns of pagan folk-religious practice remained. The intellectual flowering in Western Europe at the beginning of the second millennium AD was shaped by the growing conviction that faith and reason were to be coupled together for the glory of God. This was key to the emergence of scholasticism, or scholastic theology, one of the great developments of medieval Catholicism, which became prominent in the universities of the late eleventh to thirteenth centuries.

Theological scholarship that was public had a rich history in the catechetical schools of the East. The Crusades also brought Western scholars into contact with the intellectual approaches of the Muslim universities which drew on Aristotle. High regard for Aristotle led Christian theologians to deploy logic and dialectic approaches to debating issues and constructing an intelligible body of human knowledge. Scholastic theology mirrored the Gothic architectural style of the period, huge in scale yet packed with intricate detail, involving an array of little arguments, each building on another. To later ages it seemed dry and overcomplicated, but in its time it was fresh and exciting. It developed confidence in the potential of Christian thinking, impelled by a deep religious devotion.

Church and society in Europe

Religious and intellectual renewal took place in a society that was changing both economically and socially. Between 1000 and 1200 the population of Europe doubled. Powerful individual nation-states emerged, with their rulers increasingly involved in both social and religious affairs. It is only after 1200 that Europe was fully Christianized and can be truly spoken of as Christendom – a unified and integrated Christian society with an established hierarchy. Most people were initiated into the church by baptism soon after birth; they were married by the church and buried in the churchyard after their death. Every inch of Europe was encompassed within the parish system, with the priest the primary point of contact between church and people, teaching, if he could, the basics of the faith, administering the sacraments and visiting the sick. The church controlled much of life, was the primary source of education, and demanded an increased conformity of belief and practice, which was codified in canon law. What this meant in terms of personal belief is less clear, but rulers across Europe were able to view their subjects as in some way 'Christian'. Unity within Christendom became vital, and any who destabilized this were likely to face severe censure.

The Roman Catholic Church became the single most powerful institution in Western Europe, and also the wealthiest, as people, moved by religious impulse, gave it vast amounts of money or property. In splendid churches, tall arches now accommodated high windows, letting the light of heaven flood in to illuminate the drama of worship and ritual enacted within. Even the ordinary parish church was the largest building in the community. The pattern of the year was dictated by religious festivals – with holy days becoming holidays, and the church bell tolling the times of the services and eventually the passing of the hours.

One reason why religion played such an important role was the fragility of life. Widespread famine from 1315 to 1322 was followed by the Black Death (1347–50), claiming the lives of some 20 million people, up to a third of the population of Europe. Somewhere between 75 and 200 million perished worldwide, including half of Paris's population of 100,000. For the first time in its history, the world Christian population was subject to sudden decline. A culture and a theological system dominated by thoughts about death and the afterlife was created, with scapegoats, such as the Jewish population, sought.

The church reflected culture in affording women only subordinate positions in wider society and in the family. Men and women generally stood in different places in the church during the mass, and women were not allowed near to the altar, only into the nave. The association between reproduction and sin took hold. Women were not to enter church straight after childbirth, and the practice of 'churching' developed, by which women were purified before being re-admitted. This negative attitude towards women was somewhat countered by growing devotion to the Virgin Mary, furthered by the development of the rosary as an aid to prayer for Catholics. In some places the devotional focus was on images of the Virgin and Child; in others Mary was seated, symbolizing her status as a figure of authority.

Women reached positions of significant influence within monastic orders. Hildegard of Bingen (1098–1179), an abbess and a mystical writer, recorded a series of visions which became a devotional tool and a source of theological instruction. Julian of Norwich (c. 1342–c. 1416) reported a series of mystical visions of Jesus Christ in her *Revelations of Divine Love*, and spent much of her life exploring their theological meaning and significance. She spoke controversially of God as both Mother and Father, and of Christ also as Mother. There were universalist implications in her view that there was no wrath in God, and in her hope for the eventual salvation of all. Her famous saying: 'And all shall be well, and all manner of things shall be well', sums up her theology.

Monastic orders

In years beset by war, epidemics and a sense that the end times were imminent, a number of monastic orders underwent significant reform. These were driven by a determination to return to the original rules and lifestyle of their founders. In 910 Duke William of Aquitaine established a new monastery at Cluny in eastern France dedicated to strict observance of the original Rule of Benedict, emphasizing disciplined private devotion and corporate worship in the mass. This renewal spread widely, with many Cluniac monks becoming bishops in the church. Further Benedictine renewal began in 1098 at Citeaux in Burgundy, where a group of hermits settled in a wild and remote place. They closely followed the Benedictine principles of simplicity, austerity and hard agricultural work to support the monastery. Within the space of fifty years 360 Cistercian monasteries had been started, a third of which were in England and Scotland.

The most famous Cistercian monk was Bernard of Clairvaux (1090–1153), who entered the monastery of Citeaux in his early twenties. The monastery he established at Clairvaux became one of the most important Cistercian centres.

His successful support for Innocent II in the disputed papal election of 1130 led to privileges being showered on the Cistercian order. Bernard was a complex character. He was the greatest preacher of the twelfth century, preaching powerfully in support of the Second Crusade, yet he insisted that the true warfare of the church was through prayer, preaching, self-denial and worship. Bernard's mystical theology stressed the union between the soul and Christ the Word.

The Augustinian order proved a major medieval monastic force. It claimed its origin in the rules and advice of Augustine of Hippo, although any direct link is unclear. Augustinian monks, or Austin Canons as they became known, tended to be found in towns and cities. A significant place was given by them to the theology of Paul, and they played important roles in the developing European universities, as well as in medical care and education. The Augustinian monk Thomas à Kempis (c. 1380–1471) was famous for composing his devotional spiritual manual *On the Imitation of Christ* sometime between 1418 and 1427.

The Carthusian order founded in 1084 was named after the Chartreuse Mountains in the French Alps, where its leader Bruno started his first hermitage. Bruno was an extreme ascetic who practised self-flogging and wore hair shirts to subjugate the flesh. The Carthusians were a dedicated and otherworldly movement, with monks barely speaking, and communicating with each other by means of signs. The order's motto became 'The Cross is steady while the world is turning'.

The understanding of the ascetic life was also changing. Some rejected the idea of seclusion to engage in public ministries of preaching and pastoral care, depending directly on the voluntary contributions of their supporters. The Carmelite order, which emerged in the twelfth century, was notable for its ministry to the laity. Many lived as mendicants – begging to raise their support. The Discalced Carmelites (founded in the sixteenth century) lived barefoot. Although adopting a life of poverty, ironically it was economic growth that allowed the rise of the mendicant orders, affording the laity increased disposable income from which donations were made. It was also a reaction to the way that monasteries were becoming too engrossed in acquiring and retaining wealth.

The Dominicans, founded in Spain in 1216 by Dominic Guzmán (c. 1171–1221), grew out of the unsuccessful efforts of the Catholic hierarchy to convince heretics of their errors. Dominic was sure that preaching, debating, offering Christian instruction and living a quality of life that would inspire others was a better response than repression. The sermons of Dominic's preachers were characterized by illustrations, pithy sayings and anecdotes. Dominic's Order of Preachers, or 'Blackfriars' (after their black hoods), was officially approved by the papacy in 1216. To support their ministry of teaching and combating heresy the Dominicans lived by begging, yet offered their members the best education and a deep immersion in Catholic orthodoxy. They played a significant teaching role in the newly emerging universities. Eight years after their founder's death the pope entrusted them with the task of running the Inquisition, although Dominic would not have approved of the use of force. Dominicans were also powerful advocates of the teaching on papal indulgences which became more widespread in the thirteenth century, and attracted the strong opposition of the Reformers in the sixteenth century.

The Franciscans were founded by Francis of Assisi (c. 1182–1226) in Italy in 1209. Born to wealthy parents, Francis served in the local militia before a spiritual crisis in his twenties changed his worldview and he renounced his possessions. He stressed poverty, brotherly love and repentance, and actively engaged in preaching, raising money for the restoration of churches, and caring for the poor and sick – especially lepers. He organized his followers into an order, committed to his simple Rule. The Franciscan order was formally authorized by Pope Honorius III in 1223. Francis had no taste for leading a large-scale organization, delegating the task to others, while becoming disappointed at the institutionalization of his movement. After his retirement from the leadership of the order in 1223, it moved away from his simple ideals. The Franciscans became a major religious force in Europe, producing a number of popes.

Francis celebrated the handiwork of the Creator – communing with nature as he thought Adam and Eve had done before the Fall. He is even reputed to have preached to the birds. Work was the primary means of raising support for his monks, but when sufficient support was not forthcoming he instructed, 'Let us betake ourselves to . . . begging alms from door to door.' The focus of Francis on the sufferings and wounds of Christ was so intense that the *stigmata* are reported as appearing on his body – bleeding wounds similar to those experienced by Christ in his crucifixion. He also stressed the work of the Holy Spirit. At heart Francis was a missionary, seeking the salvation of souls not only in Europe but also among Muslim and Jewish communities. He offered a spiritual alternative to crusading,

Francis of Assisi

travelling great distances to preach, including before the sultan of Egypt, who remained unconvinced. The Franciscan Ramon Llull (c. 1230–1315) learned Arabic, wrote missionary treatises and with others undertook missionary trips to North Africa. Other Franciscan missionaries travelled as far as West Africa.

The strictest Franciscan group was the Poor Clares, an order for women, formed in 1212 by a wealthy female follower, Clare (c. 1193–1253). Her devotion emphasized the person of Christ, who was eternally rich in the presence of God but made himself poor to bring the riches of eternal life to humanity. If the richness of this world were shed, Clare believed, the richness of eternal things would become accessible.

The Franciscan and the Dominican orders did much to reinforce popular adherence to Christianity at a time when the leadership and bureaucracy of the Catholic Church was becoming disconnected from the lives of the common people, with popes and bishops living opulent and sometimes worldly and immoral lives. The laity wanted religion to be taken seriously, especially by those who had taken religious vows. The fourteenth and fifteenth centuries saw further drives for more rigorous observance by monastic orders of their original Rule. 'Observant' movements among Benedictines began in 1362, the Augustinians in 1385, the Dominicans in 1388 and the Carmelites after 1413. Observant preachers attracted large crowds to their preaching in churches and marketplaces. The threat of possible invasion from Islamic Turkish forces heightened the mood of religious intensity. From a group of radical Observants, the Capuchin order was founded in 1528. The Brothers and Sisters of the Common Life, which began in the Netherlands in the fourteenth century, also drew on the Observant desire for change, forming communities, giving up their worldly goods, and devoting their time to attending services, reading and preaching sermons, and labouring productively.

The universities

The locus for theological thought moved away from the contemplative seclusion of solitary ascetics or the monasteries, or the bitter controversies of the church councils, into the universities which emerged out of long-established cathedral schools. Here students devoted several years to theological study through a set curriculum. Bologna University traces its origins to schools in the late eleventh century which focused on the study of canon and civil law. By the start of the twelfth century, high-grade theological schools had developed in Oxford, and by 1200 the theological schools in Paris were attracting students from great distances. Before long monks were taking a key role in academic teaching.

The twelfth and thirteenth centuries saw a growing interest in the literal or historical sense of the biblical text, fuelling interest in the study of biblical languages, which was to become very important in the Reformation era. Interest in natural science as a way of exploring the mind of the Creator also deepened. The emergence of 'Summa', encyclopedic works of theological knowledge using Aristotle's systematic and comprehensive approach to observation and explanation, through gathering and analysing evidence, created a structure for what could be known. 'Scholastic' theology drew on evidence from the Bible, the Early Church Fathers or other theologians, using a series of questions to systematically consider arguments for and against a proposition, to analyse particular issues, resolve issues and propose further questions for debate. It was in some ways a scientific approach to theology.

Theological debates

Trinitarian and Christological definitions were largely settled in the first 500 years of the church's existence, and the focus now fell increasingly on the question of sin and how to deal with its consequences for the believer's relationship with God. The latent fear of death in a world overshadowed by war and the Black Death intensified such deliberations. A complex scheme of salvation emerged, centring on baptism as an infant, a regular diet of confession and penitence, and a resort to the offices of the church and the saints to bestow grace to supplement what human religious deeds were unable to accomplish. This demanded clearer expectations for Eucharistic practice, and better standards of education and pastoral care from the clergy. At the Fourth Lateran Council of 1215 Pope Innocent III called for well-trained clerical recruits to prevent the faithful from falling into the hands of heretical groups. The curriculum of the universities was increasingly shaped by the needs of preparing priests for preaching and pastoral ministry, and served by the production of textbooks suitable for teaching and examination. Scholars like Stephen Langton (c. 1155–1228) in Paris (later Archbishop of Canterbury) encouraged the teaching of moral and pastoral theology in the universities. Theology was not just to be abstract; it was to be worked out practically.

Theological reflection could also emerge from personal pastoral issues. Peter Abelard was a brilliant young theologian, born in 1079, who studied under the leading teachers in Paris. He grew frustrated with their approach and set himself up as a rival teacher. His disastrous love affair with Héloise, one of his pupils, led to the conception of a child out of wedlock, a secret marriage, and Abelard being attacked and seemingly castrated by a mob of ruffians. Abelard retreated into a monastery, his career in ruins, bitterly repenting of his conduct. Héloise was forced into a convent, from where she tragically wrote of her continued feelings for him. Abelard began to speak of the life and death of Jesus Christ as principally being a supreme demonstration of love, which should inspire the Christian to obedience to God. He rejected the view that Christ bore the penalty of sin, arguing that the Cross was not an objective work but a subjective work, not something that was done for humanity, but done because of the response it would provoke. His view became known as the 'moral influence' theory of the atonement. This left the problem of why Christ needed to die in order to demonstrate his love – could love not have been demonstrated in another way? In his commentary on Romans, Abelard conceded that Christ's death had indeed done something objective – it opened the way to paradise.

In 1140 Bernard of Clairvaux challenged Abelard's view. He stressed how, because of God's love, Christ's death had achieved something objective – bearing the sins of all and satisfying the demands of God's justice. The hymn attributed to him expresses this:

> Thy grief and thy compassion
> were all for sinner's gain.
> Mine, mine was the transgression,
> but thine the deadly pain.

However, Bernard appeared to see salvation as involving a mixture of co-operation between the love and grace of God, and the resultant activity of human beings.

Anselm (c. 1033–1109), who was consecrated Archbishop of Canterbury in 1093, emphasized the use of rational arguments to prove theological propositions, as reflected in his *Faith Seeking Understanding*. Anselm argued that faith is open to rational enquiry and so is compatible with reason: from faith flows understanding. This was different from the subjective theological emphasis of Abelard that much revelation lies beyond the grasp of reason. Anselm offered a rational 'proof' for the existence of God, as 'that than which nothing greater can be thought'. In his work *Why God Became Man* he also set out an objective understanding of the atonement of Christ. Because human sin offended the honour of God, satisfaction was required. A gift of satisfaction to an offended party would obviate the need for punishment. Jesus Christ therefore offered his sinless life in voluntary death to the Father as an infinitely perfect gift, a 'satisfaction', so that the sinner might be spared punishment.

It fell to Peter Lombard (c. 1100–60) to attempt to reconcile the approach of scholastic theology with the Early Church Fathers. In his *Sentences* he seeks to organize statements from early Christian writers around a series of key themes and to resolve contradictions between the sources he quotes. This became a standard textbook for theological students. The greatest of the scholastic theologians was the Dominican Thomas Aquinas (c. 1225–74). His philosophical theology, which is vast in scope, became known as Thomism, and is contained in treatises, Bible commentaries and commentaries on the works of other theologians. His greatest work is *Summa Theologica* (Sum of Theology), an intricate masterpiece of systematic theology in which he draws heavily on the approach of Aristotle. He argued that what is proposed should conform to reason, which is the means God has provided for us to discern the truth. Using a series of questions and answers, argument and counter-argument, he offers a series of assertions and responses to resolve contradictions. His scheme is comprehensive, covering topics from arguments for and against God's existence, to free will and grace, the church and sacraments, and questions about everyday Christian living. Aquinas equated theology to a science. By the marriage of faith and reason, grace and revelation, knowledge could be ordered and reality understood. It was in this way possible to share the mind of God. Yet, to Aquinas, reason could only lead so far. Theology rested primarily on the revelation of God in the Scriptures, which show the full reality of God. The reflections of theologians had value, but human language about God was always inadequate, and metaphor and analogy were needed. He too sought to present a rational proof for the existence of God – there must be a First Cause for the world and the goodness found in it: the root of all things must be One who is omniscient, omnipotent and omnipresent. In the great questions about salvation, Aquinas emphasized the role of grace, which comes through the work of the Holy Spirit by means of the sacraments. To this humans must respond, but their responses are also prompted by grace.

Thomas Aquinas

Others saw the role of theology differently – as not to propose comprehensive theories of knowledge or all-encompassing worldviews, but to address issues in the lives of the ordinary people of God. A fellow student of Aquinas at Paris was Bonaventure (1221–74). In 1257 he was elected master-general of the Franciscans. His desire was to put theology at the service of the church and integrate ascetic spirituality with scholasticism. He was unconvinced that reason would solve the deepest theological problems, nor would it alone achieve the ultimate purpose of theology – closeness to God. Alongside his commentaries and sermons were writings which focused on the contemplative approach towards mystical union with God.

This development of independent study and thinking in the universities increased the potential for conflicts between faith and reason. This led the Roman Catholic Church to place pressure on university authorities to limit what was permissible to believe through sanctions ranging from censure, condemnation and book burning, to removal from academic post and ultimately the loss of life. This did not stop the flow of imaginative and varied thinking into the fourteenth century, allowing scope for advances in science, especially in medicine. Some saw exploration of the material world as an extension of their study of the God who had made it. Yet the attempt to control what people thought led to those deemed heretics facing vicious harassment, persecution and even death. Unanimity in religious belief and practice was considered essential, and was backed by legal sanction and enforced by the State. Thomas Aquinas likened heresy to a contagious disease which threatened the whole community. Isolating, silencing or even executing heretics was therefore needful for the spiritual health, pastoral care and protection of society, stopping others from deviating from the accepted standards.

The Inquisition

The Papal Inquisition, which began in 1233, sanctioned the prosecution and torture of heretics, forcing those suspected of error to swear to the official understanding of the truth. It was especially strong in France and Italy, and eventually, in the fifteenth century, in Spain. Religious pluralism, or variety of expression of belief and practice, was not allowed in Europe. The difficulty in assessing just how heretical these 'heresies' were, and whether they were errors at all, is compounded by the fact that official accounts were written by the winners of the debates, who then destroyed the evidence of their opponents.

The Bogomils were one such movement which concerned the church authorities in the eighth century. Some settlers from Armenia and Syria into Thrace, north-west of Constantinople, brought with them gnostic-type teachings which spread across Asia Minor into the Balkans. The Bogomils saw the world as governed by the two opposing principles of good and evil. The visible world was seen as evil and needed to be rejected, which meant shunning sexual intercourse and avoiding eating meat, eggs, cheese, milk and wine.

Bogomil influence seems apparent in the quest of the Cathars to be the 'pure ones', or the 'perfect ones' (the name 'Cathar' coming from the Greek word *katharoi*, meaning pure). Their presence was first reported in 1140 in northern Europe, but by the 1170s–1190s they were particularly strong in Italy, and then France, where they are sometimes called the Albigensians after a town called Albi, one of their chief centres. The Cathars sought spiritual purity by separation from the controls of Catholicism, and formed their own religious hierarchy and clergy. As with the Bogomils their worldview was dualist, seeing two principles in the universe, one being Good and the other Evil. The Evil One had fashioned the present world, and imprisoned souls in the bodies of men, women, birds and animals. Souls could be released and returned to the other world God had created through celibacy, avoiding killing, and refraining from eating foods that came from sexual reproduction. Because of the view that the flesh was a bad thing, Cathar theology rejected the humanity of Christ, as well as Catholic teachings on purgatory. The Cathars had a missionary dimension, one source of attraction being their strong ethical and moral approach. When the Catholic Church's attempts to stop the spread of Cathar teaching by argument and preaching failed, an act of religious cleansing was attempted between 1209 and 1229, the Albigensian crusade. The full force of the Inquisition was unleashed, with mass burnings of any associated with the unorthodox group. Those who survived were driven underground, with leaders forced to live in isolation and constantly on the move. Crusading, which began as a battle against the opponents of Christianity, ended up with Christians persecuting Christians.

Waldensianism

Another movement that attracted a similar level of opposition was Waldensianism. It began as the Order of the Poor of Lyons, started by the rich citizen and businessman Valdes (Peter Waldo). After a conversion experience around 1175, he gave away much of his money to the poor and took up itinerant, Scripture-based preaching, gathering a group of followers. From Lyon the movement spread into France and northern Italy, and eventually as far as Spain, Poland, Bohemia and Hungary. Waldensianism, which grew at a time of pastoral crisis in the Catholic Church, was strongest, and safest, in the Alps. Waldensians rejected the teaching of purgatory, saying masses for the dead, and seeking the intercession of departed saints. The movement's spiritual ideals were high, stressing the Sermon on the Mount, the importance of vernacular Bible reading, and a literal approach to biblical interpretation. Members placed a strong emphasis on social care for the whole community, taking vows of poverty, chastity and obedience, and espousing pacifism. The Waldensians were excommunicated en masse in 1184, and faced significant opposition and inquisition for over a century. One surprising legacy of the time remains in common use. The Waldensians of Nîmes (*de Nîmes*) were weavers of a tough, hard-wearing cloth, now known as denim. The movement proved as tough and resilient as their cloth, surviving through to the Reformation. When that began it was embraced by most Waldensians.

The Waldensian call for a purer, simpler, Bible-based spirituality reflected a growing pre-Reformation critique of the official Catholic Church, deemed to have lost the ideals of the poverty and humility of Christ. These motives were not so different from the appeal for simplicity and purity found in the new religious orders, such as the Franciscans. The line between orthodox practice and what was deemed heretical could be very fine. Yet, because it was a very religious age, debates about change and reform were taken very seriously and penalties were extreme. The medieval world was changing, and the church was struggling to keep up.

11. GROWING, CONTRACTING, QUESTIONING

Lifeline

543 – Coptic missionaries sent to Nubia
c. 1190 – Lalibela becomes priest-king in Ethiopia
1245 – John of Plano Carpini begins mission to the Mongols
1314–44 – mass Ethiopian conversions to Christianity under King Amda Sion
1377 – Gregory XI returns papacy from Avignon to Rome
1384 – death of Wycliffe
1415 – Hus executed
1453 – fall of Constantinople
1498 – Savonarola executed

As they move into adolescence children can often have periodic growth spurts. However, rarely does growth turn to contraction, until extreme old age. Although little is known about some aspects of Christianity outside Europe during the medieval period, it was in fact more a world religion than ever before, and reached places that would not again be reached until the nineteenth and twentieth centuries. The Church of the East grew to stretch from the Mediterranean to India and China. In Africa Christian influence reached into Ethiopia and as far west as Darfur, almost halfway to the Niger. But then, growth turned to contraction lasting several hundred years. Nonetheless, for the first thirteen centuries of its existence, Christianity should more properly be spoken of as a world faith than a Western one.

Nubia and Ethiopia

For centuries the story of the Nubian church (in modern Sudan) remained largely forgotten until archaeological work in the 1960s revealed its existence. Christianity arrived sometime in the fourth century, brought by merchants, travellers and refugees journeying along the River Nile. They were followed, in 543, by Coptic missionaries sent at the encouragement of Theodora, wife of the emperor Justinian. A church was established in the capital Faras, a bishop consecrated, and the king and a number of the aristocracy baptized. Within fifty years Christianity had spread at least 400 miles further south into the kingdoms of Alodia and Soba. Although the Nubian church was divided, with different expressions in its three kingdoms, in 641 an Arab attack was repelled. Nubian kings funded the building of significant cathedrals, which were magnificently decorated, as well as a large number of village churches. A painting of Bishop Petros from the late tenth century shows he was an African, indicating the existence of some indigenous leaders, although other clergy were not local. Connections with the church in Ethiopia were also important, and Christian influence extended west into Sudan.

Over time the Nubian churches slowly declined, before many were literally submerged under the sands of the desert. This was, however, only after some 800 years of existence. The beginning of the end came with the conquest of Nubia in the early sixteenth century by Islamic invaders. One part of the kingdom retained Christian rulers until the eighteenth century, but much of the populace had only a superficial understanding of Christianity. As society changed from a settled agricultural pattern to a nomadic lifestyle, intermarriage with Arab nomadic families progressively weakened Christian influences.

In Ethiopia Christianity was miaphysite in form. By the end of the thirteenth century it found itself surrounded by Muslim states, with about half of what is now Ethiopia under the influence of Islam. King Lalibela (1190–1225) of the Zagwe dynasty built his capital at Roha in the Lasta Mountains, where he served as a priest-king figure. Under his direction twelve churches were carved out of the red volcanic rock. Monks travelled extensively to baptize people in the waters of local springs, where they built churches, as Coptic missionary Christianity was gradually transformed into an indigenous Ethiopian church. Under the Solomonides dynasty after 1270, much use was made of the *Kebra Negast* (Glory of the Kings) document to assert the rulers' claims to be the legitimate successors to the kingdom. This took the biblical account of the Queen of Sheba's meeting with King Solomon and added to it the legend that she embraced his faith and bore him a son, who in adulthood, as Menelik I, took the ark of the covenant to Aksum (Axum) in Ethiopia. This account became central to Ethiopian Christianity. Churches were built on the pattern of the Jerusalem temple, with the altar stone (*tabot*) as the most holy and precious religious item.

Under the rule of the Solomonide king Amda Sion (1314–44) there were mass conversions to Christianity, accompanied by further significant building of churches and monasteries. A deepening and extending of Christian influence was continued under Zar'a Ya'qob (1434–6), who enhanced the concept of sacral kingship in Ethiopia, giving to the monarchy an aura of mystery and ritual.

As in Europe, the medieval church in Ethiopia saw its own movements of monastic revival, demanding higher and more rigorous standards of Christian living in all levels of society, from the royal family to the peasantry. The 'Holy Men' (who also included women) were people of prayer; they celebrated the Eucharist, carried the cross, sang psalms and made use of holy water. Some were renowned as healers and exorcists. Converts expressed their faith by professing their trinitarian belief, undergoing baptism and taking a new name. The Ethiopian church proved to be a lasting, African version of Christianity. Its churches and monasteries were architecturally notable, possessing beautiful works of art and precious manuscripts.

Christianity also enjoyed a period of growth in the East in this period, despite great difficulties and political uncertainties. Here any form of Christian mission was fraught with danger. Monks travelling from Syria to China needed to cover 5,000 miles, those from Europe even further. It was an arduous and perilous journey across Asia, taking up to twelve months. Meaningful communication with leaders in the West was extremely difficult. At the start of the second millennium there may have been 38 million people in Europe who had been baptized into the church. There were possibly a further 12 million Christians in the East, widely scattered. They faced centuries of relentless repression with peaks of violent persecution. They lived out their faith surrounded by the adherents of other well-developed religions found in Asia – Buddhism, Confucianism, Hinduism and Islam. Christian survival depended on rulers whose policy of tolerance was fitful at best; most were fiercely anti-Christian.

China

Following the arrival of Alopen in the seventh century, Christianity was allowed to develop in China during the Tang dynasty (618–907). This foothold lasted for only two centuries, but it was restored by Roman Catholic missionaries during the Mongol or Yuan dynasty (1271–1368). Although the famous Genghis Khan (c. 1162–1227) married a niece of a Christian Kerait ruler, the Mongol threat to Europe was considered very great. Mongol invasions, such as that of Russia, sparked fear across Europe, but also deeper interest in mission to the Mongols, who ruled the largest empire in the world.

The first Franciscan missionary to the Mongols, John of Plano Carpini, arrived in 1245. He was followed by other Franciscans and Dominicans who sought permission to work among this much-feared people. They observed little official interest in their message, but they did discover Buddhist temples and mosques in the Mongol capital. They also found a small but well-established community in the East Syrian tradition. Roman Catholic missionaries rejected its Nestorian tendencies, as well as a syncretistic tendency to draw elements of Buddhism and even local cultural superstitions into their practice. They also felt that the morality of the East Syrian clergy was severely lacking. In turn, the East Syrians viewed the Catholic missionaries as schismatic.

The East Syrian Church had gained a measure of official acceptance in the Mongol empire, but its divisions and the lack of clarity of its message prevented it from taking full advantage of the opportunities available. Nonetheless, in the thirteenth century, the East Syrian patriarch exercised ecclesiastical power over a greater geographical area than the pope. East Syrian Christianity remained the dominant expression of Christianity in Asia well into the fourteenth and fifteenth centuries. A report from 1330 suggested there were 30,000 East Syrian Christians in China, with well-decorated churches and enjoying privileges from the emperor. Reports that East Syrian Christianity reached Korea, Japan, Thailand, the Philippines and Java between the thirteenth and fifteenth centuries are hard to verify, especially the further south and east the claims go, but there may have been East Syrian Christians on the Chinese–Korean border before 1000.

Kublai Khan, who in 1279 became the first Yuan emperor of China, had a Christian mother. His pragmatic policy of toleration of all religions allowed for a small Christian presence in China, which was offered some protections. Marco Polo (c. 1254–1324), who served as the only Western advisor in the court, felt that although Kublai Khan showed respect for Christianity, the ignorance and poor standards of the East Syrian clergy held back its advance. The missionary efforts of educated Buddhist monks were far more successful and eventually led to Buddhism being accepted as a Chinese religion, not a foreign one. However, the popes were more preoccupied with internal matters, and the last vestiges of the Crusades, than in major investment in mission to the Far East, and the opportunity passed. The death of Kublai Khan in 1294 signalled the end of the Mongolian Empire which had encompassed China, Central Asia,

Persia and Russia, and thereafter the wind decisively turned against the churches in the East. Toleration gave way to persecution.

The dark clouds did not roll in immediately. The Franciscan missionary John of Montecorvino was able to build a church in Beijing in 1299, and by 1305 reported up to 6,000 converts. For his success he was made Archbishop of Beijing (an office no-one held again until the twentieth century). Other monks joined him, many being converted Buddhists, but their level of adherence to Christian tenets and practice was limited. By the time of his death (c. 1328–33), the phase of liberty he had benefited from was fading. Churches were not self-sustaining, beset by bitter divisions between Catholics and East Syrians. It was nearly 300 years before Catholics returned to China in any force.

The Ming dynasty, which commenced in 1368, proved resistant to all outside influence. By 1400 the vestiges of the Catholic and East Syrian churches, starved of support from further west, had seemingly disappeared, just as they had done after the end of the Tang dynasty nearly 400 years earlier. Only a residual consciousness of Christian teaching remained, especially around the former imperial capital Xi'an, something which Catholic missionaries in the sixteenth and seventeenth centuries appealed to. When they did return, they found the Middle Kingdom's Confucian-based and Buddhist-infused culture deeply resistant to Christian influence.

The conversion to Islam of the Ilkhan Ghazan (who ruled from 1295 to 1304) in Persia rendered the fate of Christians in the East even more precarious. Ghazan's first decree was to destroy all churches, synagogues and Buddhist temples. Islam was to be the only religion allowed in his empire. The East Syrian patriarch was tied up by a Muslim crowd, suspended upside down, his mouth filled with ashes, and repeatedly beaten and ordered to convert to Islam. Bravely he refused, before he was rescued by the ruler himself. Although the later years of Ghazan saw the repressions lessen, matters worsened for Christians in the East under the rule of Timur the Great (1336–1405), or Tamerlane, whose dream was to revive the Muslim caliphate and crush all infidels. He slaughtered Christians ferociously, repressing Christian Georgia, and sacking Smyrna and slaughtering its people. Vengeance was also wrought on other Muslims whom he considered 'not faithful': he is thought to have massacred 90,000 people in Baghdad in 1401. Surprisingly, a few Christian traders survived, including some in Tamerlane's capital Samarkand, but only a tiny number of churches in the larger cities remained. The already struggling Christian community in Persia was all but eliminated.

By 1500, when the Western Church again became serious about mission, the faint light of the ancient churches of the East had almost gone out. Constantinople fell to Muslim invaders in 1453. What has been called the first age of world Christianity was over, although seemingly America and Oceania had not been reached. While it had lasted it had been a world church of many languages, cultures, forms and divisions – Graeco-Roman, Coptic, Syriac, East Syrian, Armenian, Nubian and Ethiopian. It had many regional centres but no single focal point. There remained some sense of global Christian identity, although the division between East and West was noticeable, as was that between churches that accepted Chalcedonian teaching, and Miaphysites and Nestorians. Christians in the old Roman Empire had already moved apart from many in Asia and Africa, before their own bitter division in 1054.

Persecution, inability to adapt to the challenges of other religions, lack of numbers and an over-reliance on state protection (which could all too easily be quickly withdrawn) – all contributed to the end of this first age of world Christianity. So too did the failure of churches in the West to seize the opportunities for mission that periodically appeared in the East. Christian communities in the East were left inward-looking. A noticeable Christian presence remained in Syria and among the St Thomas Christians in the south of India. Operating in survival mode, these churches found it hard to break out of their ethnic identities to reach other Asian peoples. Divisions among Christian groups undermined any tolerance they were shown. Persian missionaries appear to have translated only a few portions of the New Testament into Chinese, a failing in a culture where literature was important to identity. There was some Christian writing in Chinese, but no foundation for a Chinese Christian theology was laid, with instead suggestions of syncretistic borrowing of concepts from other religions.

As the light in the East faded, the churches in Europe were called to deal with a number of fundamental issues, the outcomes of which would shape the next great age of world Christianity. Even by the medieval period, the work of mission in Europe and Eurasia was not finished. In 863 the Patriarch of Constantinople sent the brothers Cyril and Methodius to Slavs who had moved into provinces south of the Danube. Confronted with a language that existed only in oral form, they invented an alphabet and translated portions of Scripture, and liturgical texts, into Slavonic. This was opposed by church leaders in Bavaria, who insisted that only Latin should be used for the liturgy. After an appeal to Pope John VIII the Slavonic liturgy was accepted, but after the deaths of Cyril and Methodius it was again condemned. Their disciples took refuge in Bulgaria, where the Slavonic liturgy and Cyrillic alphabet were accepted.

Russia

Although legends link the apostle Andrew with the introduction of Christianity into Russia along the north coast of the Black Sea, in the ninth century

Christianity was taken to what is now Ukraine, Belarus and Russia by Greek missionaries from Byzantium. The first Christian bishop was possibly sent to Novgorod from Constantinople in around 866–7. By the mid-tenth century many around Kiev had embraced Christianity, although the majority of the population adhered to paganism.

According to the *Russian Primary Chronicle* (about which there are a number of historical questions), Vladimir I (c. 956–1015), the prince of Kiev, was baptized and adopted Byzantine Christianity in 988, a date sometimes seen as the official birthday of the Russian Orthodox Church. The residents of Kiev were called to travel to the river to be baptized, or risk 'the Prince's displeasure'. Vladimir married a Byzantine princess, Anna, forging an alliance with the Byzantine emperor. Although maintaining some distance from the Greek Orthodox leadership, the first Christian clergy were Greeks, and the first churches built in Byzantine style. In 1039 the patriarch sanctioned the appointment of a metropolitan (regional leader) in Kiev for the surrounding Christianized lands.

From 1236 to 1241 much of Russia was invaded by the Mongols, and Kiev, the heart of Russian Christianity, was destroyed. Yet, under Mongol rule from 1250 through to the fifteenth century, the Russian church enjoyed a favoured position, with a remarkable growth of monasticism. Gradually the centre of political and ecclesiastical power shifted from Kiev to Moscow. The Russian Orthodox Church also increasingly began to develop independently from that in Byzantium, with a series of distinct national features.

Challenges within Catholicism

In Western Europe the papacy's vast bureaucracy was only sustainable by means of huge financial inflows, and a measure of stability and unity. This became difficult in the face of social change and a growing sense of individual identity among both people and nations. Local political boundaries were clarified in the fifteenth and sixteenth centuries with the ending of the Hundred Years War in Europe, the Wars of the Roses in England and the expulsion of the last Muslim forces from Spain in 1492. In the emerging nation-states local rulers paid increasing attention to internal affairs, which included religious matters. The claims of the papacy, and the Holy Roman Empire, began to be viewed differently.

Although only 5% of Europe's population could read, literacy in the towns was 30%, bringing growth in the capacity for greater individual thought and expression. The desire to assert individual rights provoked a series of peasants' revolts which were brutally repressed, increasing antagonism towards landlords and also the clergy when they supported such measures. Growing anticlericalism in the fourteenth century was exacerbated by the behaviour of those in the highest office. In 1309 the papacy moved to Avignon in France, where it remained for nearly seventy years through the reigns of seven popes, owing to the volatile political situation in Rome. This was coupled with extravagant papal lifestyles, nepotism and exacting levels of taxes.

The death of Pope Gregory XI in 1378, the year after the papacy returned to Rome, provoked prolonged political infighting and the election of two popes by rival cardinals. When the Council of Pisa was called in 1409 to find a solution, a third pope was elected. It took the Council of Constance (1414–18) to resolve the unseemly wrangle, which severely damaged the credibility of the papacy as a unifying force. Matters were little improved by the notorious behaviour of some fifteenth- and sixteenth-century popes. Paul II (1464–71) spent vast sums as a patron of the arts, rather than supporting the needs of the poor and needy. Alexander VI (1492–1503) came from the infamous Borgia family and, ignoring the requirement of celibacy to hold such office, had many mistresses and fathered at least eight children, including the notorious Lucrezia Borgia. Alexander's successor, Julius II (1503–13), led the papal armies into battle dressed in armour, using military force to further his political power in Italy. Leo X (1513–21) famously declared, 'Now that God has given us the papacy, let us enjoy it.' At a local level, the behaviour of some bishops and priests mirrored that of the hierarchies. Many parish clergy also did not know the basics of the faith and could not recite the Ten Commandments. The sense of a need for renewal and change was growing.

Roman Catholic teaching emphasized two sources of authority: Scripture and tradition. The latter allowed elements of innovation in doctrine. One such was the teaching of transubstantiation, an early version of which was promoted from 831 onwards by the French-born monk and abbot Radbertus (785–865). According to this doctrine, during the mass the celebrant priest repeated the sacrifice of Christ, and a miraculous change occurred in the wine and the bread (wafer). Although externally the elements appeared the same, internally their substance was turned into the body and blood of Christ. This teaching was officially sanctioned in 1215 by the Fourth Lateran Council. Priestly celibacy was also extensively promoted after 1139, although many clergy struggled to live up to the ideal. In 1439 purgatory became official Roman Catholic doctrine, teaching of the need for a period of purgation after death to deal with issues of sin that remained unresolved before the end of life. From the sixth century onwards the teaching also developed that it was possible, through the performance of certain religious activities, to secure an 'indulgence', a remission of the temporal punishment due for sin, as a result of which the superabundant merits of Christ and the saints could be applied. These religious teachings fuelled an intensely religious era.

Two major schools of theological thought dominated Western Europe. The *via moderna*, the modern way of the nominalist school, grew from the teaching of William of Ockham (c. 1285–c. 1349). This school was optimistic about human nature and took the view that people could contribute in some way to their salvation: put simply, 'Do your best and God will do the rest.' In contrast to this, the *schola Augustiniana moderna* followed the line of Augustine that, because of the reality of sin, human capacity in contributing to salvation should be downplayed. Humans should look instead to the grace of God for saving power, which came through the church. During his personal spiritual struggle, Martin Luther was to move between these two schools of thinking.

Wycliffe

In England John Wycliffe (c. 1330–84) sought to break down the clerical monopoly on Bible reading. As master of Balliol College, Oxford, Wycliffe was an intellectual heavyweight and distinguished academic philosopher. Using the scholastic method, he made intellectually coherent and articulate calls, based on Scripture, for reform in official teaching on the papacy, the church and the sacraments. These alarmed the Roman Catholic authorities, especially when he invited the laity to be part of this process. He saw huge contrasts between the pattern of Christ and the apostles, who lived in poverty and simplicity, and the opulence and power of the church of his day. Wycliffe believed that the recent innovation of transubstantiation was a distortion of the true meaning of the Eucharist.

John Wycliffe

To Wycliffe the Bible was the key source of authority because it was the expression of divine truth. Among his extensive writings are two complete translations of the Bible, one literal and the other idiomatic, a collection of 294 sermons, many commentaries, and polemical and theological works. He wanted the laity to be able to read the

Bible and interpret it. This *doctor evangelicus* attracted followers, the 'poor preachers', also known as the Lollards, although the latter term was more widely used for those who challenged religious authority. The extent to which they drew directly on Wycliffe's teaching is unclear, but they echoed his themes in seeking to preach the Bible, place it in the hands of the laity and promote Bible study. Persecution forced Lollardy into a nonconformist, underground movement, meeting in isolated barns and secret locations. Its influence was surprisingly extensive, such that universities in England and Scotland resorted to requiring students to swear an oath that they would not attend Lollard meetings.

In 1382 Wycliffe was removed from his teaching position at Oxford. He turned to parish ministry in Lutterworth where he died two years later. The primary tool at the disposal of the Catholic Church in response to such challenges was to stigmatize Wycliffe with the charge of heresy. In 1407 all versions of the Bible in the English vernacular were banned, something no other country resorted to. After his death Wycliffe's views were condemned at the Council of Constance. Nonetheless, his work inspired that of others, such as Richard Rolle's *English Psalter Commentary*, and the *Pore Caitif*, a collection of treatises which sought to give spiritual direction on Christian obedience and virtue. The teaching of Wycliffe and the Lollards shook both church and society.

Hus and Savonarola

The fears of the Catholic authorities that the teachings of Wycliffe would spread were justified. One of those into whose hands his works came was Jan Hus (1372–1415), who became Dean of Faculty at Prague University in Bohemia. He was deeply concerned for the needs of the laity and preached against abuses in the church. He was especially interested in Wycliffe's emphasis on the grace of God and use of the Bible as the basis of Christian teaching. In the view of the church authorities the use of the vernacular scriptures would only encourage heresy and rebellion, and in 1412 Hus was excommunicated. He appealed against this to the Council of Constance and was given a promise of safe conduct

Jan Hus

from the Holy Roman Emperor Sigismund to attend. The promise counted for nothing as Hus was condemned in 1415 as a heretic and burned at the stake. He met his death with immense fortitude, singing hymns of praise to God, reflected in his dying words: 'Christ, Son of the living God, have mercy on me.'

The death of Hus was greeted with outrage in Prague, where he was viewed as a national hero. A religious and political uprising followed, in which the independence of the Bohemian church was proclaimed, reflecting Bohemian nationalist sentiment. However, the support of the nobility for the reforming movement was not consistent and the country descended into civil war. Eventually, the papacy launched a crusade against the Hussites and by 1452, after a long and bitter struggle, the church had been forced back under papal authority. A number of radical reformers, espousing pacifist sentiments, chose to withdraw from the mainstream of society and lived in separate settlements. Scattered by persecution, some settled in Moravia, before further persecution drove these Moravians to seek shelter in Germany, a move which was to prove influential in the eighteenth-century Evangelical Revival. The Hussite movement was also of significance for the Reformation, although the views of Hus were not entirely identical with those of the Reformers. The fusion of religious views with nationalistic sentiment made the Hussites a distinctly Bohemian movement.

Calls for reform in both church and society were also heard in Italy, the country at the heart of the Catholic structure. The Dominican monk Girolamo Savonarola (1452–98) undertook preaching work in several cities before settling in 1490 in Florence, and became renowned for his urgent and dramatic sermons. Deeply burdened for the salvation of souls, and with an apocalyptic sense of imminent judgment about to fall, he lived a simple life, wearing coarse clothing and eating little food. He called for repentance on the part of the city leaders, especially the wealthy Medici family, and voiced the cries of the poor and oppressed. People wept profusely during his powerful sermons.

Girolamo Savonarola

When in 1494 Italy was invaded by the French king Charles VIII, Savonarola led a delegation out to plead with him that Florence might be spared. His courageous pleas were successful. In the power vacuum after the invasion, Savonarola prophesied that Florence would be a catalyst for reformation and renewal throughout Italy. His supporters steered a programme of moral reform through the council and extended democracy to all citizens. He called for a 'bonfire of the vanities', with gambling equipment, cosmetics, wigs and immoral books consigned to the flames. Calls for tax reforms and aid for the poor were highly popular with the common people, but the higher orders of society were less convinced. When Savonarola denounced the failings of the church he was eventually threatened, then excommunicated and arrested. Under arrest he wrote *The Triumph of the Cross*, exploring the victory over sin and death brought by the Cross and outlining what it means to be a Christian. After being terribly tortured, he was burned at the stake. Martin Luther was later to praise his emphasis on faith and grace. Savonarola's calls for church and society to reflect the kingdom of Christ on the earth failed in the fifteenth century, but they were a persistent cry of reform-minded individuals in the following century.

The Renaissance

The period of rapid intellectual, cultural, scientific and social advance between the fourteenth and seventeenth centuries has become known as the Renaissance, suggesting a rebirth of what had been lost from the classical past. The church struggled with how to respond to such challenges. When the Polish astronomer Nicholas Copernicus (1473–1543) proposed a heliocentric theory of planetary motion, which described the earth as rotating each day on its axis, and revolving each year round the sun as did the other planets, the effect was indeed revolutionary. In 1616 the Roman Catholic Church belatedly condemned this cosmological theory which had overturned the worldview that the earth was at the centre of the created order. Similarly, in 1633 the Italian Galileo Galilei (1564–1642) was condemned by the Roman Inquisition, found 'vehemently suspect of heresy'

Nicholas Copernicus

Johannes Gutenberg

and forced to recant. His life was spared, but he spent the rest of his days under house arrest. Nonetheless, Galileo's work on planetary motion, based on detailed observation of empirical evidence, laid a foundation for the European Enlightenment.

Two other events with equally revolutionary impact also took place during the Renaissance. Around 1439 Johannes Gutenberg developed a way of printing books by using a movable typeface. Coupled with the use of sheet paper (before then it took a whole goatskin to produce six pages of parchment), the possibilities for communication were transformed. Then in 1453 Constantinople, heart of the Orthodox Church, fell to Islamic invaders. This unleashed a wave of apocalyptic speculation that the Last Days would occur sometime in 1492–3, thought to be the end of the seventh millennium since creation. Although that event failed to materialize, for the next three centuries the possibility of an invasion of Europe by Muslim forces hung over society. The collapse of Constantinople, the great centre of Christian thinking, led to a flood of refugees into Western Europe, including scholars who brought precious manuscripts and study skills. Change was coming to the churches of Western Europe.

12. DIVISIONS

Lifeline

1517 – Luther's 'Ninety-Five Theses'
1521 – Diet of Worms
1524 – Peasants' Revolt starts in southern Germany
1529 – Marburg Colloquy
1530 – Augsburg Confession
1534 – Henry VIII's Act of Supremacy
1536 – Calvin starts ministry in Geneva
1536 – execution of Tyndale
1546 – death of Luther
1560 – Scots Confession
1572 – St Bartholomew's Day massacre, France
1598 – Edict of Nantes

Change can be painful. Some families handle it well and grow stronger through the process. Others are torn apart when contentious issues are raised, or by a growing sense of self-identity among family members. The Reformation represents one of the most profound, and difficult, periods of change within the biography of Christianity. The inability of the Roman Catholic Church to deal with a series of important challenges provoked a profound split in Western Christendom.

Humanism

Humanism, an important scholarly approach during the Renaissance, emphasized exploring the human condition through the great classics of literature, reading them in their original Greek and Latin. Art began to depict scenes using highly realistic linear perspective. This turned pictures into windows on to events, bringing scenes, often of biblical events, vividly to life, and often provoking an emotional response. *The Lamentation of Christ*, an early Renaissance painting by Giotto (1267–1337), evokes profound pathos as the broken body of Christ is tenderly lifted from the Cross by his grief-stricken followers. Michelangelo's (1475–1564) statue of Moses is of a strong man with well-formed biceps, veins on his hands, and the curls of his hair and beard individually picked out.

When the humanist cry of *ad fontes*, 'to the sources', was applied to Christianity, documents from the early church were read in their original languages in an attempt to get close to what the first Christians believed. This raised inevitable questions about how things had become so different. A catalyst for religious change was Desiderius Erasmus (c. 1466–1536). Inspired by humanist scholarship he produced a Greek edition of the New Testament in 1516, which proved essential to the work of Luther and Tyndale. He lamented the 'translator's clumsiness or inattention' in earlier Bible translations: Matthew 4:17 had been rendered 'Do penance, the kingdom of God is at hand', rather than 'Be penitent' or 'Repent'. Erasmus also criticized aspects of the Catholic Church, especially in his works *In Praise of Folly* and *Enchiridion Militis Christiani*. He lamented papal militarism, believing the weapons of the true Christian were prayer and the Bible. Erasmus believed it a mortal sin to give to richly endowed monasteries and shrines while 'Christ's living temples', the poor, starved.

Although it has been suggested that Erasmus 'laid the egg that Luther hatched', he never broke with the Catholic Church, and differed from the Reformer on key issues, including arguing that human works had a contribution to play in salvation. To some Erasmus is the apostle of common sense, calling for moderation in theological dispute; to others he failed to follow through the implications of his ideas.

Luther

It fell to Martin Luther (1483–1546) to take to a new level the challenges Erasmus had raised. Luther dramatically abandoned his hoped-for legal career after a lightning strike threw him to the ground during a thunderstorm, and he vowed to become a monk. Despite suffering deep anxieties (*Anfechtung*) about his spiritual state, Luther's career as an Augustinian monk was a considerable success. He became a doctor of theology in 1512, and by 1515, aged just thirty-two, he was district vicar, with oversight of ten monasteries. Influenced by the views of the *via moderna* theological school that he should do his best in the religious sphere and that God would make up what was lacking, Luther's acute mind raised questions. What if he did not do his best? Lack of assurance of acceptance with God plagued him.

Martin Luther

After becoming lecturer in biblical theology at Wittenberg University, Luther regularly taught directly from the biblical text. His view of God gradually changed from fear of overwhelming judgment and condemnation, to reliance on mercy and grace. Sometime between 1513 and 1519 his 'breakthrough' occurred. Key was Romans 1:17 – 'The righteous will live by faith.' He realized that this righteousness was not earned through a religious life but that it was the gift of God, which came by faith in the work of Christ. Luther rejoiced: 'At this I felt myself straightaway born afresh and to have entered through the open gates into paradise itself.'

A range of factors, from monastic politics to psychological and family pressures, have been postulated as lying behind this change, but at its heart lay a transformed theological understanding, rooted in deep scriptural study. Its outcome shaped not only Luther's career path but also the religious, political and social shape of significant parts of Europe. A series of influential writings followed. His 'Ninety-Five Theses' (1517) challenged the Roman Catholic Church's teaching on indulgences. In 1520 Luther published three widely read treatises. His *Open Letter to the Christian Nobility of the German Nation* called for Germany's leaders to take responsibility for reforming the church. In the *Babylonish Captivity of the Church* he proposed reducing the sacraments from seven to two: the Eucharist and baptism. *The Freedom of the Christian Man* explored the relationship between faith and works, stressing that good works do not create the transformed life but flow from it.

In June 1520 the papal bull *Exsurge Domine* condemned Luther's views. When he refused to recant he was excommunicated as a heretic. Luther's life was now on the line. At the Diet (imperial parliament) held in Worms in 1521, Luther resolutely affirmed his conviction as to the supreme authority of Scripture in matters of belief and practice, declaring, 'Here I stand; I can do no other.' It was a profound statement of the rights of individual conscience and of interpretation of Scripture.

This was a pivotal moment for the Western Church. It had accommodated previous monastic reforming movements, but Luther's call to rethink doctrine and practice was rejected. He was spared death only by the intervention of Frederick, the elector of Saxony. By 1522 Luther was back in Wittenberg, where the Reformation of the church had begun. Luther's translation of the Bible into German (the New Testament was completed in 1522 and the Old Testament in 1534) became the rock on which German Protestantism was built. Other German cities began to adopt the Reformation model, led by Nuremburg, and then Strasbourg. In 1525 Luther broke with clerical celibacy and married a former nun, Katherine von Bora.

Prompted by Luther's assertions of the equality of all before God, a peasants' revolt broke out against oppressive landlords. Faced by impending social collapse, Luther called on the nobility to end the rebellion, which they brutally did. Luther recognized that alongside having access to reading Scripture, the laity needed trained pastors to teach them and help them interpret it. In 1529 he lamented, 'Dear God, help us! . . . the common man, especially in the villages, knows absolutely nothing about Christian doctrine.' In the same year he published the Larger and Smaller Catechisms as a teaching tool for both adults and children.

The spread of Lutheranism

The protection afforded to Luther by the authorities in Saxony resulted in an institutional Protestant state-church. Wittenberg became the intellectual heart of a pan-European religious culture, eventually stretching from Germany to Denmark and Sweden, sending out a steady stream of pastors to meet the demands from many territories and cities. The German Reformation was by no means Luther's work alone. Philip Melanchthon (1497–1560) was a brilliant theologian in his own right, deputizing for Luther in key debates including the 1530 Diet of Augsburg, where a conciliatory position with the Catholic authorities was sought. Of different order was the Croat Matthias Flacius (1520–75), named 'Illyricus', professor of Hebrew at Wittenberg before lecturing in Magdeburg, Jena, Regensburg and Frankfurt. He dismissed Melanchthon's approach as meek and compromising.

In 1529 a group of princes at the Diet of Speyer issued a 'protestation' against the imperial condemnation of Lutheranism, from which the term 'Protestant'

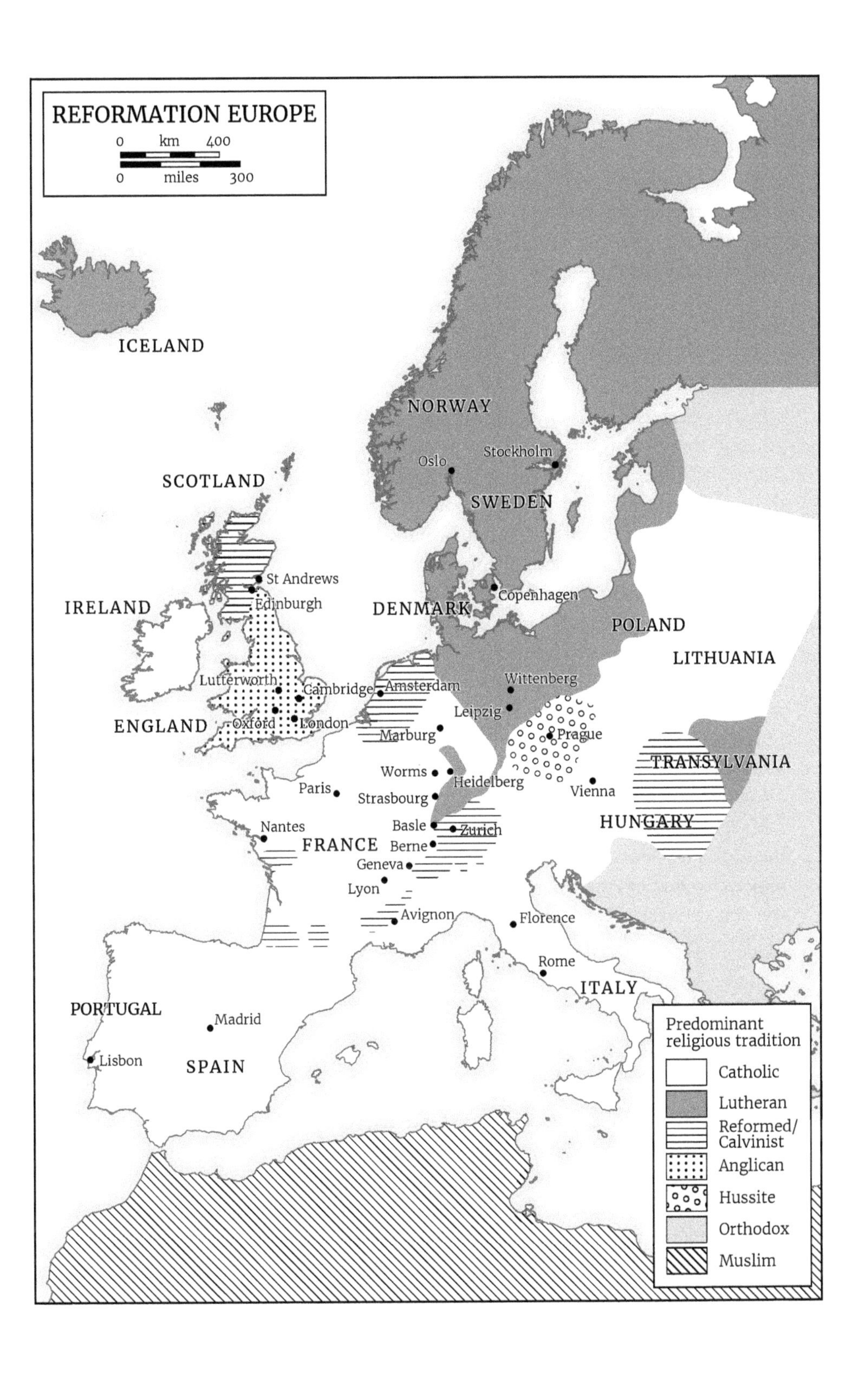
REFORMATION EUROPE
0 km 400
0 miles 300
ICELAND
NORWAY
Oslo
Stockholm
SWEDEN
SCOTLAND
St Andrews
Edinburgh
IRELAND
DENMARK
Copenhagen
POLAND
LITHUANIA
Lutterworth
Cambridge
Amsterdam
Wittenberg
Leipzig
ENGLAND
Oxford
London
Marburg
Prague
TRANSYLVANIA
Worms
Heidelberg
Paris
Strasbourg
Vienna
Nantes
Basle
Zurich
HUNGARY
FRANCE
Berne
Geneva
Lyon
Avignon
Florence
Rome
ITALY
PORTUGAL
Madrid
Lisbon
SPAIN
Predominant religious tradition
Catholic
Lutheran
Reformed/ Calvinist
Anglican
Hussite
Orthodox
Muslim

derives. Lutheranism was formally defined by the 1530 Augsburg Confession. This was followed in 1531 by the formation of the Schmalkaldic League, a defensive alliance of Lutheran states. Yet, in the years before his death in 1546, Luther lamented how shallow the adherence of many to his teaching was, and how the spiritual renewal of the Reformation had slipped into confessionalization.

The late 1540s saw debate descend into periodic war between German states which adopted Lutheranism and those which remained Roman Catholic. The Peace of Augsburg (1555) sought a resolution, deciding that the religious complexion of an individual state would be determined by the ruler's personal religious practice. This brought competition and instability over the right to educate the children of the ruler. Some lands were 'reconverted' on several occasions. By 1576 Lutheranism was established in three German electorates, thirty-four principalities, and other counties and cities. Maximillian II (1527–76), a German prince who also ruled Bohemia, Hungary, Croatia and parts of Austria, and was Holy Roman Emperor from 1564 to 1576, tolerated the spread of Lutheranism and other Reformed groups in his lands.

Gustav Vasa was elected king of Sweden in 1523, and in 1527 he took control over the national church, separating from Rome over the pope's interference in the Swedish church. Gustav declared that the 'pure Word of God' was to be preached in the churches and taught in the schools, sanctioning the spread of Lutheranism. In Denmark, under Frederick I (1523–33), Lutheran Reformers gradually came under protection. A key figure was Hans Tausen (1494–1561), a former monk who returned to Denmark in 1525 to preach an evangelical message to large crowds. In 1536 the national assembly ended the authority of the Roman Catholic bishops, and King Christian III ruled as a Protestant monarch. Here Johann Bugenhagen (1485–1558) took a leading role in reforming the state church. From 1560 to 1700 only 'pure' Lutheranism was permitted in Denmark.

Zwingli

Whether Luther's works were read by the Swiss Reformer Ulrich Zwingli (1484–1531) before his public adoption of Reformation approaches is unclear, but he was one of many European Christian leaders who at the same period were determined on the need for religious change. Zwingli was greatly influenced by humanist scholarship, and read Erasmus's New Testament in Greek in the year of its publication, also studying Hebrew and the works of the Early Church Fathers. After serving as a parish priest, Zwingli was in 1518 elected 'people's priest' in Zurich's Great Minster. The following year Zwingli fell seriously ill during a plague epidemic in the city, an occurrence which seems to have been part of his unfolding spiritual crisis. He began to preach through the New Testament, and asserted that Scripture alone should be the basis for church practice and teaching. In 1522, with reforming sentiment growing, matters reached an unlikely crisis point over eating sausages.

Ulrich Zwingli

This seemingly innocuous event took place in Lent, when Catholic church law forbade the eating of meat. Zwingli does not appear to have eaten the offending sausages, but he argued that decisions on fasting should be left to the individual. In 1522 he also broke with priestly celibacy and married. In 1523 the first of a series of 'disputations' (public debates) began over the reforms Zwingli had started in Zurich, with the city council voting that they could continue. Zwingli's pattern of gaining popular approval for change through the council brought his reform closer to the people than the Lutheran model, which operated on a top-down basis.

For some the pace of change was too slow. Zwingli had emphasized the importance of Bible study, and some began to adopt very literal, and radical, readings of Scripture. They argued against infant baptism and military service. In 1525 the council resolved that parents who refused to have their children baptized were to be arrested and fined. After George Blaurock (c. 1492–1529) was baptized as a believer by Conrad Grebel (c. 1498–1526), the Zurich council in 1526 declared rebaptism also an offence against the State, punishable by death by drowning. The term Anabaptist (or 'rebaptizers') was used of this radical group, although they contended that their baptism was the one true baptism. In the following year Felix Manz (c. 1498–1527) was found guilty of the capital offence of rebaptizing and executed by drowning. Tragically, a reforming council resorted to oppressing other reform-minded opponents over a matter of biblical interpretation, simply repeating the policy of the Roman Catholic Church of persecuting opponents. It did not convince radicals to change their views, and their ideas spread across Switzerland, Austria and Germany.

In 1525 Zwingli began training preachers in Zurich Cathedral, emphasizing that their ministry was to study and expound Scripture. The Reformed pattern spread steadily: Berne and St Gall embraced it in 1528, and Basel in 1529. In 1529 Philip of Hesse (1504–67), a ruler who had converted to Lutheranism, summoned the Marburg Colloquy of representatives of the German and Swiss Reformation movements, seeking to forge an alliance. Here Luther, Melanchthon and Zwingli agreed on fourteen out of fifteen articles, but not on the Eucharist. Both sides rejected the sacrifice of the mass and transubstantiation but disagreed over the way in which Christ was present when partaking the Eucharist. Luther stressed that Christ was really present with, and under, the elements of bread and wine. Zwingli stressed the real spiritual presence of Christ, seeing the bread and wine simply as memorials of the death of Christ. Philip of Hesse allowed both views to circulate, but the opportunity for a united theological and political front between reform-minded states was lost.

Zwingli was condemned as a heretic in 1526 by the Catholic authorities. In 1531, in the midst of growing tensions, forces from the Swiss Catholic cantons crossed the border and defeated the poorly equipped army of Zurich. Among the dead was Zwingli, who had accompanied the army. The intervention of forces from Berne ensured that Zurich was not lost to the Reformation. Although Protestantism was strong in the city-states, Catholicism tended to predominate in the rural cantons.

The radicals and Anabaptists

Events in Zurich highlight the significance, and potential challenges, of granting the right to interpret the Bible to the individual. Others went much further than the Swiss radicals. The term 'Radical Reformation' is used to describe a wide range of interpretations of the Bible. Thomas Muntzer (c. 1488/9–1525), a radical who supported the Peasants' Revolt in Germany, believed that the kingdom of God would be established on the earth. The Zwickau prophets, an Inspirationalist group who arrived in Wittenberg in 1522 and were condemned by Luther as 'fanatics', caused considerable disturbance by proclaiming the imminent end of the world, claiming direct prophetic inspiration and revelation from the Holy Spirit. In 1534, in the German city of Münster, a radical group led by the apocalyptic preacher John of Leiden proclaimed the 'new Jerusalem'. All books except the Bible were burned, property was held in common and polygamy was permitted. A terrible massacre followed when the city was captured by Catholic forces in 1535. Thereafter, radical sentiment was discredited by association with Münster, even though such extreme views were utterly discountenanced by most Anabaptists.

The Rationalists were the most theologically radical group, using the freedom to interpret the Bible to challenge foundational Christian teachings. Michael Servetus (c. 1509–53), a gifted Spanish scholar and scientist (the first to describe accurately the process of pulmonary circulation), actively promoted anti-trinitarian teaching. The Italian Faustus Socinus (1539–1604), who spent his later years in Poland, also rejected the doctrines of the Trinity, original sin and justification by faith alone. He proposed that Christ's death was a moral example to Christians rather than a substitutionary act of atonement, strongly influencing the development of Unitarian theology.

Most Anabaptists remained orthodox and evangelical in their beliefs, taking the text of the Bible literally. Opposed by both Catholic and Protestant authorities, they became a semi-secret, semi-underground movement. Their leaders served as a powerful missionary force, willing to embrace martyrdom for the sake of the gospel. George Blaurock left Zurich to work in the Tyrol, where he was eventually burned at the stake; Balthasar Hubmaier (1480–1528), a former Catholic preacher and theologian, worked in Waldshut in Austria and then in Moravia, before being executed in Vienna. Conrad Grebel's work in St Gall brought a remarkable response, with 200 people baptized in the river one Palm Sunday and possibly up to 400 more over the next six weeks. In southern Germany Michael Sattler (c. 1490–1527), a former prior, began a theological search which took him to Zurich, where he became an Anabaptist. Sattler played an important role in producing the Schleitheim Confession (1527), which set out core Anabaptist beliefs, order and practice. Sattler was arrested and horribly tortured before being burned at the stake, signalling to his followers from the flames that he had sustained his faith.

Some 700 Anabaptists were executed at the hands of the Roman Catholic authorities, and around eighty in Protestant regions in the 1530s, with many others arrested and imprisoned. Both Catholic authorities and Protestant Reformers, such as Luther, Zwingli and Calvin, who depended on the sanction of the State for their reforms, upheld the Christendom concept of a Christian society held together by the glue of universal infant baptism and the church–state connection. To reject this was to destabilize society, as was refusal to fight in the army or hold office, such as that of magistrate. Therefore, although Anabaptists rejected violence and political engagement, desiring a spiritual kingdom not an earthly one, their apoliticism was viewed as highly political.

Persecution did not eradicate Anabaptist belief but scattered its adherents to Moravia, Hungary, Holland, England and eventually America. A key figure among the Dutch Anabaptists was Menno Simons (1496–1561). After twelve years as a Catholic priest he adopted Anabaptist views, undertaking an active and highly successful ministry in Holland and parts of Germany. Dutch Anabaptists became known as Mennonites, and his influence is seen in the Waterlander Confession (1577). In order to separate from the pollution of the world, other Anabaptists, such as the followers of Jacob Hutter (c. 1500–36), embraced communal living and a community of goods, based on Acts 2. Hutter's Bruderhof at Nikolsburg was one of some 100 communities established, echoing the desire for separation and spiritual purity found in some medieval Catholic orders.

Calvin

In 1536 the Genevan authorities voted to 'live henceforth according to the law of the gospel and the word of God and abolish all papal abuses', after four years of work by the French Reformer Guillaume Farel (1489–1565). The decision was largely political and economic, and in his quest for a genuine spiritual transformation Farel invited a young French scholar, John Calvin (1509–64), to assist him. Calvin was thoroughly schooled in humanist scholarship at the universities of Paris and Orléans. Of his conversion to Protestantism, which probably took place in 1532–3, Calvin simply records, 'God subdued and made teachable an unteachable heart.' The French king, Francis I (r. 1515–47), had initially been open to reform-minded humanism, but when demands for changes in the mass became overt, persecutions followed, and many Protestants, including Calvin, fled Paris.

John Calvin

The task in Geneva was made difficult by the desire of the civil authorities to retain control of both church and society. Calvin sought to work in partnership with them, but in the face of profound disagreements with the city council over issues related to reform, he and Farel were forced to leave Geneva. Calvin went to Strasbourg, where between 1538 and 1541 he worked with Martin Bucer (1491–1551), the 'fourth man' of the Reformation. Bucer proved highly influential on Calvin and the subsequent reforms in Geneva.

When the Genevan council invited Calvin to return, he presented the *Ecclesiastical Ordinances*, his plan for the reformed structure of the church. Its fourfold leadership model, of pastors (ministers), doctors of theology (lecturers in theology), lay elders (often chosen from among the civic leaders) and lay deacons (to minister the church's social care and concern), was largely adopted by churches in the Presbyterian tradition. Yet it was 1553 before Calvin saw real success in his work, largely achieved through regular preaching, and teaching of both adults and children. The Genevan Academy, which opened in 1559, served primary and secondary levels and also functioned as a Reformed university, attracting students from across Europe. Calvin's *Institutes* became a core statement of Reformed theology, synthesizing biblical, historical and patristic sources, and ideas from other Reformers. It was a framework for biblical interpretation, to 'open a way for all children of God into a good and right understanding of Holy Scriptures'. He placed at the heart of wisdom two things: 'the knowledge of God and of ourselves'. His genius was to bring structure and order to the Reformed system.

Of the Reformers, Calvin has become one of the most controversial. He taught predestination, but so did Luther, Zwingli, Augustine and Paul. It was perhaps the clear focus that he gave to the teaching that has attracted attention, although his successor Theodore Beza (1519–1605) rendered it more systematic and rigid. Also controversial was the trial and execution of Michael Servetus, for rejecting the Trinity and the deity of Christ. The execution was not Calvin's decision but that of the Genevan council. Servetus would have faced the same outcome in any Protestant or Catholic city. Calvin tried hard to persuade him of the error of his thinking, but he accepted the prevailing idea that to stop the destructive effect of false teaching, which left hearers in danger of eternal condemnation, heretics should be put to death. A third controversial area was the attempt to reform the social and moral lifestyle of Geneva's populace. To modern eyes this appears intrusive, yet church control of private lives was an accepted part of the Christendom concept, held by both Protestants and Catholics alike.

The Reformed churches of Europe

Geneva became the centre of the non-Lutheran Reformation, attracting some 5,000 refugees from across Europe. Calvin encouraged and promoted an extensive network, training over 200 pastors for the Reformed churches of France and writing many treatises and letters in French. Despite severe persecution, by 1562 the French Protestant (Huguenot) church numbered perhaps 10% of the French population, with a further 20% in sympathy. A period of severe repression culminated in the St Bartholomew's Day massacre of August 1572 when at least 5,000 (some estimates say 30,000) Protestants were killed by Catholics. The conflict ended when Henry of Navarre, a Huguenot, converted to Roman Catholicism in order to ascend to the throne as Henry IV. His pragmatism is famously summed up in the (now questioned) comment attributed to him: 'Paris is well worth a mass.' In 1598 he issued the Edict of Nantes, granting Protestants a limited measure of toleration and civil rights, a rare example of religious pluralism in Europe. Protestantism in France never fully recovered from the persecutions, whereas renewed Catholicism became the 'first daughter of Rome'.

The Reformed churches made significant headway in the highly urbanized Low Countries. Here Protestants faced some of the severest repression anywhere in Europe, with over 1,300 victims between 1523 and 1566. They survived by forming underground churches, but the situation descended into rebellion. By 1609 the seven northern provinces had become an independent Protestant country (the Netherlands). The southern provinces (Belgium) remained largely Roman Catholic.

In 1561 the elector Palatine, Frederick III, adopted Calvinism, and his capital, Heidelberg, became the centre of the Reformed faith in Germany. The Heidelberg Catechism of 1563, composed by Caspar Olevianus (1536–87) and Zacharias Ursinus (1534–84), became the Reformed equivalent of the Augsburg Confession. In the next thirty years a significant number of smaller German territories moved from a Lutheran to a Reformed position.

The network of Reformed churches shared theological and political ideas, and a common sense of identity. The Reformed tradition was often a grassroots movement well before it was officially endorsed. The state church became Reformed quickly in Scotland and more slowly in the Netherlands. In Hungary the majority of the population had embraced Protestantism by the end of the century, with Reformed Protestants around 40–45% of the total and Lutherans about 25%. However, the intense efforts of the Counter-Reformation in the seventeenth century saw the majority revert to Catholicism, leaving a significant Protestant minority. In Poland, Lutheranism gained followers among German-speakers in the 1520s and 1530s, while the Reformed churches also made progress during a period of relative toleration. John à Lasco (1499–1560), a native Polish nobleman, spent the last years of his life advancing the cause. At the height of its strength, over half of the members of the upper house of the Polish Diet were Protestants. This brief Protestant flowering was ended during the reign of King Sigismund III Vasa (1587–1632), who was strongly influenced by the Jesuits. In 1666 apostasy from Catholicism was banned and deemed punishable by death.

England and Scotland

The Reformations in England and Scotland were shaped by the religious preference of the monarch, political considerations, dynastic complications and genuine popular movements for religious change. Institutional weaknesses in the church included absenteeism by bishops and clergy, low levels of morality and poor education. Yet acceptance of Roman Catholic teaching on heaven, purgatory, hell, prayers and masses for the dead was widespread, although often mixed with folk belief and superstition.

The humanist scholarly approach, so influential in mainland Europe, was also significant in England. Erasmus taught in Cambridge for several years. John Colet (1467–1519) lectured systematically through the Epistle to the Romans at Oxford University. William Tyndale (1490–1536) was much influenced by humanism. His determination to translate the Bible into English, so that the 'boy at the plough' could understand the Scriptures, met with opposition from the English church hierarchy. Tyndale took his work to Europe, hunted by the Catholic authorities for his endeavours. By the time of his final arrest in 1535, he had translated the New Testament, the Pentateuch and the historical books of the Old Testament into English. It was reported that his dying prayer as he was executed in 1536 was 'Lord, open the king of England's eyes'. When, in 1535, Miles Coverdale (1488–1568) published a complete Bible in English, he used much of Tyndale's work. In 1538 Tyndale's hope was fulfilled when King Henry VIII permitted the printing of Bibles in English, and ordered a copy to be placed in every church.

Henry VIII's desperate search for a male heir, and the refusal of the pope to annul his first marriage, led to his growing estrangement from the Catholic Church. Although Henry remained a Catholic, he encouraged pro-Lutheran voices in England as he sought to pressurize the papacy. In 1534, following Scandinavian precedents, Henry declared himself the supreme head of the English church, making the formal break with Rome complete. Inspired by the new Archbishop of Canterbury, Thomas Cranmer (1489–1556), and the Lord Chancellor, Thomas Cromwell (c. 1485–1540), a series of cautious reforms followed.

Henry was succeeded in 1547 by his ten-year-old son Edward VI, who had been educated by Protestants. Cranmer, supported by preaching and reforming bishops, introduced liturgical reforms including, in 1549, the Book of Common Prayer. This process of reformation was cut short by the death of Edward VI in 1553. He was succeeded by his Catholic half-sister Mary Tudor who swiftly undertook a work of counter-reformation, restoring Catholic practice. Her repression of Protestants earned her the title 'Bloody Mary'. Nearly 300 were martyred, including Cranmer.

When Mary died unexpectedly in 1558, she was succeeded by her half-sister Elizabeth I, reared as a Protestant. She displayed astute political sense during her long reign through volatile times, including an attempted invasion of England by the Catholic Spanish in 1588. Her 'Elizabethan Settlement' steered a middle course between Protestant and Catholic emphases, producing an episcopal church leadership, a largely Protestant theology in the Thirty-Nine Articles, and elements of Catholic practice retained in the liturgy.

In Scotland, closely tied to Catholic France, calls to deal with problems with clerical discipline and morality went unheeded. The influential Archbishop of St Andrews, David Beaton (c. 1494–1546), had at least eight illegitimate children. Protestantism filtered into Scotland through merchants, lawyers and academics. In 1528 Patrick Hamilton, aged just twenty-four, was burned at the stake outside the University of St Andrews for promoting Lutheran teaching. The same fate befell George Wishart (c. 1513–46), whose Protestantism had attracted a significant group of followers. Among them was a former Catholic priest, John Knox (c. 1513–72), who was captured by the French authorities after a mini-rebellion in St Andrews. After his release Knox travelled to England and then to Geneva, where he found what he called 'the most perfect school of Christ since the time of the apostles'.

Knox returned to Scotland in 1559 to lead a popular Protestant uprising. When Scottish noblemen overturned the Scottish–French alliance in 1560, he was invited to draw up the Scots Confession for the church. It was followed in 1562 with the Book of Common Order, establishing the pattern for worship services, and then the Book of Discipline. They owed much to what he had seen in Geneva. Knox envisioned a comprehensive church order, embracing education and social concern.

Through much of the 1560s the outcome of the Scottish Reformation remained unclear. Mary Queen of Scots returned from France in 1561 to rule as a Catholic monarch of Scotland until she abdicated in 1567. She was succeeded by her one-year-old son, James VI, who was reared as a Protestant by the Scottish leaders. When Elizabeth I of England died in 1603, unmarried and childless, the English and Scottish crowns were united under James. Bitter disputes over the nature of the Scottish church continued until 1690 before Presbyterianism was legally established by the crown.

Thus was drawn the religious map of most of Europe. Significant parts remained strongly Roman Catholic, largely unchanged by the Reformation. In the East the Orthodox churches of Russia, Greece and the Balkans were similarly substantially unchanged by the Reformation, although there was some periodic dialogue with the Reformers which influenced some Orthodox leaders. Protestantism remained almost entirely a European phenomenon, whereas political and economic considerations would enable Catholicism to re-engage with global mission.

13. CONTINUITY AND CHANGE

Lifeline

1492 – surrender of Granada to Christian forces
1540 – papal recognition of the Society of Jesus
1545 – Council of Trent opens
1552 – death of Francis Xavier
1556 – death of Ignatius Loyola
1559 – first Jesuit mission in Japan
1565 – permanent Spanish settlement in the Philippines
1580 – Jesuits establish mission in China
1614 – Japanese government begins efforts to suppress Christianity

For some, times of transition and debate lead not to the rejection of inherited and established views but to holding them even more resolutely. In the sixteenth century there were significant calls for reform not only from those who eventually left Roman Catholicism but also from those who remained within its fold. Some, like Erasmus, urged reform but stayed faithful to Rome, despite being uncomfortable with the prevailing system. Others, aware of a need for change, experienced a deeper and more intense sense of devotion to Catholicism. A number of internal Catholic reforms dealt with the issues the Reformers highlighted; others drove Protestants and Catholics further apart.

That this process of internal change took place at a time when Catholicism was afforded opportunities to spread globally proved deeply significant. The work of Columbus and Vasco da Gama did not change the shape of the world, but they made it look a different, far more accessible, place. The sense of responsibility to proclaim the Christian message to hitherto unknown peoples became deeper.

The Inquisition renewed

Sanctioned by papal commissions in the thirteenth century against the Cathars and Waldensians, the Inquisition long predated the Reformation. It was renewed with the Spanish Inquisition in 1478, followed by that in Portugal in 1536. This brutal episode was marked by deep-rooted suspicion of other cultures and a desire to eradicate any taint of Muslim or Jewish influence. The Inquisition shaped the spirituality of many seeking a deeper and more intense devotional life, inspiring more ardent Catholic practice, accompanied by crusading militaristic images of discipline and spiritual warfare.

Around a third of all Jews in Spain were massacred after a wave of anti-Jewish preaching in 1391, with something like a third of the rest forcibly converted to Christianity, although the loyalty of these *conversos* was often doubted. The first Grand Inquisitor of the Spanish Inquisition, the Dominican Tomás de Torquemada (1420–98), ruthlessly punished thousands accused of continuing to maintain Jewish practices. By 1500 more than 1,500 had been executed for Judaizing; others suffered lesser punishments and up to 100,000 Sephardic Jews fled abroad. The pattern was repeated in Portugal with the forcible baptism of many Jews in the 'Great Conversion' of 1497, and executions of those who continued Jewish practices.

Spanish forces completed the Reconquista in 1492 with the capture of the final Islamic stronghold of Granada. The forced conversion of remaining Muslims was ordered in Granada in 1500 and Castile in 1502. In 1526 all remaining Muslims in the rest of Spain were forcibly baptized, but these *moriscos* remained suspect. Some 8,000 of them were tried by the Inquisition, with around 200 executed. As late as 1609, in a stark act of ethnic cleansing, 300,000 *moriscos* were expelled from Spain. In total, between 1540 and 1700 Spain witnessed more than 40,000 inquisitorial trials, with a further 13,000 in Portugal.

Desire for purity in the Spanish nation was matched by desire for purity in the church. After Cardinal Ximenes (1436–1517) became Inquisitor-General in 1507, clergy were forced to live in their parishes, and monks to embrace their vows of poverty; 'purity of blood' had to be demonstrated to achieve promotion. By the time of Philip II of Spain (1527–98), the Inquisition had ensured that to be Spanish was to be a traditionalist Catholic.

Such a strong reassertion of Catholic culture gave little room for emerging Protestantism to make headway. Those even suspected of humanist-minded reform, such as Bartolomoé Carranza (1503–76), Archbishop of Toledo, were silenced. He spent seventeen years in prison before his death. Ironically, his catechism was the basis of that approved at the Council of Trent. A Spanish 'Confession of Faith', with marked Lutheran and Reformed elements, was in existence in 1560, but underground networks of Reformation sympathizers were a target of inquisitorial efforts. The Vatican's Congregation of the Index, founded in 1571, censored books containing unacceptable teachings, destroying thousands of copies of Reformed writings. By the end of the century the Inquisition had largely cleared Spain, Italy and Portugal of Protestant influence. In Spanish-controlled Flanders the Inquisition was especially vigorous, with large numbers of Protestants executed. After jurisdiction over heresy was given to the secular courts in most of northern Europe in the sixteenth century, more than 3,000 Protestants, many of them Anabaptists, were burned there for heresy.

Catholic reform

This heightened religious atmosphere, with its desire for a purified form of Catholic devotion, fed into the intense, mystical spirituality of Teresa of Avila (1515–82), who joined a Carmelite convent in 1533. In her quest for a simple devotional life of spiritual perfection, she spoke of visions and described her heart feeling as if it had been pierced by a spear of divine love. She sought to return her order to its origins in the wilderness: her 'Discalced' Carmelites walked barefoot. Another Spaniard whose spirituality was distinguished by mystical images and whom Teresa encouraged to join the order was John of the Cross (1542–91). His famous meditation *The Dark Night of the Soul* explores the painful hardships and difficulties met on the journey towards union with God, battling against the world, the devil and the flesh.

Around the time of Luther's crisis between 1514 and 1517, the Oratory of Divine Love was formed by Giovanni Carafa (1476–1559). This intense, austere movement of priests who upheld monastic vows inspired deep devotion to Catholic Church order, and established orphanages, hospitals and charities for the relief of the poor. It attracted high-calibre recruits and has been called a 'nursery of bishops'. Its members loved Roman Catholicism and abhorred deviations from it – whether Muslim, Jewish or Protestant.

Teresa of Avila

In 1536 a papal commission undertook a thorough review of the Catholic Church. Its findings substantiated some of the Reformers' concerns about unqualified clergy, clerical non-residence in many parishes, poor levels of church discipline and low moral standards in some religious orders. Yet those who made sustained calls for wholesale change from within Catholicism, such as Cardinal Contarini (1483–1542), were suspected of Lutheranism. In 1511 Contarini had undergone a spiritual crisis similar to that of Luther. With others, like the Capuchin monk Bernardino Ochino (1487–1564), and Pietro Martire Vermigli (1499–1562), later known as Peter Martyr, he advocated an emphasis on the grace of God which came through faith, with a devotional attraction to the Cross of Christ. In 1541 Contarini attempted to negotiate a doctrinal compromise with Melanchthon and Bucer at the Colloquy of Regensburg. Although his venture nearly succeeded, after its failure he found himself under house arrest. Within a year he had died, and Vermigli and Ochino fled north to join the Reformers.

After the death of Pope Paul III in 1549, there was a possibility that the reform-minded English cardinal Reginald Pole, living in exile in Italy, might succeed him. Pole sympathized with Erasmus and inclined towards Contarini's views, but Carafa swiftly intervened with suggestions of heresy against him. Had the opportunity to find a *via media* been embraced, the religious outcome for Europe might have been different. Instead Carafa, now a cardinal, moved into the ascendancy. He commenced the Inquisition in the Italian Papal States in 1542 and served as Inquisitor-General. Copies of the Talmud were burned. Jews were forced to live in ghettoes and to wear yellow stars or hats. There were more than a hundred heresy executions before 1620, mainly of Protestants. Carafa's authoritarian approach to reform dominated the Catholic response to Protestantism after he became Pope Paul IV (1555–9).

Ignatius Loyola and the Jesuits

One leader of renewal within Catholicism who typified the rigorist Spanish approach was Ignatius Loyola (1491–1556). Born to a noble family in the Basque region, his life as a courtier was dramatically ended when a cannonball shattered his leg during the siege of Pamplona. During his months of convalescence he underwent a profound religious experience through reading the lives of Catholic saints, including those of Francis and Dominic. His crisis led him towards a life of deeper devotion within the Catholic Church. He resolved to apply his courtly chivalric code to the service of 'Our Lady and her Son'. During a time of fasting and penitence Loyola reported visions and religious experiences, which became the basis for his *Spiritual Exercises*, a syllabus for deepening the Christian life through prayer, self-examination and self-surrender.

Ignatius Loyola

Despite being in his late thirties, Loyola spent the years 1528–35 as a student in Paris (when Calvin was also in the city) and gathered around him a group of male followers who became the core of the Society of Jesus. They readily lent obedience to their nobleman leader, adopting a life of preaching, catechizing and hearing confessions, seeking to deepen the adherence of others to Catholicism. Although highly educated they lived a life of poverty, wearing a black gown rather than a monastic habit. The Society of Jesus developed a highly flexible structure. It was not a closed monastic order confined to a religious house, nor was there daily communal worship or a requirement for all members to be ordained. For the Jesuits, as they soon became known, study and action took precedence over ascetic practices.

In 1540 the Society of Jesus received papal authorization. Loyola was elected as the order's superior in 1541, aged fifty-five. Every member offered unconditional obedience to the rulers of the order and the pope: if the church hierarchy declared that white was black, a Jesuit would accept it. The pope quickly recognized the potential for such a group of zealous, committed men, many from noble families, and by the time of Loyola's death in 1556 there were some 1,000 members.

Candidates were carefully selected. Training was rigorous, practical, intellectual and theological, lasting six or seven years. Jesuits who progressed to the elite rank known as 'professed of the fourth vow' offered direct obedience to the pope. At the heart of the Jesuit system was education, and its members also engaged in charitable care and foreign mission. By 1542 a missionary training college had been established in Portugal. In 1622 Loyola was canonized by the Catholic Church, along with Francis Xavier (1506–52) and Teresa of Avila.

Xavier, another son of a noble Spanish family, became renowned for his work in foreign mission. One of Loyola's seven initial devotees, Xavier had shared a room with him when a student in Paris. An intense figure, he subjected himself to rigorous personal discipline and self-punishment. In Paris he encountered both the Renaissance and the Reformation and decisively rejected, indeed hated, both. His admiration was reserved for medieval theology: Xavier may never have carried a Bible with him on all his missionary journeys, nor did he base sermons on scripture texts. Over a span of fifteen years he reached Goa, Sri Lanka, Indonesia, Malaysia and Japan. Jesuits claim that through the influence of Xavier and his associates 700,000 people in various lands were introduced to Catholicism. He died in 1553 in Macao, just across the straits from China, his next intended destination. The accounts of Xavier's missionary journeys stirred deep interest in Catholic mission to unreached territories.

Within Europe the Jesuits were in the vanguard of efforts to combat the spread of Protestantism. The resolution in the Peace of Augsburg (1555) that a nation's religious complexion would follow that of its ruler offered them a strategic route, and they sought out opportunities to teach the children of noble and royal families. In Portugal, which was to become a rich source of recruits, Simon Rodrigues became a confidant of the king, and tutor to his son. In the south of Germany, Jesuits helped ensure that the sons of princes were educated as Catholics. A number of Protestant areas in Germany and Austria were won back to Catholicism through Jesuit efforts. The Jesuits could display a ruthless streak, advising rulers that those guilty, or suspected, of 'heretical impiety' should be treated in a rigorous manner through exile, confiscation of property and even summary executions.

The Council of Trent

In 1545 a council of the church was summoned to meet at Trent (Tridentum in Latin) in northern Italy. It lasted, on and off, until 1563. Of 270 bishops who met, 187 were Italians, ensuring that conservative Catholicism held sway. The papal curia closely controlled proceedings. Many of the Council's decrees were straight rebuttals of the teaching of the Reformers. An emphasis on Scripture alone as the source of Christian teaching and practice was countered by the Council of Trent's resolution that both Scripture and tradition were authoritative, and that the right of biblical interpretation remained with the Catholic Church. Indeed the Council largely restated the core of medieval Catholic doctrine. The Vulgate (Latin) Bible, including the Apocrypha, was accepted as authoritative. Justification by faith alone was rejected; purgatory was reaffirmed, as was transubstantiation. Celibacy was reasserted as the core of the priestly role. The Council resolved that the liturgy and the mass were to be only in Latin, not the vernacular, hence the dominance of the Tridentine mass until the Second Vatican Council in the 1960s. Roman Catholic worship was to be led by priests in a special religious language which only the educated could understand.

Catholicism into Africa

This renewal of Catholic devotional practice coincided with the beginnings of a remarkable expansion of Catholicism. At the heart of both developments were Spain and Portugal. Their ships carried the soldiers and missionaries who turned Catholicism into a global movement. Despite a population of fewer than 2 million people, Portugal's maritime expansion was prodigious, assisted by technological advances in sail power. In a series of papal bulls from the 1440s to the 1480s, successive popes created the Portuguese *padroado*, authorizing the king of Portugal to found churches and monasteries in all the territories his people conquered, and to supply them with clergy or monks. In 1452 Pope Nicholas V, in a move that was to profoundly affect black Africans, also authorized the Portuguese to conquer and enslave the peoples of Guinea. The Portuguese were voracious traders, trawling the west coast of Africa for gold, ivory and slaves.

In 1488 Bartholomé Dias navigated the Cape of Good Hope, and Vasco da Gama reached India in 1498, seeking 'pepper and souls'. By 1513 the Portuguese had navigated round the Chinese coast. Pedro Álvarez Cabral 'discovered' Brazil in 1500. In their wake a series of Portuguese trading settlements was developed, the bare bones of an empire strung around the ocean rims. With trade and colonization came a quest to impose religious views on their settlements.

During an expedition to the Gambia in 1458, Diogo Gomez debated religious matters with the chief, Nomimansa, who showed interest in Christianity. Gomez persuaded Catholic missionaries to follow, and further Portuguese settlements

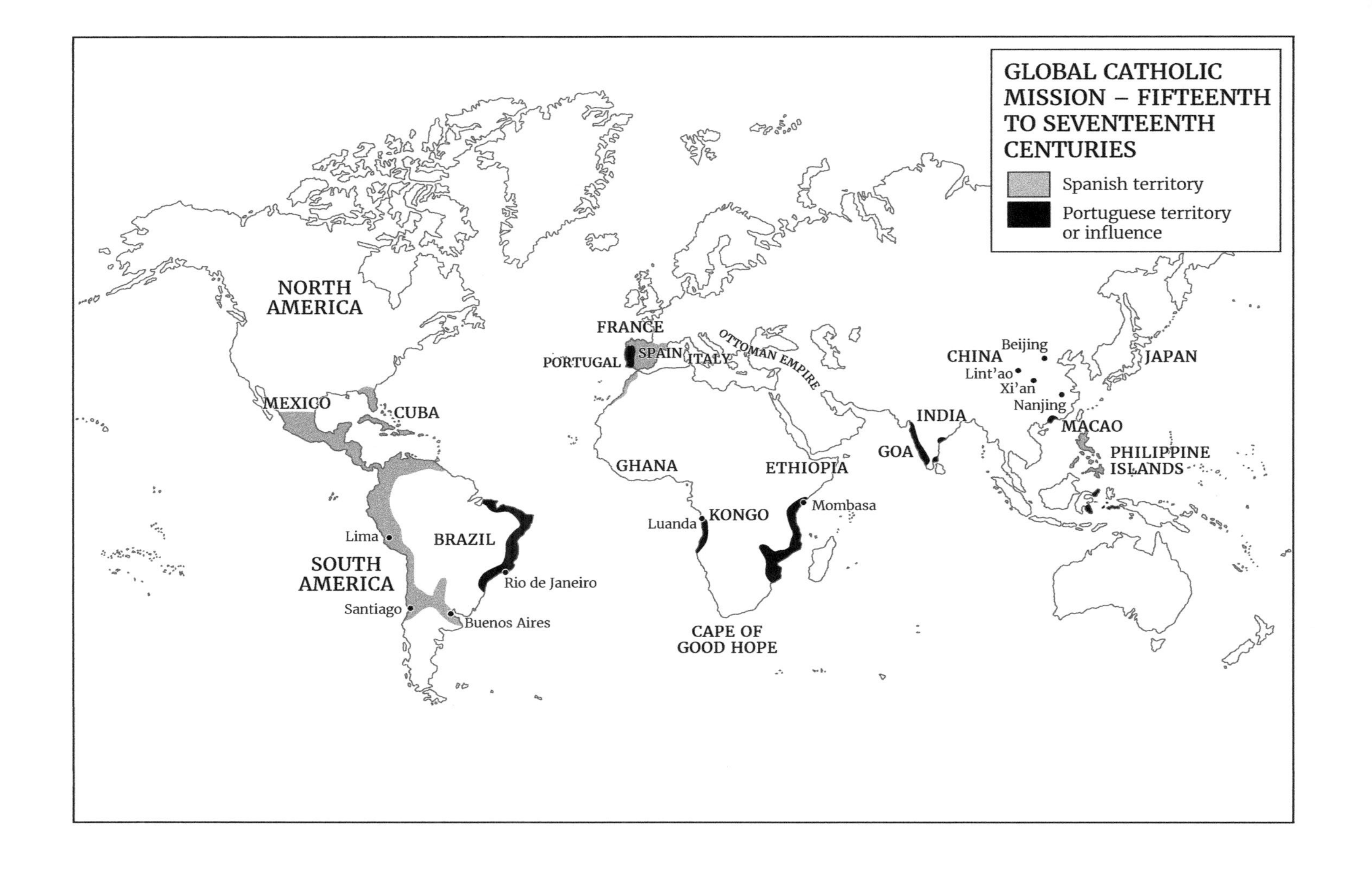
GLOBAL CATHOLIC MISSION – FIFTEENTH TO SEVENTEENTH CENTURIES
Spanish territory
Portuguese territory or influence
NORTH AMERICA
MEXICO
CUBA
SOUTH AMERICA
BRAZIL
Lima
Santiago
Buenos Aires
Rio de Janeiro
FRANCE
PORTUGAL
SPAIN
ITALY
OTTOMAN EMPIRE
GHANA
KONGO
Luanda
ETHIOPIA
Mombasa
CAPE OF GOOD HOPE
GOA
INDIA
CHINA
Beijing
Lint'ao
Xi'an
Nanjing
MACAO
JAPAN
PHILIPPINE ISLANDS

were established on the Gold Coast (Ghana), where a number of chiefs brought their people to be baptized. Christian mission in Africa centred on Portuguese trading posts, but, lamentably, this included slave trading, building on the vast internal African trade. Some 3.5 million slaves were taken in Portuguese ships to Brazil alone. Some priests spoke against this, but many others were complicit. Mass baptisms of slaves before they left Portuguese-controlled ports in West Africa were common, but the message was deeply compromised and they were afforded little subsequent teaching. The papacy used slaves to man its galleys in the Mediterranean until the late eighteenth century.

By 1483 the Portuguese were trading on the Congo River. Here they encountered Mvemba Nzinga, ruler of the kingdom of Kongo, who was to become one of the most significant Christian rulers in African history. He opened schools, built a cathedral, and his son was consecrated as a Catholic bishop. By the time of his death half of his population had been baptized – perhaps 2 million people. The Capuchin order supplied 440 friars working in Kongo and Angola between 1645 and 1835. Mass baptisms, claimed to number over 340,000, often at the behest of local rulers, were reported. Key to the spread of Catholicism were the Kongolese interpreters, who offered basic Christian teaching to children and young people. Yet the relationship with Portugal was troubled, and war in 1655 saw the capital city, and its churches, largely destroyed. Although the Kongo kingdom was still formally Catholic early in the eighteenth century, the church gradually faded away.

Jesuit missionaries established a college in Luanda, Angola, in the early 1550s, and reached Mozambique in 1560, where they baptized a young ruler and several hundred of his people, before travelling further up the Zambezi River. Some of the ruling family of Zimbabwe were baptized in the seventeenth century after military action in which Dominicans had taken part. Catholic mission along the Kenyan coast began after the Portuguese erected 'Fort Jesus' in Mombasa in 1591, and by 1597 there were some 4,000 converts. A backlash followed in the early 1630s as Mombasa fell under Muslim control, with 250 Portuguese and African Christians martyred, and others enslaved.

In 1541 Portuguese forces helped Ethiopian rulers defeat Ahmed Gragn (1506–43), who had declared an Islamic holy war on Ethiopia and its church. However, the later Jesuit missionaries proved critical of aspects of Ethiopian Orthodox teaching, and during a hostile reaction in the 1630s they were expelled from Ethiopia. The work of the German Lutheran medical doctoral Peter Heyling (1607/8–c. 1652) proved very significant when he translated part of the New Testament into Amharic, leaving an important legacy for later evangelical missionaries.

Catholic missions to the Americas

Christopher Columbus, on an expedition to find a new route to China and the East Indies, landed instead in what we now know as the Bahamas in 1492. Suddenly the 'West Indies' and the Americas were on the European map. His party included a number of priests intent on spreading Spanish culture and religion. This discovery of a vast new continent galvanized missionary thinking. Pope Julius II granted the Spanish and Portuguese the exclusive rights to preach the gospel in the new territories, in consequence of which Spanish became one of the dominant languages of Christianity.

The Catholicism that reached America was shaped by European events, including the Inquisition. It was often enforced by rulers whose policy was to enslave and brutalize local peoples. The military adventures of Hernán Cortés against the Aztecs in Central America, and Francisco Pizarro against the Incas in Peru, unleashed events of genocidal proportions. The indigenous peoples were decimated by both military actions and the death of thousands from smallpox, which may have been deliberately spread. The first epidemics saw around half of the indigenous population of the Americas perish – in Mexico perhaps 90%. There were probably more victims of these actions of the *conquistadores* than of the Holocaust. Policies of cruel labour exaction followed, and forced resettlement into towns and villages.

Some settlers protested against such vicious treatment, among them the Dominican friar Bartolomé de Las Casas (1484–1566). His attempts to defend humanity and hence the legal rights of the indigenous peoples of South America earned him the title 'Protector of the Indians'. Las Casas argued that the gospel should be extended by 'reason and human persuasion', not by force of arms. In 1537 Pope Paul III finally asserted that indigenous peoples of the Americas were rational human beings with the same rights as the colonists, although their mistreatment continued.

When Cabral landed in Brazil and claimed it for the king of Portugal he was accompanied by a number of priests and fifteen Franciscan monks. The arrival of the Jesuits in 1549 brought a focus on mission to the indigenous peoples which included study of local languages and culture, although this was hindered by the ruling that the Christian message should be preached only in Portuguese. Jesuit policy in Latin America was to gather groups of indigenous peoples into large settlements to 'protect' them from exploitation. The Jesuits ruled over these as benevolent dictators, leaving them highly vulnerable after their order was expelled in the eighteenth century.

By 1550 some 10 million people in the Americas had been baptized as Catholics. Although some were trained as catechists and assistants, native South

Americans were not brought into the priesthood until the eighteenth century. The flamboyant and lavish decoration of Catholic churches appealed to the local populace, as did great religious festivals, such as that on Corpus Christi Day. Images of the Virgin Mary and the saints were prominent, perpetuated by local stories of apparitions and miracles.

One dreadful mistake Las Casas made in his attempts to stop the indigenous people of America from being enslaved on plantations was to suggest that Africans be used instead. A labour force was needed which could survive the climate, diseases and relentless hard work, and so a forced one from Africa was sought. Despite the baptism of many African slaves on embarkation for South America, and others adopting Catholicism on arrival, their African culture and religion was not forgotten. Some slaves merged Catholicism with traditional spiritualities to produce syncretistic religious expressions such as Vodou in Haiti, Candomblé in Brazil and Santería in Cuba. At times the religious practice of folk Catholicism was hard to distinguish from these new spiritualities.

Catholic missions in Asia

In Asia, Catholic missionaries operated without the military backing of the colonial authorities found in South America. Priests and monks travelled with successive Portuguese fleets to minister in the nation's trading outposts. The first Catholic church in India resulting from the new wave of mission was consecrated in Cochin in 1503. After Goa's capture in 1510, it became the headquarters of Portuguese work in India, where Franciscans saw 800 conversions within a year: the first bishop of Goa was consecrated in 1538. Catholicism was presented in a visually attractive form, with splendid processions, ornamented statues and pictures, and use of incense, in ways that appeared similar to Hindu forms. After thirty years of Portuguese rule the majority of Goa's inhabitants remained Hindus or Muslims, but in the early 1540s the more aggressive 'rigour of mercy' policy was adopted, and by the end of the decade all the Hindu temples had been removed.

Francis Xavier established a Jesuit base on Goa in 1542. The college of St Paul, the major training centre for Jesuits in the East, had such influence in the region that they become known as 'Paulists'. Xavier translated the Lord's Prayer, the Apostles' Creed and the Ten Commandments into Tamil, but no chapters of the Bible, and much educational work was rote learning of Catholic teaching. His rigorist Iberian roots were not forgotten, and before his death in 1552, Xavier had recommended the introduction of the Inquisition to Goa against the ancient Thomas Christians. In general, Catholic missionaries showed little respect for the historic churches they encountered in Asia, which lessened the attractiveness of Christianity in the eyes of the local populace, and many converts became as much Europeans as Christians.

Apart from in small territories such as Goa, Catholic missionaries operated in often hostile circumstances and in cultures in which religion was deeply interwoven. In India, Hindu converts to Christianity automatically lost caste. This created a significant barrier for higher castes, so most missionary success was enjoyed among the lowest castes. A notable ministry was undertaken by João de Cruz, a Hindu merchant who had converted to Christianity and adopted a Portuguese name. After he introduced the Paravas (or Bharathas) – pearl-fisher folk of south India – to Catholicism, they accepted Portuguese protection, and around 20,000 were baptized in 1537. Through their influence Catholicism spread to Sri Lanka.

By the middle of the sixteenth century Catholicism was established in India, mainly in areas of European influence, especially in the south-west of India. Together with the Paravas and the Thomas Christians, Christians in India numbered some 150,000, a small fraction of the total population. Progress was hampered by a limited supply of European missionaries who understood local languages, a reluctance to ordain Indian priests and a lack of books. There were attempts at mission to Muslims, including to the court of Akbar, the Great Mogul, in modern Pakistan, where some openness to Catholic missionaries was shown. Although work in the court came to nothing, a number of poor people were attracted to Catholicism.

Under the Chinese emperor Zhu Di (1360–1424) China became one of the most powerful empires. His armada, the largest in the medieval world, explored the seas south of China, westwards towards the Gulf of Aden, and to Madagascar. After his death China turned inwards, making it difficult for Western missionaries to reach the vast Chinese population of 150 million, which dwarfed Europe's 60 million in the early seventeenth century. Between 1581 and 1712, 376 Jesuits sailed for China, although 127 of them died before arrival. Chinese authorities only granted missionaries permanent residence in mainland China in 1583, but the country was then open for nearly a century until the Manchu defeat of the Ming dynasty in 1666. After this, churches in the provinces were again closed and Christianity suppressed. The years of openness saw Christianity progress steadily, with around 2,500 Chinese Christians in 1610, and 70,000–80,000 in 1665. The Jesuits led the way, although Spanish Franciscans and Dominicans arrived in the 1630s. Only one Chinese priest was known to be active, the Dominican Luo Wenzao (1616–91), who was ordained in the Philippines in 1654.

A key figure in Catholic mission to China was the Italian Jesuit Matteo Ricci (1552–1610). Building on significant interest in Western sciences in the late Ming dynasty, the Jesuits published and printed books on theological and moral issues, and also on astronomy, mathematics, geometry and geography. They believed these would open elite literate minds to questions about the meaning of the cosmos and the nature of the Creator. Some missionaries served as technical advisers to the emperor, ensuring that the Chinese court protected Christianity. Yet the fruit of this was meagre: in 1636, of 38,300 Catholics in China, just fourteen were high-level officials. Over time the Jesuits adopted the dress of Confucianist scholars, emphasizing the value of 'practical' learning. They identified similarities between Christian and Confucian norms, studying and translating the Chinese classics, which shaped culture, moral values and social order. This Confucian–Christian synthesis was also found among seventeenth-century Chinese Christian scholars, such as Zhu Zongyuan (c. 1616–60), and the brothers Han Yun and Han Lin (c. 1600–49).

The Chinese language lay at the heart of the missionary process, allowing Christian ideas to be expressed using Chinese thought patterns. Ricci worked on a translation of the Bible into Chinese, although he fell foul of Rome for using the Chinese word for 'King of Heaven' for God. Eventually official versions transliterated the word *Deus* into Chinese characters, leaving Chinese Christians called 'Deusts', condemned for following the religion of foreign 'devils'. Any such accommodation was strongly opposed by Dominican and Franciscan monks, who had been schooled in the confrontational approach of the Latin American mission.

Christianity spread quickly to the major centres, first to Nanjing in the south, then Beijing, and the Fujian and Shanxi regions. Well-known converts included Xu Guangqi (1562–1633), who held the position of Grand Secretary, one of the highest positions in the civil administration. These converts helped produce a number of writings known as 'Heavenly Studies' (*tianxue*), covering theological, philosophical, ethical, and scientific topics, and offering answers to key life questions. Over time the missionaries turned their attention to the lower officials and common people, where the most enduring acceptance of Christianity occurred. Here Christians had a reputation for charitable works and social harmony. Most were illiterate, maintaining a simple devotional life and keeping Sunday, although their religious practice sometimes looked akin to Buddhism. With so few priests, the laity played a key role, including serving as catechists. Women were central to maintaining religious practice within the family. This locally embedded belief and ritual allowed Catholicism to be sustained even when missionary leaders were expelled. Despite severe obstacles, by the late eighteenth century the Catholic community in China still numbered some 200,000.

The work of the Jesuits in Japan began as a great success and ended in disastrous failure. Xavier and other Jesuits arrived in Japan in 1549. Within thirty years there were some 130,000 baptized Japanese, and perhaps 300,000 by the end of the sixteenth century. An attempt was made to create a church well adapted to Japanese culture and society, with a clergy drawn from the higher orders. The Jesuits had been able to take advantage of a period of instability among the feudal lords, but when the powerful Tokugawa family emerged as the dominant political force, they turned against the missionaries. A number of Franciscan friars who had arrived in 1593 were executed, and in the early seventeenth century all Europeans were expelled from Japan, leaving only one small trading post. One of the most brutal campaigns of persecution against Christians in history followed, reducing a thriving church to a handful of Catholic believers who met in secret. They somehow survived until the 1850s when Japan once again opened up to foreign influence.

When the Portuguese explorer Ferdinand Magellan reached the Philippines in 1521, he found a group of scattered peoples without centralized power. Colonization and trade was accompanied by Christianization, with significant missionary effort by Augustinian friars, Dominicans and Franciscans. The name Las Islas Filipinas was given to the archipelago in 1543 by the Spanish explorer Ruy López de Villalobos in honour of the king of Spain, and in 1565 the first Spanish settlement was established. The Philippines were part of the Spanish Empire for more than 300 years. Spanish colonization created the only major country in Asia that was predominantly Catholic.

In the sixteenth and seventeenth centuries Catholicism became a global phenomenon through the determined and courageous work of its missionaries. Yet for a long time it was never truly indigenous in its mission fields because of a reluctance to train native clergy or entrust them with significant leadership roles. A church structure emerged that was dominated by European influences and which worked only when there was a ready supply of European clergy. A jolt was to come in 1773 with the papal suppression of the Jesuit order, but widespread training of local leaders did not happen until the twentieth century.

14. DESIRES FOR PURITY, ORTHODOXY AND PIETY

Lifeline

1448 – Russian bishops elect Metropolitan of Kiev and all Rus
1589 – head of Russian Church appointed as Patriarch
1604 – Hampton Court Conference, England
1620 – Pilgrim Fathers sail to America
1642 – beginning of Civil War in England
1648 – Peace of Westphalia
1649 – execution of Charles I of England
1653 – Oliver Cromwell becomes Lord Protector
1660 – restoration of Charles II
1685 – revocation of Edict of Nantes
1721 – Peter 'the Great' begins reform of Russian Church

Self-image and issues of truth and purity can be major challenges for young people entering adulthood, the outcome of which helps to shape their future identity. Key debates in sixteenth- and seventeenth-century Europe related to the nature of the 'true faith', religious 'purity', inner piety and the structure of the church. They were themes that had recurred in the Eastern and Western churches from the fourth-century ascetics onwards, but they now saw significant expression within Protestantism. The outcome was often dissatisfaction with a range of religious establishments.

The Eastern Orthodox churches remained convinced that theirs was the expression closest to early Christianity and therefore the purest form. However, apart from in Russia, their power and treasures were steadily denuded. Crusader attacks on Constantinople at the start of the thirteenth century brought systematic looting of the city, with Christian relics seized, including the reputed crown of thorns, which quickly found their way into Western monasteries and churches. Constantinople was restored to Eastern control in 1261, but as the authority of the Byzantine emperors steadily declined, Orthodoxy was freed from the political fortunes of the empire, and the authority of the Orthodox Patriarch increased. In the late fourteenth century he declared himself 'leader of all Christians found anywhere on the inhabited earth ... the father and teacher of them all'. Orthodox churches in other countries were also permitted more autonomy. The first archbishop of the autocephalous (ecclesiastically independent) Church of Serbia was appointed in 1291. Throughout the fourteenth century Byzantine territory was gradually encircled by the Ottomans, forcing Orthodoxy to become more adaptable in areas under Islamic control.

A last major attempt to heal the Orthodox–Roman Catholic schism of 1054 came with the Florentine Union (1438–9), negotiated between Roman Catholic and Orthodox leaders as part of the Eastern Church's appeal for help as the armies of the Turks threatened Constantinople. Although a form of agreement was reached by the embattled Byzantine emperor, it was widely rejected and the Orthodox synods refused to ratify it. Prince Basil II of Moscow rejected the concessions in 1452. The fall of Constantinople the following year elevated the status of Moscow to a 'third Rome', with claims to be a genuine successor to the Byzantine capital. Indeed the negotiations at Florence probably pushed the two traditions further apart. In 1453 the city of Constantinople capitulated to an army of over 60,000 soldiers, followed by murder, rape and looting. The dream of Islamic rulers of an empire mirroring Constantine's Eastern empire, based on Constantinople, with Islam as the predominant religion, appeared to have been achieved. For more than 200 years, until Ottoman forces were driven back from the gates of Vienna in 1683, the possibility of Islamic advance into Western Europe was a significant threat.

Although the sultan appointed a new Ecumenical Patriarch, slowly the Christian presence under Islamic rule was suppressed. Many churches became mosques, including the famous Hagia Sophia. Christians were reduced to an inferior status: missionary work became impossible, and theological training difficult. As the percentage of Christians in the former Byzantine Empire steadily declined, it took a significant amount of negotiation and diplomacy by the patriarch and leading Christian citizens to maintain the few diminishing rights of Christians and their properties. In the 1330s the patriarch had declared that if Orthodox believers chose not to express their faith publicly in Muslim controlled areas, it would not entail loss of salvation. Many chose to conform outwardly to what the Muslim authorities required, while privately maintaining their faith. Monasticism proved crucial to Orthodoxy's survival.

Russian Orthodoxy

However, a new heartland for Orthodoxy developed in north-east Europe. After the death of Metropolitan Peter in Moscow in 1326, he was declared a saint, enhancing the claims of the city to spiritual ascendancy. By the fifteenth century Grand Prince Vasilii of Moscow was pronouncing himself 'Sovereign of the whole Russian land'. In 1441 he headed the church council which chose the next Metropolitan of Kiev, without even consulting the Orthodox leadership in Constantinople. Seven years later, Russian bishops elected their own Metropolitan of Kiev and all Rus without gaining the consent of Constantinople, effectively declaring the Russian Orthodox Church as autocephalous.

Orthodoxy in Russia developed in a very different cultural context to the classical past of Constantinople. Settlements were smaller and more isolated, the environment harsher. Russian Orthodoxy strove for purity through meditation, prayer, past tradition, community and corporate life. With settlements expanding over vast territories, creative and flexible responses were needed. Mission was often in the hands of monks, sometimes living as hermits, or wandering holy men who were treated with reverence by the poor and operated somewhat outside the control of the church hierarchy. Followers were formed into monasteries.

The collapse of the 'second Rome', Constantinople, and the non-appearance of the expected apocalypse in 1492–3, were taken by the leadership of the Russian Orthodox Church as signifying God's sanction for the claims of Moscow to be the Third Rome. A huge wave of church building in Russia followed in the next century, producing churches with characteristic 'onion' domes. The Cathedral of the Dormition in the Moscow Kremlin was rebuilt, symbol of the triumph of Orthodoxy under a Christian ruler, the Tsar. The contrast with the struggles of Orthodox churches in Islamic or Catholic contexts was sharp, although harmony between church and state was by no means absolute. With up to a quarter of Russia's cultivated land owned by the monasteries in the sixteenth century, fears arose similar to those which had fuelled monastic dissolutions in Western Europe. However, a careful alliance with Russian rulers was built by church leaders. The status of Moscow as the Third Rome appeared confirmed in 1589 by the visit of the Ecumenical Patriarch

Jeremias II, raising funds for the Church of Constantinople. He rewarded his hosts by promoting the Metropolitan of the Russian Church to Patriarch.

The church played a restraining role during the rule of Ivan IV ('the Terrible'). He became ruler in 1533, aged just three. Reared in a court riven by suspicion, feuding and bloodletting, Ivan ruled through sadistic terror. The Metropolitan Makarii steadily pressed on him the importance of the Christian faith and the welfare of his soul. Ivan reorganized the affairs of church and state, and gave instructions for the building of St Basil's Cathedral in Red Square in 1552, but the death of his first wife and of Metropolitan Makarii in 1560 was followed by a spate of violence and killing which left tens of thousands dead. His remaining years were spent mixing bitter repentance for his behaviour as a 'stinking hound' while founding new monasteries, with terrorizing his people and murdering one of his own sons. Out of the turmoil that followed his death in 1584, the Romanov family came to power in 1613, and ruled until 1917. The church–state alliance was cemented when the father of Tsar Mikhail Romanov became Patriarch of Moscow in 1619, claiming to be the leader of Orthodox Christians around the world. The state-supported reforms of the Russian Orthodox Church in the seventeenth century were fiercely resisted by a series of breakaway groups, who became known as the Old Believers, creating the biggest and bitterest schism in Russian church history. They grew in strength considerably in the eighteenth century.

In 1721 Peter I, 'the Great', proclaimed himself 'Emperor of all the Russians'. Through the eighteenth and nineteenth centuries an empire stretching from Europe to the Pacific was created, one of the largest ever. He filled his capital, St Petersburg, with churches, although personally inclined to a secular path. Absolute obedience to the Tsar became central to Russian identity. Peter controlled the leadership of the church, which was ruled by a twelve-strong College of Spiritual Affairs (soon renamed the Holy Synod) presided over by an appointee of the Tsar. The Church became an organ of the State, powerfully influencing the lives of ordinary Christians. In 1722 Peter decreed that priests should report to security officials any conspiratorial talk or insults to the Tsar heard in the confessional.

Peter 'the Great'

The Orthodox churches of the Balkans and the East increasingly looked to the Third Rome for direction and protection, a process which contributed to the disastrous events of 1914. The Balkans and the Danube region remained contested religious territory. In the mid-fifteenth century up to 20% of Bosnia's population was Catholic, and Polish Catholic religious policy created tensions within the Orthodox Church in Ukraine and Belarus.

Some Protestant leaders showed interest in Orthodoxy. Luther argued that the Orthodox Church demonstrated that churches could exist without submission to the papacy. Protestants' efforts for the conversion of the Orthodox in south-eastern Europe saw little fruit, although Hungarian Calvinists saw more success in Transylvania. One notable exception was the Orthodox Patriarch Cyril Lukaris, who around 1613 accepted Calvinist views and attempted reforms in the Orthodox Church, later publishing his Calvinist 'Confession of Faith'. He was Patriarch in unstable times: the sultan ordered his execution in 1638, and his religious views were subsequently refuted by Orthodox Church councils. A Protestant community emerged in Russia in the mid-sixteenth century, which numbered around 30,000 by the 1670s, but most Orthodox adherents had little understanding of Protestantism.

Consolidation of European Catholicism

Although there are reports of Christian mission to Lithuania from the eleventh century onwards, it was the end of the fourteenth century before Lithuania became identifiably Christian, the last European country to do so. A condition of the Lithuanian king Jogaila (Jagiello) taking the Polish throne was his baptism, which took place in 1386, and marriage to the heir to the throne. He returned accompanied by Catholic bishops, and his country entered the Roman Catholic fold. Paganism remained strong among the peasantry: across Europe it took the work of the Counter-Reformation in Catholic areas, and Pietism and Puritanism among Protestants, to consolidate Christianity among the populace.

When Henri of Anjou, brother of King Charles IX of France, took the crown in Poland-Lithuania in 1573, a clause on religious freedom was agreed. His brother's sudden death in 1574 meant Henri acceded to the French crown, and his stay in Poland was necessarily brief. His replacement, Stefan Bathory, encouraged the foundation of Jesuit colleges in both Poland and Lithuania, attracting the children of many of the gentry and nobility, including Protestants, and bringing a steady stream of conversions to Catholicism. In the 1660s the Trinity-rejecting Socinians were expelled. Despite growing political influence over Poland from Prussia, Russia and Austria, the Catholic Church remained the place in which Polish and Lithuanian identity continued to be expressed – even into the communist era of the twentieth century.

Catholicism sought to intensify the devotional practice of the faithful. The confessional box was created, containing a small window with a grille separating the priest from the confessant. A set of catacombs discovered beneath Rome in 1578 contained the bones and relics of early Christians, which were exported across Europe, becoming the focal point for Catholic devotion in churches and monasteries. The power and magnificence of Catholicism was asserted as churches were extensively renovated, extended and lavishly decorated: the re-development of St Peter's in Rome was completed in the early seventeenth century with a huge frontal piazza emphasizing its splendour. Pope Gregory XIII even asserted his authority over the regulation of time by reforming the Julian calendar in 1582. In vain the Lutheran astronomer Johann Kepler (1571–1630) defended the scientific necessity of the revisions: it was 1752 before England accepted the new dating system.

The simmering dispute between Catholic and Protestant rulers in the Holy Roman Empire descended into the Thirty Years War (1618–48), which left much of Germany devastated. The Treaty of Westphalia (1648) created a framework for confessional coexistence by recognizing the right of sovereign states to self-determination. Protestants were accepted as a legitimate religious community, and Protestant princes were recognized as heads of churches, some Lutheran, others Reformed. The by-no-means neat religious boundary lines of Western Europe were set. The Thirty Years War weakened the Holy Roman Empire and the papacy.

In 1682 the French king Louis XIV promoted the 'Gallician Liberties', freeing his nation from the interference of the pope in all temporal, and some ecclesi-astical, affairs. But this did not mean a weakening of Roman Catholicism. In 1685 the Edict of Nantes was revoked, making Catholicism the only legal religion in France and forcing the expulsion of some 400,000 Huguenots (French Prot-estants) into exile. Habsburg rulers in east-central Europe, Bohemia, Silesia and Hungary also placed increased pressures on Protestants. In Silesia 1,200 Prot-estant churches were claimed for Catholic worship, and around 200,000 Lutherans emigrated; others attended secret Lutheran services in the woods. It was as late as 1782 before the Habsburg Empire passed a 'Toleration Edict'.

Pietism

Protestant churches also sought to consolidate their identity and deepen the devotion of their adherents. In Switzerland, Protestant cantons were forced into war to defend their confessional autonomy. Emerging state bureaucracies assumed increasing control over church affairs; in some Lutheran and Calvinist territories this was through consistories serving as representatives of the prince in his position as the head of the church. In other countries this role was played by bishops; in Lutheran Sweden it was the Archbishop of Uppsala.

In Lutheran Germany communion was still called mass, clergy wore vestments and Luther was deeply respected. Out of tensions created by the way the German Reformation had developed, the movement known as Pietism emerged, helping shape seventeenth- and eighteenth-century European Protestantism. At its heart was the work of Philipp Jakob Spener (1635–1705). Disturbed by the empty religious formality of members of his Protestant congregation in Frankfurt, he formed those who lived consistent lives of devotion and practice into an *ecclesiola in ecclesia*, his *collegia pietatis*. This core group within the larger body of church attenders met for Bible study and spontaneous prayers, serving as a model and motive force for the reform and renewal of the church from within. In 1675 Spener wrote his *Pia Desideria* (Pious Wishes), setting out the key principles of Pietism, but was opposed for potentially creating a two-class Christianity. He advocated an optimistic post-millennialism, expecting a long period of advance in the kingdom of God before the return of Christ. Spener presented something many Lutherans seemed to lack, arguing that through repentance came new birth, evidence of sanctification and assurance of eternal salvation.

Although controversial, Spener was steadily promoted, becoming court preacher in Dresden in 1686, before moving to Berlin in 1692. Spener argued for social reforms alongside spiritual renewal, offering support to the poorest in society, and a system of pastoral care and visitation. By the time of his death in 1705, he led a Europe-wide Pietist movement, characterized by devotional practice and expressed in a burst of hymn writing. Opportunities for lay leadership were a significant feature, including a role for women. Attempts to suppress this spontaneous, international revival movement only served to increase its fervency.

After he became a professor at the newly founded University of Halle, August Hermann Francke (1663–1727) built on Spener's work. With the support of the Hohenzollern court, Francke developed the social concern of Pietism, founding an orphanage, primary and secondary schools, a teacher-training college, a medical dispensary and a facility to print tracts and Bibles. The schools at Halle were of such high standing that members of the Prussian aristocracy sent their children there. Halle-trained teachers fanned out across Europe, even reaching India as missionaries in 1706. When Frederick William I became king of Prussia in 1713, he sought to restrict the international activity of the Pietists, but they remained a network reaching to Hungary, Bohemia, Latvia, Lithuania, Denmark, Russia, and even Siberia and India. John Wesley was later to pay an influential visit to Halle. Pietism moulded a confident, outward-looking Lutheranism that made an impact on world Christianity.

After the death of Calvin and his successor at the Genevan Academy, Theodore Beza, debates developed over the true nature of Calvinism. Jacobus Arminius (1560–1609) promoted the view that Christ died for all, rather than just for the elect, and that the election of the believer was on the basis of foreseen faith. He argued that saving grace is resistible and that Christians can fall from grace. When his followers set out his views in the Remonstrance of 1610, it split the Dutch Reformed Church. The traditional Calvinist response, outlined at the international Synod of Dort (Dordrecht) in 1618–19, spoke of total depravity (fallen humans cannot choose to serve God because of sin); unconditional election through God's grace alone (not dependent on any human action); limited atonement; the irresistibility of God's grace; and the final perseverance of true believers to glory. These 'five points' of Calvinism were later formed into the mnemonic TULIP. Calvinists argued that God in eternity in his wisdom chose to save, out of pure grace, a number known only to himself of those justly condemned for their sin. Moses Amyraut (1596–1664), a French Protestant, subsequently set out the Amyraldian *via media* position, a form of hypothetical universalism, which suggested that the atonement of Christ was sufficient for all, but was efficient (i.e. personally applied) only for the elect. Amyraut taught that God decreed to provide a universal salvation through the work of Christ, to be offered to all on condition that they had faith. However, seeing that of themselves humans would not believe, by a subsequent decree God elected some to eternal life and granted them the grace of repentance and faith.

Puritanism

Within the Church of England a strong group felt that the Reformation was but 'halfly' done. Their endeavours for the reform and purification of the church earned them the title 'Puritans'. They sought biblically ordered local church structures matched by personal reformation. This involved prayer, Bible reading, a godly home life, consistency in public life and morals, and clear understanding of doctrine.

During the reign of Elizabeth I those who met independently of the parish church for worship or prayer fell under the suspicion of the authorities, potentially facing forfeiture of property, imprisonment, exile or even death. When

James I ascended the throne in 1603 he was already reigning as James VI of Presbyterian Scotland, and royal permission was granted for a new 'Authorized' version of the Bible, later known as the King James Bible, issued in 1611. Although James's survival in 1605 of the 'gunpowder plot' to blow up him and his Parliament prevented a return to Catholic ascendancy, it became clear that further reform would not come from the top down. The Puritan mission therefore became a work of reformation from the bottom up, starting in homes, families and parishes.

Civil war

Puritanism was also associated with calls for increased political expression. These demands were opposed by Charles I, who ruled from 1625 to 1649. He believed in the divine right of kingly rule and reigned, in absolutist fashion, for long periods without calling Parliament. His high-handed decision to impose an episcopal church order and prayer book on Scotland, through the work of William Laud, the much-disliked Arminian Archbishop of Canterbury, provoked an uprising in 1638. Charles mismanaged events badly, and when he eventually called Parliament to raise an army and funds for the campaign, and to settle a rebellion in Ireland, he faced considerable opposition. In 1642 this precipitated a civil war between his forces and those of the Parliament. Among the Parliamentarian leaders was Oliver Cromwell (1599–1658), who had experienced a strong religious conversion when aged around thirty, becoming a Member of Parliament in 1628. He proved an able military leader, establishing the 'New Model Army', promoting the most godly and able as officers. He ensured the spiritual care of his men: his military chaplains included the notable Puritans Richard Baxter and John Owen. After the Parliamentary victory in the Civil War, Charles I was accused of treachery against his own people and executed. A 'Commonwealth' was proclaimed, with Cromwell becoming Lord Protector – he refused the offer of the crown.

Oliver Cromwell

The support of Scotland in the war against Charles I brought an expectation that Presbyterianism would be introduced into the Church of England. While the Civil War raged, theologians met to draw up the Westminster Confession and the Westminster Directory, to establish the worship and doctrine of the future church. However, during the war Cromwell had allowed considerable liberty of religious expression within his army – including for Presbyterians, Independents and Baptists. Cromwell therefore drew back from imposing Presbyterianism, fearing, in the words of John Milton, that 'New Presbyter' would become 'but Old Priest writ large'. Instead, in a remarkable ecumenical experiment, he permitted local congregations meeting in parish churches to decide their own church order, as long as each remained doctrinally orthodox and not Catholic. Along with Presbyterians, some 194 Congregationalist and nineteen Baptist churches operated within the establishment, with an even larger number outside it.

Others moved in radical religious directions – such as the Quakers, who spoke of the 'inner light', emphasizing the impulse of the Spirit rather than the Bible. The 'Ranters' went even further, arguing that the saved were freed from any obligation to keep the law. Extreme antinomians were reported running naked down the street. The 'Diggers' and the 'Levellers' called for common ownership of property. Another experiment was the creation of a Christian Parliament from representatives of gathered churches, an attempt at the 'rule of the saints'. Nicknamed the 'Barebones Parliament', it was soon dissolved amid major disagreements.

Cromwell was a complex character. Deeply religious and enlightened in many ways, he permitted the resettlement of Jews in England 350 years after they were banished. Yet he consented to ruthless warfare, including terrible bloodshed in the siege of Royalist Drogheda in 1649, part of his brutal attempt to pacify unrest in Ireland. Within two years of Cromwell's death in 1658, the monarchy was restored.

Charles II's promises of toleration were empty words, and in 1662 an Act of Uniformity compelled all ministers to submit to ordination by a bishop and use the Book of Common Prayer. Two thousand and twenty-nine ministers with Presbyterian, Independent and Baptist views held true to their consciences, refused to conform, and in the Great Ejection were deprived of their livings. These 'Nonconformists' included Richard Baxter (1615–91), who had conducted a remarkable ministry of preaching and family catechizing, seeing much of the town of Kidderminster converted. He was imprisoned for five years under the new regime. Another was the great theologian John Owen (1616–83), formerly Dean of Christ Church, Oxford, and Vice Chancellor of Oxford University. Fines and imprisonment for those who refused to conform were severe. The refusal of the Baptist preacher John Bunyan (1628–88) to desist from preaching without Anglican ordination or licence left him imprisoned for twelve years. From prison came Bunyan's most famous book, *Pilgrim's Progress*. In Scotland Samuel Rutherford (1600–61), a pastor and devotional writer, who later became Principal of St Andrews University, was imprisoned for resisting the attempts of the crown to control the church and for defending the rights of individual citizens. He died before he could be tried on charges of high treason. Famously, his last recorded words were, 'Glory, glory dwelleth in Immanuel's land.'

The Independent and Separatist church groups, in existence since Elizabeth I's time, suddenly saw their numbers boosted by the events of 1662. But Puritanism was no longer a political force: the path of dissent was a route to ostracism and often persecution. The Restoration period brought a libertine reaction to the Puritan past. Charles II was renowned for his mistresses and extravagant lifestyle. He was briefly succeeded by his brother, James II, a Roman Catholic, who continued the repressions, especially of the Covenanters in Scotland. They resisted the intrusions of the crown into church governance. Many died and others were exiled in the 'Killing Times'. Rebellion broke out in south-west Scotland.

James II alienated almost everyone, and in 1688 the English Parliament summoned a Dutch Protestant prince, William of Orange, to their assistance. William had married Mary, daughter of James II, and in the largely bloodless 'Glorious Revolution' they took the throne as James fled. Within a year William had passed the Toleration Act, giving Nonconformists freedoms of worship and expression, subject to certain conditions. In 1690 he resolved the religious conflict in Scotland by accepting the Church of Scotland as Presbyterian. James II raised an army, including French and Irish supporters, but he was decisively defeated in the same year at the Battle of the Boyne.

The spiritual dynamic of Puritanism sustained it in difficult times. Puritans were determined that what was preached should be biblically and theologically informed: sermons emphasized the sovereignty of God, the inclination of the human heart towards sin, and the work of Christ. They followed the 'regulative principle' that church practice should conform to the pattern set out in Scripture. Puritan sermons were lengthy but filled with illustration and application. They were earnest – Baxter preached 'as never sure to preach again, as a dying man to dying men'. Congregations were sometimes inclined to introspection, but were high in biblical and theological literacy: ploughmen were heard debating the complexities of predestination. Theology was 'the doctrine of living to God': it affected church, home and workplace. Preaching was consolidated through catechizing and pastoral counselling. Pleasure was to be found in God-pleasing ways: under Cromwell's regime people were instructed not to observe Christmas because of the excesses during the celebrations and its association with the Catholic past.

North America

Catholicism reached North America through the work of Spanish settlers into Florida in 1513, before they moved into Texas, New Mexico, Arizona and California. French settlers in the early sixteenth century brought Catholicism to their trading posts and forts in Quebec, around Detroit and in New Orleans. British settlers into Maryland, founded in 1632, were also initially Roman Catholic.

Protestant settlement from England into North America began in the 1580s, initially in Virginia where Anglican worship forms were established, and resumed after 1607. During the first half of the seventeenth century many Puritans left England for the freer religious air of New England, intent on creating a godly Christian society, free of persecution. One group of just over a hundred settlers, known as the Pilgrim Fathers, sailed from England in 1620, although they survived only after great privations, with half their number dying within a few months of arrival. Nonetheless, by 1630 there was an established community of some 300 people. During the 1630s a further 20,000 followed them to the New World, embracing their vision of a 'Commonwealth'. The first governor was the Puritan John Winthrop, who declared his intention to build 'a city on a hill' (Matt. 5:14), that all might learn from it. As early as 1636 a college to train clergy had been started in Cambridge, Massachusetts, named Harvard in honour of the Cambridge-educated Puritan John Harvard, a major donor.

New World Puritanism bore many similarities to that in England, with desire for a purer worship form and greater emphasis on the Bible and the Psalms. The early Puritan settlements formed into the colonies of Massachusetts, Connecticut and New Hampshire. New Amsterdam, initially a Dutch outpost, was taken over by the English in 1664 and renamed New York. In Quebec, the first resident bishop, François-Xavier de Montmorency Laval (1623–1708), established the basis for an enduring Catholic culture. Puritan Congregationalists, Virginian Anglicans and the Catholics in New France all sought to operate a form of religious establishment. In Pennsylvania, formed in 1682, William Penn (1644–1718) granted freedom of religion for all monotheists and attracted a religious rainbow of migrants, including the Amish from Switzerland who arrived in the early eighteenth century and sought thereafter to maintain unchanged their inherited religious and social patterns.

Settlers from Scotland founded Presbyterian churches in Pennsylvania and New Jersey, and on Long Island. The first American presbytery was formed in

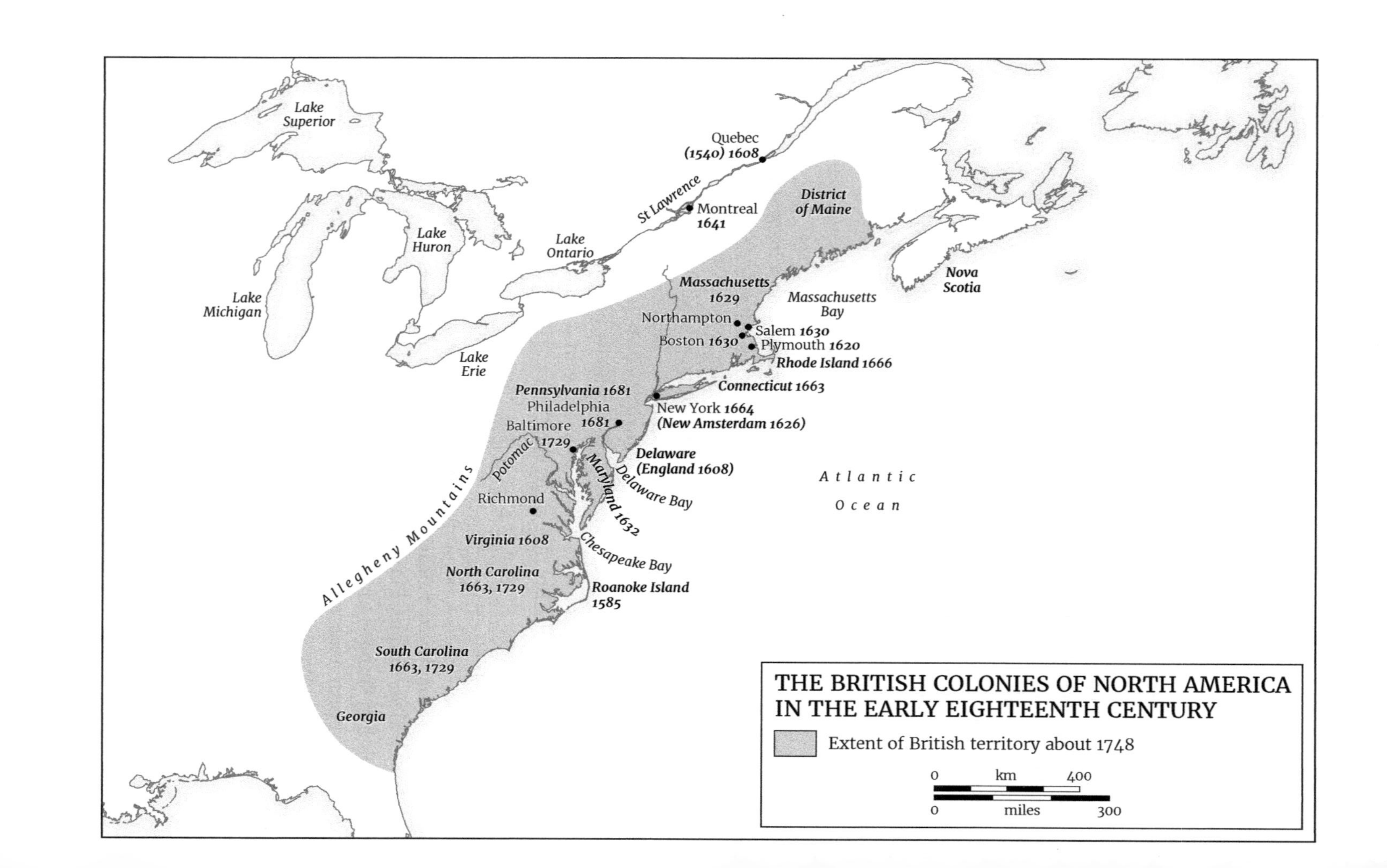
THE BRITISH COLONIES OF NORTH AMERICA
IN THE EARLY EIGHTEENTH CENTURY
Extent of British territory about 1748
0 km 400
0 miles 300
Lake Superior
Lake Michigan
Lake Huron
Lake Ontario
Lake Erie
Quebec (1540) 1608
St Lawrence
Montreal 1641
District of Maine
Nova Scotia
Massachusetts 1629
Massachusetts Bay
Northampton
Salem 1630
Boston 1630
Plymouth 1620
Rhode Island 1666
Connecticut 1663
Pennsylvania 1681
Philadelphia 1681
New York 1664
(New Amsterdam 1626)
Baltimore 1729
Delaware (England 1608)
Potomac
Maryland 1632
Delaware Bay
Atlantic Ocean
Richmond
Virginia 1608
Chesapeake Bay
Allegheny Mountains
North Carolina 1663, 1729
Roanoke Island 1585
South Carolina 1663, 1729
Georgia

1706. Baptist churches took root in New England, New York and further south. German-speaking immigrants included Mennonites, Moravians and Brethren, but most were Lutheran and Reformed. A plurality of small orthodox and non-orthodox religious groups also settled in the New World, providing a vibrant religious mixture not possible in Europe.

In 1636 what became the colony of Rhode Island was founded by Roger Williams on a policy of complete religious toleration, such that 'all men may walk as their consciences persuade them'. Late seventeenth-century Britain only reluctantly conceded toleration to Christian minorities alongside an established church, but the practice of the American colonies was pluralism with free, although not always happy, competition between all religious groups.

Unlike the Catholic missionaries in Latin America, and early Jesuit efforts in Canada, the Puritan settlers proved slow at undertaking mission to indigenous American peoples. Pocahontas, daughter of the Algonquian chief, accepted Christianity at Jamestown in 1614 but only lived on for another three years. John Eliot (1604–90) and Thomas Mayhew Jr (1621–57) led the way. Between 1646 and 1663 Eliot translated the Bible into the Algonquian language. By 1674 there were some 3,600 'praying Indians', although over time they were left marginalized. A further complicating dimension was the widespread importation of Africans as slaves: in 1710 they outnumbered whites in South Carolina. Here, when slaves sought Christian baptism, they were required to promise they were not requesting this to free themselves from their 'duty and obedience' to their masters.

By the end of the seventeenth century Europe and its colonies were more closely regulated and more intensively Christian societies than ever before. Despite Pietist and Puritan efforts, Europe had also probably become more Catholic and, after the revocation of the Edict of Nantes, less tolerant. By the early eighteenth century Britain had become the premier Protestant power in Europe, followed by the new Kingdom of Prussia, counterbalancing the influence of the Catholic rulers in the old Holy Roman Empire. Conflicting visions of what was true and pure competed. The vision of global obedience to a true church, ruled from Rome, fuelled Catholic mission. Russian Orthodoxy presented Moscow as the new Rome, claims endorsed by its Christian emperor. The Puritan vision of the godly and more democratic commonwealth eventually provoked a willingness to take up arms in its defence and make heroic sacrifices, including transatlantic voyages in tiny vessels. Quests for purity and orthodoxy reduced toleration of non-Christian viewpoints. Catholic and Protestant were united in their abhorrence of the occult. Between 1400 and 1800, over 50,000 people were executed on charges of witchcraft.

15. ENLIGHTENMENT

Lifeline
1695 – Locke's *Reasonableness of Christianity* published
1711 – Ziegenbalg completes translation of Bible into Tamil
1713 – papal condemnation of Jansenist teaching
1724 – Catholic missionaries expelled from China
1734–5 – Awakening at Northampton, Massachusetts
1738 – John Wesley's heart 'strangely warmed'
1742 – Cambuslang and Kilsyth revivals
1751 – publication of the *Encyclopédie*
1773 – pope dissolves Jesuit order
1783 – Yi Seung-hun baptized in Beijing and returns to Korea
1802 – Paley's *Natural Theology* published

'Enlightenment' refers to a decisive moment of understanding or maturity in a person's development, associated with a cultural rite of passage or a decisive turn in life. Adults often search for such enlightenment earnestly. Joseph Wright's painting *An Experiment on a Bird in the Air Pump* (1768) captures the fascination and fear associated with the remarkable advances in science in eighteenth-century Europe. It depicts a natural philosopher's experiment surrounded by onlookers, some of whom watch in eager curiosity, while others half-look or turn away in horror. In a darkened room, the light falls on the spectators' faces in a way that is normally associated with religious illumination, but which here evokes the dawn of a new age of scientific understanding. The Enlightenment was an optimistic age, one of supreme confidence in human reason: it had a profound impact on politics and society, literature and philosophy. Theology and church life could not escape untouched. Enlightenment influence was felt in distant colonies and mission fields.

During the Enlightenment, natural philosophy (science) began to challenge theology as a route to 'gnosis'. Although many scientific leaders held profound Christian beliefs, gradually the basis of authority shifted from revelation to reason. The universe was to be comprehended in material terms. Francis Bacon (1561–1626) laid a foundation with empiricism, stressing the faithful collection and recording of data from which theories and models were extrapolated.

Faith, science and reason

The Royal Society, founded in London in 1660, promoted knowledge of the natural world through observation and experiment. Its co-founder Robert Boyle (1627–91), who has been called the 'father of modern chemistry', underwent a profound conversion experience, after which he dedicated his life and talents to Christ. Alongside financing Bible translation projects, he viewed science as God's 'second book' in which were revealed his power and wisdom. Boyle's mission was to convince people that God's two books were in harmony. Another devout, if somewhat theologically unorthodox, believer was Isaac Newton (1642–1727), who viewed each scientific discovery as a gift from God. He depicted a universe functioning by natural and rationally understandable laws. The order evident in planetary motion pointed to a divine Author: 'It is unphilosophical to seek for any other Origin of the World, or to pretend that it might arise out of Chaos by the mere laws of Nature.' Similarly, his law of universal gravitation explained planetary motion but not who set the planets in motion: 'God governs all things and knows all that is or can be done.' Newton is widely known for his *Principia Mathematica* (1687), the development of infinitesimal calculus, and work in optics.

In *Natural Theology* (1802) William Paley argued that the intricacy and complexity of nature pointed to the work of a Designer, as the existence of a watch presupposed a watchmaker. However, this emphasis on a universe sustained through scientific laws produced a reticence, fuelled by Deism, to speak of God intervening miraculously in the natural world. Once the watchmaker had wound up the watch, he need not interfere with its operation.

The seeds for a radical discontinuity had been sown by René Descartes (1596–1650), a French Catholic mathematician. He proposed a division between what could be felt and measured (matter) and the world of consciousness (thought or 'spirit'). This 'Cartesian dualism' threatened the comprehensive Christian worldview, potentially separating faith from reason. A significant critique of revealed Christianity emerged in the eighteenth century: the enthronement of reason superseded the emphasis on the reasonableness of Christianity.

John Locke (1632–1704) argued that knowledge is determined by experience and derived from sense-perception. In *The Reasonableness of Christianity* (1695) he asserted that faith was rational assent to something reasonable – God's existence is self-evident and provable. The Deist John Toland, in *Christianity Not Mysterious* (1696), responded with a set of principles founded on the laws of nature, coining the term 'pantheism'. The emphasis on reason reduced the space for dogma: Deists rejected doctrines such as the Trinity because they did not appear 'reasonable'. Unitarianism became an attractive option.

Benedict Spinoza (1632–77), an Amsterdam Jew expelled from his synagogue for heretical views, spoke in pantheistic terms in his *Ethics*, proposing only one infinite substance (as opposed to creator and creation). God was conflated with Nature. Spinoza prefigured modern biblical criticism by presenting the Bible as the product of irrational human minds. His ideas were adopted by Dutch radicals. In *Traité des trois imposteurs* (1710–11), Jesus, Moses and Muhammad were depicted as the three great impostors. As traditional mores were overthrown, heretical and pornographic material flowed off French, Dutch and Swiss presses. In France Montesquieu and Voltaire passionately promoted anticlerical and anti-dogmatic opinions in the 1720s. A stout defence against these views was led by the abbé Noel Antoine Pluche in *Le Spectacle de la nature* (1732), affirming God as the only active, self-willing, self-sufficient and eternal being: matter only moves because God acts on it. His views were more widely read than Voltaire's, but the 'Pandora's box' of radical critique of the Christian worldview was open.

The French word for 'philosopher' emerges from the 1740s tract *Le Philosophe*. It claimed that God's existence was the most deeply ingrained of 'all the prejudices'. In *De l'esprit* (1758) absolute atheism was promoted. The *Encyclopédie* (1751) presented knowledge through a functional alphabetical system, each entry of equal intrinsic merit rather than being ranked according to theological importance. An influential group of freethinkers across Europe practised radicalism in religion, politics and personal morality: life was to be lived for pleasure, including sexual liberty. The freethinking and free-living morality of Erasmus Darwin (1731–1802) was widely known, and he presented an early statement of evolution long before his grandson Charles. Some rising industrialist families lived without the formal practice of Christianity. Others held non-orthodox views. Joseph Priestley (1733–1804), pioneer of the discovery of oxygen as a gas, was a Unitarian minister.

Catholicism and the Enlightenment

The rise of European nation-states weakened papal influence on individual countries, leaving Catholicism dependent on royal favour to maintain its confessional privileges. In some nations this required the papacy to cede organizational control and the right to appoint bishops and higher clergy, making Catholicism an attractive proposition for rulers. During the seventeenth and eighteenth centuries up to fifty-one German princes converted to Catholicism. Local parish priests acted as agents for promoting loyalty among the population, reading out royal edicts from the pulpit. After 1767, in the Habsburg Empire, an administrative department was created to implement ecclesiastical legislation and ensure reform of the Catholic Church. After 1780 the education of parish clergy was led by the State. Although European rulers were inclined to absolutism, this began to be tempered by the values of the Enlightenment.

Roman Catholicism still retained its vision for a reunited church, which would be achieved by the absorption of other churches, or force, rather than through practices of toleration. In Bohemia adherence to Protestantism was punishable by death during Charles VI's reign (1711–40). Religious nonconformity was associated with political nonconformity, making the situation of non-Catholics precarious, especially after 1685 in France. Only after the accession of Louis XVI in 1774 did France begin to reflect the wider trend for toleration across Europe, and in 1787 restricted rights were granted to French Calvinists.

There was little interest in religious toleration in Spain. After concordats between the Bourbon dynasty and the papacy in 1737 and 1753, the crown controlled 12,000 benefices and the nomination of archbishops and bishops. The Portuguese crown's efforts to assert its authority over the church strained relations with the pope. Relationships were particularly difficult in Italy, with the Papal States repeatedly invaded by foreign armies as the temporal power of the papacy steadily eroded. German Catholic monarchs balanced their sovereignty with respect for the spiritual (but not political) supremacy of Rome.

The Enlightenment forced Catholicism into a post-Tridentine world, highlighted in the Jesuit and the Jansenist controversies. The Jesuit order's conservatism, and the influential position Jesuits held in court circles as royal confessors and controllers of much higher education, sat uncomfortably with increasingly independent and Enlightenment-minded rulers. A dramatic policy shift in 1759 saw the first expulsions of Jesuits from Portugal and its colonies, followed by Spain and its colonies in 1767. Some Jesuit leaders were imprisoned, mission fields were abandoned and schools lost their teachers. In a domino-like fashion, expulsions spread to Naples in 1767 and Parma in 1768. Finally, in 1773, the pope yielded to pressure and dissolved the Jesuit order.

Jansenists and Jesuits

Dissatisfaction with the Tridentine formulas, especially over faith and grace, divine initiative and human responsibility, surfaced in the Jansenist controversy. In *Augustinus*, published in 1640, two years after the death of its author Cornelius Jansen (1585–1638), the bishop of Ypres, an interpretation was offered of Augustine's theology of grace which stressed conversion, original sin and divine predestination, and stood against the view that Christ died for all. Jansen retained a place for 'good works' in salvation rather than the Reformers' emphasis on justification by faith alone, but he stressed it was impossible to fulfil God's commands and perform good works without the disposition, which was conferred by grace. Similarly, the sacraments were not in and of themselves efficacious but needed to be transformed by the obedience of the recipient which came through God's grace. The Jansenist emphasis that absolution in penance should only be offered after signs of change in the individual, motivated by grace, stood in contrast to the lax confessional practice of which the Jesuits were accused. Many academics, clerics (especially in Paris) and lay Catholics were drawn to the Jansenist devotional approach. One adherent was the philosopher, scientist and mathematician Blaise Pascal (1623–62), who in 1654 was transformed by an overwhelming sense of God's presence, as he recorded: 'FIRE. The God of Abraham, the God of Isaac, the God of Jacob. Not of the philosophers and intellectuals. Certitude. Certitude. Feeling. Joy. Peace.' Pascal's new perspective is reflected in his *Pensées*.

The Jesuit accusation that Jansenism was a new form of Calvinism proved damaging, especially in a France haunted by previous Catholic–Calvinist blood-letting. Louis XIV and other Bourbon monarchs, prompted by their Jesuit confessors, pictured Jansenism as a 'republican' threat. Papal condemnations of Jansenist teaching culminated in the bull *Unigenitus* in 1713. French clergy, religious orders, seminaries and universities were purged of any Jansenist sympathizers; despite strong protests from the press, many were imprisoned in the Bastille in Paris. The French monarchy's 'plague on both your houses' policy banned both Jesuits and Jansenists, but the anti-Jesuit consensus lasted only until Napoleon's time, whereas French policy remained strongly anti-Jansenist.

By the eighteenth century Catholicism was represented across significant parts of the globe. In Latin America magnificent churches, dripping with gold ornamentation, soared above towns, and colourful processions threaded through the streets on notable saint's days. The Virgin Mary and the saints remained the devotional focus. As European monarchs sought to promote a more rational and orderly religious practice, reports from the colonies reached Spain and Portugal of poor clerical standards, superstition and over-emotionalism among the laity.

In cultures beset by fear of illness, death and the devil, comfort was found in local patron saints, well-known ritual and locally made images, combining Catholicism with elements of traditional belief and practice. In the Andean highlands, adherence to the ancestor spirits was pervasive. Many black slaves and former slaves freely merged Catholicism with traditional African beliefs and practices.

The regimes in Spain and Portugal viewed the wealth of the colonial Catholic churches enviously and between the 1750s and 1800 subjected them to heavy taxation, before in 1804 demanding that most assets be handed over. Some 10.5 million pesos were collected from Mexico alone. Taxation policy drove a secularizing wedge between church and state. Efforts were also made to reduce the heavy dependence of Catholicism in the New World on the religious orders: a third of parishes were controlled by the Franciscans, Dominicans, Augustinians and Jesuits. In 1749 all parishes controlled by religious orders were handed over to secular clergy and placed under the control of bishops who could be more easily influenced. This created a chronic shortage of priests, especially in rural areas, and after the expulsion of the Jesuits missionary and educational work among the indigenous population of Brazil collapsed. In the 1760s the assets of other orders were seized.

Missions continued to remote locations in California, Texas, Chile, the Amazonian regions, Argentina and Patagonia. Tragically, some who accepted the missionaries found themselves subsequently enslaved by European settlers, and efforts to get converts to engage in settled farming resulted in disease and malnutrition. The acceptance and understanding of Catholic teaching was patchy. The wars of independence in Latin America further damaged an already weakened mission system. Many local clergy appointed to replace the missionary priests felt little loyalty to the colonial order and supported revolutionary efforts, accelerating secularizing tendencies in the nineteenth century.

Catholicism in Asia

Between 1660 and 1815 South and South-East Asia were beset by political, cultural, economic and religious conflicts. As Western powers began to exercise increased influence, new opportunities for missionary engagement developed. Only in the Philippines did Catholicism become widely established, largely through colonial influence. Indigenous peoples, pacified under the system of feudal-style land grants to colonizers, proved responsive to the mass evangelism of Catholic missionaries, who allowed a measure of continuity with existing belief structures. Women played an important role in Filipino society and the church, but there was resistance to them joining the religious orders until the eighteenth century. After the Jesuits were expelled in 1768–9, bishops took control of local parishes and installed hastily trained Filipinos, many of whom proved unready for such duties, which considerably weakened Catholicism.

In China divisions among the missionaries and papal interference threatened the willingness of the authorities to accept even Christians who were prepared to remain subordinated to the Confucian state. In 1704 the pope forbade the Jesuit-sanctioned participation in Confucian ceremonies, and the use of Chinese terms *shangdi* ('lord on high') and *tian* ('heaven') for God, requiring instead *tianzhu* ('Lord of heaven'). This placed Catholics at odds with the Chinese emperor, who in 1706 declared that only missionaries following Matteo Ricci's practice of accommodation would be granted imperial permits. The papacy refused to concede ground, and in 1724 Christianity became a proscribed religion in China; foreign missionaries were deported, and churches in cities gradually closed. Christianity was left in the hands of Chinese believers, as periodic persecutions continued throughout the eighteenth century.

The arrival of Catholicism in Korea came through Korean Confucians reading Jesuit works on science and Catholicism they had obtained in China, and seeing a compatibility with their Confucianism. In 1783 Yi Seung-hun met with Catholic priests in Beijing and was baptized, returning home to preach to his friends and relatives. The first Korean Catholic church was established in 1784. By the end of the eighteenth century there were some 10,000 Korean Catholics, despite periodic persecution. In Japan persecution was even more severe after it became a closed country in the early seventeenth century. Christianity was forbidden, and policies of exterminating the remaining 150,000 Japanese 'secret Christians' (*senpuku Kirishitan*) were ruthlessly applied.

Portuguese missionaries in India had sought to align the ancient Syrian-influenced Thomas Christians with the Roman tradition, and in 1662 the majority of them accepted communion with Rome, becoming the Syro-Malabar Catholic Christians. Other Thomas Christians became an autonomous church under the West Syrian patriarchate. Mission work in outlying areas was attempted. The Capuchins worked in Lhasa between 1707 and 1745, before retreating to Nepal. Jesuits had reached Tibet in the seventeenth century and made further attempts in 1713. They withdrew from their work in Goa in 1760 after their suppression in Portugal the previous year.

Protestant missions in Asia

The first significant Protestant missionary engagement with the Indian subcontinent was the Lutheran Pietist mission at Tranquebar in south India, staffed by Halle-trained pastors and led by the Dane Bartholomaus Ziegenbalg (1682–1719). By 1711 he had translated the Bible into Tamil. Between 1720 and 1740 three Indian catechists were ordained as pastors, and lay participation was encouraged. A leading role was also played by Christian Friedrich Schwartz (1726–60), who learned Tamil, Telugu, Marathi, Persian and Sanskrit, and proved a capable preacher, teacher, diplomat. Large congregations were formed at Chennai, Tranquebar, Tiruchirapalli, Thanjavur and Palayamkottai.

Despite the official withdrawal of priests from Sri Lanka after the Dutch conquest in 1658, by the end of the eighteenth century there were still some 67,000 Roman Catholics. The Dutch East India Company officially promoted Protestantism, and in 1722 it was claimed that there were nearly 425,000 Protestant Christians on the island, but nominalism was widespread. In Vietnam Christian activity had been forbidden by royal edict in 1533, but Jesuit missionaries arrived in 1615. Persecution was ended by French intervention in 1788, and by 1802 there were 320,000 Catholic communicants.

Catholics and Protestants in Africa

The steady decline of Catholicism in Kongo in Africa, after its seventeenth-century flowering, was punctuated by the early eighteenth-century popular renewal movement led by the twenty-one-year-old Donna Beatrice (Kimpa Vita). A reputed healer and prophet, she called for people to burn their charms and even their crucifixes. Viewed as politically subversive, in 1706 she was burned to death for heresy. European priests continued their visits: between 1759 and 1774 Cherubino da Savona claimed to have baptized 700,000 people. But 1835 saw the departure of the last of the Capuchin monks, who had served in Kongo since 1645. The Jesuit dominance of Luanda, playing a key role in education and training local clergy, continued until the removal of the order in 1760. The Jesuits baptized Princess Nzinga, leader of the Kimbundu people, but her efforts to end slave trading meant she endured harsh measures from the Portuguese after 1648.

European trading in the Cape of Good Hope (later part of South Africa) brought local Africans into contact with Christianity. The year 1652 saw the arrival of 126 Dutch settlers to the Cape, and the first reported convert was Eva, a young Khoikhoi girl, but spreading the Christian message did not rank high on the settlers' agenda. A few Khoikhoi were baptized in 1737 through the work of the Moravian George Schmidt (1709–85). By 1793 the slave population equalled the white population; although slaves could obtain freedom by being baptized, few were allowed to do so.

Religious revival in Europe

A number of factors militated against religious revival among Protestants in the eighteenth century: some continued to endure severe persecution; the Enlightenment emphasis on reason made deepened interest in personal religious experience, founded on the Bible, inherently unlikely; and the wider social and moral context appeared averse to religious awakening. William Hogarth's print of an etching, *Gin Lane*, graphically depicts the evils of the gin-drinking craze. People were 'drunk for a penny, and dead drunk for tuppence'. Nonetheless, revival did take place, and initially in unlikely areas.

Repression by Catholic Habsburg rulers forced Protestant worshippers into isolated locations. Among the miners and rural workers of Silesia there were so few churches that Protestant congregations gathered in the open air: some 40,000 met in the hills surrounding Teschen, Upper Silesia. Johann Adam Steinmetz (1689–1762) arrived in 1720 with a team of Halle-trained assistants, holding all-day meetings in different areas as crowds flocked to hear preaching, singing hymns as they waited. In Catholic Salzburg, Jesuit-led persecution also kindled the fires of awakening. In 1731 all Protestants over the age of twelve were expelled from the region without notice. They scattered across Europe – some 20,000 going to Prussia and others reaching North America. Their experiences of awakening, lay leadership and informal networks travelled with them. Around the Baltic area, and in the Tyrol, further revivals were reported outside the formal church system. The intense evangelical spirituality of the European revivals, drawing on elements of mysticism, emphasizing the love, beauty and glory of God, the excellence of Christ and the denial of self, is reflected in the writings of Gerhard Tersteegen (1697–1769), whose hymns were widely sung.

The leading figure among third-generation Pietists was Count Ludwig Nikolaus von Zinzendorf (1700–60), who had studied at Halle and allowed pious Protestants to settle on his estate at Herrnhut. They included refugees from Moravia, spiritual descendants of Jan Hus, who had endured persecution and scattering across Europe. In 1727 revival broke out during a service at Herrnhut: participants reported that 'an overwhelming flood of grace swept us all out into the great ocean of Divine Love', leaving them unsure whether they were in heaven or on earth. Numerous conversions and spontaneous prayer meetings followed. The Moravians were transformed into an international Protestant missionary movement: within twenty-five years a community of fewer than 2,000 people had sent out 100 missionaries. Their heroic mission endeavours included work among the Inuit (Eskimos) in Greenland, and African slaves in the West Indies.

The Great Awakening

By 1750 there were a million white settlers in the thirteen American colonies, including some 120,000 German-speaking immigrants. Henry Melchior Mühlenberg (1711–87) brought them a Halle-influenced Lutheranism, filled with evangelistic zeal, intense spirituality and tireless energy in itinerancy, matched by considerable organizational ability. By 1776 he had gathered 126 congregations, consolidating Lutheranism in North America. Theodorus Jacobus Frelinghuysen (1691–1747), a Dutch minister who emigrated to New Jersey, similarly introduced the emphasis on spiritual awakening: revival was reported under his eloquent preaching in the 1720s. His association with the Tennent family, of Irish Presbyterian background, proved important. William Tennent (1673–1746) founded a seminary in New Jersey in 1726, derided by opponents as the 'Log College', which supplied preachers for the revival in the middle colonies. His son, Gilbert Tennent (1703–64), united Calvinistic orthodoxy with a stress that conversion must be followed by genuine piety and holiness. He challenged Presbyterian formalism, publicly deploring unconverted ministers. Many Log College men served on the board of the College of New Jersey which began in 1746 and moved to Princeton in 1756.

In Puritan New England, as the 'godly commonwealth' ideal weakened, low levels of church membership became commonplace, punctuated by periods of religious intensity. A climate of hysterical fear and suspicion led to the famous Salem witch trials, in which twenty people were executed for the crime of witchcraft in 1692–3. The old world of Puritan awakening was not entirely lost: Solomon Stoddart (1643–1729) reported five periods of 'reaping' between 1679 and 1718.

The person most synonymous with the Great Awakening in the American colonies is Jonathan Edwards (1703–58), Stoddart's grandson. After succeeding his grandfather at Northampton, Massachusetts, and a short missionary pastorate at Stockbridge among the Native Americans, he was briefly President of Princeton College, before his untimely death aged fifty-five. He was one of America's greatest intellectuals, his sermons and writings demonstrating considerable capacities as a theologian, philosopher, man of science and pastor. Edwards offered a coherent Christian response to the Enlightenment, raising profound questions about how humans know things. Locke's emphasis on empirical observation and personal experience is reflected in Edwards' *Treatise Concerning Religious Affections* (1746). He argued that religious feeling needed to be set alongside external evidence such as the Bible and faith in the historic work of Christ. In his *Freedom of the Will* (1754) Edwards challenged simplistic understandings of self-determination.

Jonathan Edwards

Edwards' ministry at Northampton was punctuated by periods of religious awakening. Of the 1734–5 revival he reported, 'Not one family that I know of, and scarcely a person, has been exempt.' His subsequent *Faithful Narrative of the Surprising Work of God* was widely read in Europe. Edwards' theological interpretation of events helped shape the outward-looking, evangelistic and experiential Calvinism important to the Awakening. By the 1740s a series of parish-based revivals had crystalized into the Great Awakening. A unifying figure was the Anglican preacher George Whitefield (1714–70), who arrived in 1740 and preached extensively across the New England colonies. Whitefield had been dramatically converted as an Oxford undergraduate, and his first preaching endeavours in 1736 were attended by extraordinary success. His messages were delivered with dramatic vividness, emotional intensity and often tears, from a Bible he believed was God's Word. He emphasized repentance, conversion, new birth and a direct personal encounter with God, which were striking themes in a Deist and Enlightenment-influenced society. After 1737, as Anglican pulpits closed against him, he took extemporary preaching into marketplaces, open spaces and even the drawing rooms of the aristocracy. Some 10,000 came to hear him preach to the hitherto unreached miners of Kingswood, Bristol. Congregations of 20–30,000 were reported in London at Moorfields and Kennington Common.

Whitefield's success was repeated in the American colonies, vast crowds attracted by word-of-mouth accounts of his message and by preparatory advertising. Whitefield's work consolidated the Great Awakening as an intercolonial, transatlantic movement, and made him an international celebrity. Although a committed Anglican, he declared in 1742 his determination to preach the gospel to 'all that are willing to hear me, of whatever denomination', even the pope if he was invited to do so.

The Great Awakening helped root evangelicalism in American culture, proving a cohesive force across the colonies that later constituted the United States. Yet by 1744 its peak was over. Revival brought division. Some claimed that the dramatic religious manifestations associated with the revival – falling to the ground, crying out and shaking – were real evidence of a work of God, while others argued the opposite. In their radical critique some, such as Charles Chauncy (1705–87), moved in liberal and Unitarian directions.

The Evangelical Revival in Britain

Religious awakening had been experienced in seventeenth-century Ireland and Scotland. The legacy of the intense spirituality of the Covenanting tradition, with its illegal conventicle meetings, remained strong in the Scottish lowlands. In north-east Scotland revival was noted after 1730. There were stirrings in the lowlands through the work of Ralph and Ebenezer Erskine who seceded from the Church of Scotland in 1733. Their protest reflected a combination of the beginnings of spiritual awakening, Enlightenment thinking as to liberty of individual conscience (expressed in demands for congregations to choose their own minister), and frustration at rationalism and Moderatism in the Kirk. Within thirty years their Associate Presbytery had gathered over a hundred congregations. The Church of Scotland ministers William MacCulloch (1691–1771) in Cambuslang, and James Robe (1688–1753) in Kilsyth, saw revival begin in their parishes in 1741. Whitefield preached to 20–30,000 at open-air 'communion seasons' held at the zenith of this movement in 1742, gatherings marked by their emotional intensity, with some people crying out in spiritual distress or falling to the ground.

John Wesley (1703–91), reared in the Anglican High Church tradition, saw his religious life intensify at Oxford University through the 'Holy Club', a society of zealous young Anglicans devoted to prayer, devotional Bible reading, self-examination, and visiting prisoners and the sick. For their regular religious lifestyle they were derided as 'Methodists'. In 1738, at a Moravian meeting in London, as someone read from Luther's *Preface to Romans*, Wesley felt his heart 'strangely warmed', and he found the assurance and certainty of trust in Christ alone that he had long sought. Wesley was introduced to open-air preaching by Whitefield and began widespread itinerancy, travelling thousands of miles each year on horseback, including visiting the north-east of England on forty-eight separate occasions. Like Whitefield he was capable of drawing crowds of up to 20,000. Wesley gathered his followers into societies for mutual encouragement and teaching, with a significant place for lay preachers on the circuits he created. The Methodist network spanned Britain and Ireland, and eventually North America. Wesley's famous missionary dictum 'I look upon all the world as my parish' put him at odds with the territorial Anglican parish system, and in 1787 Methodists were forced to register their buildings as 'dissenting meeting-houses'.

John Wesley's brother Charles (1707–88), who also experienced evangelical conversion, proved a very capable preacher, but is best known for writing more than 5,000 hymns.

John Wesley

Wesley followed Whitefield in combining evangelical spirituality with social concern, especially care for orphans. Both were thoroughgoing evangelicals, but instead of the evangelical Calvinism which Whitefield believed, derived from the Anglican Thirty-Nine Articles, Wesley retained the Arminianism of his High Church upbringing, convinced that believers could fall away from their faith and that Christ died for all. He also added an emphasis on 'scriptural holiness', or 'Christian perfection'.

Evangelicalism in Britain had an impact on those in the higher echelons of society, including Selina Countess of Huntingdon (1707–91). An evangelical stream of clergy developed within the Church of England, including Henry Venn in Huddersfield; William Grimshaw of Haworth, near Bradford; and William Romaine in London. In Wales the Anglican rector Griffith Jones saw revival under his ministry in 1713 and ran itinerant schools which by his death had taught over 158,000 pupils to read the Bible. Daniel Rowland (1713–90) and Howel Harris (1714–73) were the pre-eminent preachers of the 'Welsh Revival', preaching extensively in the open air. Their converts were formed into Religious Societies, of which 433 had started by 1750. Close contact with Whitefield ensured that Methodism in Wales was Calvinistic rather than Arminian. Calvinistic Methodism became the denomination of preference for the majority in Wales. English Dissenters did not sit in the mainstream of the Evangelical Revival, although some, such as Philip Doddridge (1702–51), were active supporters. They tended to benefit indirectly as many converts found a spiritual home in their chapels.

Evangelicalism became a movement spanning denominations. One frequently used definition of evangelicalism sees it as unified by several themes: conversion as the definitive Christian experience; the Bible as the basis of Christian life; the Cross of Christ as the heart of the Christian message; and a conviction that Christianity should be active. There was willingness to disagree on secondary matters, including church governance. Evangelicalism stood both in continuity and discontinuity with the Enlightenment, making the gospel appeal rationally, promoting humanitarianism and assessing spiritual experience empirically, while emphasizing the new birth, revealed religion and direct personal encounter with God. Evangelicalism's full social and cultural impact would be felt in the following century.

16. REVOLUTION

Lifeline
1787 – Constitution of the United States signed
1789 – French Revolution
1793 – Carey arrives in India
1799 – van der Kemp begins work in the Cape Colony
1807 – abolition of slavery in British ships
1813 – Judson arrives in Burma
1816 – death of Francis Asbury
1838 – final emancipation of slaves in British colonies
1860 – election of Abraham Lincoln

Revolution involves widespread and fundamental change which is deep and irreversible. For individuals involved, all aspects of life are affected, whether they personally harbour revolutionary or counter-revolutionary sentiment, or are just caught up in events. Revolutions profoundly influence life and faith, as well as wider church structures. Such revolutionary change had shaped church and society after the conversions of Constantine and Martin Luther, but events from the late eighteenth to the early twentieth century were equally momentous. Not just one revolution, but a series, shook Europe and North America, the seeds of which had been sown in the Enlightenment. Political events in America and France were the most outwardly dramatic, but revolutions in science, philosophy and theology were also hugely significant.

Revolution and religion in the USA

In 1776 thirteen American colonies declared their independence from British rule, precipitating a protracted war. Success in this cause initially seemed unlikely, and when it came some religious leaders attributed it to the hand of God, believing it a portent of the global spread of freedom and knowledge. It deepened convictions that God had a special purpose for America. Yet, when the Constitution of the new United States was drawn up in 1787, it made almost no mention of religion. No religious test was to be required to qualify for public office. The First Amendment of the Constitution enshrined both freedom of religion and also a 'wall of separation' between church and state, ensuring there would be no established government-supported national church, although individual states had liberty over such matters within their own borders. Although the Declaration of Independence announced that 'all men are created equal' with the inalienable rights of 'Life, liberty, and the pursuit of Happiness', those who were black, female or Roman Catholic had genuine cause to doubt the seriousness of this claim for many years.

The Founding Fathers used the term 'the Creator' freely, and valued virtue and a moral code to prevent social chaos, but the views of Thomas Jefferson and George Washington were predominantly Deist. A broadly Christian republic emerged, creating an open field of free competition between different religious groups. The churches with the most flexible and outward-looking structures, and with the most dynamic leadership, would succeed, especially the Methodist, Baptist and Disciples of Christ churches. Their religion tended to be small-town or rural, emotional, conversionist and often apocalyptic. Congregationalism, Presbyterianism and Episcopalianism remained important but did not grow quickly.

Among American Methodists, Francis Asbury (1745–1816) paralleled John Wesley's abilities in organization and itinerancy, travelling 270,000 miles and preaching 16,500 sermons. He helped make Methodism the leading religious force in America for a century. The 200,000 American Methodists at the time of Asbury's death had become 1.5 million by 1855, out of a population of 23 million. Women played a key role, especially in Methodist class meetings. The Baptist churches similarly adapted well to post-revolutionary society. The 460 Baptist churches of 1780 had increased to 12,000 by 1860, with over 1 million members in 1860. They were particularly strong in the South.

One major feature of the new America was the presence of some 500,000 African Americans, the vast majority of them enslaved. Many proved responsive to the Christian message, but when the Methodist Episcopal Church attempted to rid its societies of slave holders in 1784, it was forced to back down in the face of Southern opposition. Black Christians in mainline churches were often forced to sit in segregated areas. As a result, separate churches were formed, such as the African Methodist Episcopal Church, which started in 1816 and had 20,000 members in 1860. By 1800 there were also 20,000 in independent African American Baptist churches in the South. These churches represented a quiet religious rebellion against racial discrimination and the failure of Christians to live out the egalitarian implications of their profession. They also reflected the attractiveness of the Christian message of spiritual liberation and its promise of eternal life. It offered the dispossessed self-worth and dignity in the eyes of God. Leading among African American preachers was Richard Allen (1760–1831), a converted slave.

The opening up of the American West in the nineteenth century created opportunities to exploit the territory, promoting a vast effort in mission to reach the scattered settlers. But it also brought suffering for Native Americans, who faced a catalogue of broken treaties and land confiscations. Unsurprisingly, attempts at Christian mission to them met with a mixed response.

The Second Great Awakening, which began in America in the 1780s and lasted to the 1830s, produced church growth of astonishing levels. It Christianized the institutions and social habits of the new nation, and rooted evangelicalism firmly into American culture. Revivalism became a significant dimension of nineteenth-century American evangelicalism, a feature of which was the camp meeting. The most famous example was held at Cane Ridge, Kentucky, in 1801, attended by some 20,000 people and marked by passionate and emotional preaching with highly exuberant manifestations. Revivalism offered a contextualized expression of Christianity – voluntary, egalitarian, individualistic, yet functioning within a community structure. In a physical environment needing to be tamed by determined personal exertion, theology shifted in an anti-intellectual and Arminian direction. Based on his own experiences, Charles Finney (1792–1875) systematized revivalism in his *Lectures on Revival* (1835). By 1845 some 40,000 ministers served the USA's population of 20 million, but many had limited training. Their preaching was unpretentious, plain and practical: populism replaced learning, deference and patronage. Liberty became a sacred cause, inseparable from notions of Christianity.

The French Revolution

The cry for 'liberty', coupled with that of 'equality and fraternity', was at the heart of the very different revolution in France, where inequalities were very great. When Enlightenment thinkers like Voltaire (1694–1778) called for an overthrow of the 'superstition' of the past, the Catholic Church, owning perhaps a third of all the land in France, was an obvious target. When the French state faced bankruptcy in the late 1780s, the absolutist monarch Louis XVI was forced to call a meeting of the Estates-General, which had not sat since 1614. Pent-up forces were unleashed, and in 1789 a National Assembly was formed which transferred power from the king to the people, released prisoners from the Bastille fortress in Paris and claimed the Catholic Church's vast wealth for the nation. The 'Declaration of the Rights of Man and the Citizen' issued by the revolutionaries asserted that 'men are born free and live free and equal under the laws'. Roman Catholicism was drastically reformed under the Civil Constitution of the Clergy passed by the Assembly in 1790. By 1792 Christianity had become equated with opposition to the revolution, provoking attempts to eradicate it. Sunday was abolished, a ten-day week instituted, the teaching of Christianity in schools was forbidden and marriage replaced by a civil ceremony. Through 1793–4 the 'Terror' raged, an orgy of stabbings, lynchings and guillotinings, in which most of the royal family and aristocracy, and over 2,000 clergy, were executed. By 1794 just 150 out of 40,000 pre-1789 churches were still celebrating mass, although other services were held in secret. It was the first state-sponsored policy of de-Christianization in Europe since the days of Diocletian. By 1795 the worst was over, priests and nuns were released, and worship resumed.

In 1799 Napoleon Bonaparte, a revolutionary general, staged a coup d'état in France. Through military conquest he built an empire that stretched to Germany, Spain, Portugal and Italy. Napoleon realized the social usefulness of the church. A concordat set out the terms of the new relationship between the papacy and France, with Catholicism acknowledged as the religion of 'the great majority of French citizens', but not as the state religion, and bishops were selected by the head of state. In return bishops were to declare their loyalty and pray for the Republic. The Église de France was free to worship, but closely overseen by the State, which also controlled education. Protestants (around 2% of the French population) were also given freedom of worship, as were Jews. In 1804 Pope Pius VII was in Paris to witness Napoleon's coronation as emperor, but unlike Charlemagne, it was the emperor who placed the crown on his own head.

The defeat of Napoleon by the armies of the European allies in 1815 saw the Papal States restored to the pope, and the monarchy to France, but the Gallican Church had lost its glory. Church attendance, especially among men, declined, except at major religious festivals. Yet the survival of Christianity through the Terror was remarkable, owing much to the quiet courage of the laity, especially women, in retaining traditional beliefs and practice in the home.

Religion and the Industrial Revolution

That Britain was spared revolution in the years after 1789, and again in 1848 when revolution rocked many European countries, has raised important questions. Was it, for instance, the impact of the Evangelical Revival which turned the working classes away from political revolution because their energies had been absorbed by spiritual revolution? The reality was more complex, for there had already been revolution in the seventeenth century, which had redressed the balance between crown and Parliament, and shifted some power away from the aristocracy. Britain's revolution was instead industrial, bringing associated revolutions in transport, agriculture and commerce. By 1851 over half the population lived in urban areas and 42% worked in manufacturing, mining or the building industry. Market towns like Manchester, Birmingham and Bradford mushroomed into industrial cities.

Such rapid change placed great stresses on the inflexible parochial system of the established churches which survived from the medieval period. Urbanization meant some parishes contained 150,000 people, far beyond the ministry capacity of a single clergyman. A rapid programme of church building in urban areas followed, together with a restructuring of clerical hierarchies: the See of Manchester was created in 1836. It was, however, the Nonconformist churches, with their looser organizational structures, which adapted most quickly and efficiently to population change and growth; buildings were quickly erected in areas of most need, funded by the voluntary giving of members.

Within Anglicanism a strong and growing Evangelical Party emerged alongside the High and Broad Church parties, as a legacy of the eighteenth-century Revival. By 1833 possibly 30% of clergymen were considered Evangelicals. A key figure was Charles Simeon (1759–1836), for over fifty years minister of Holy Trinity Church, Cambridge, and Fellow of King's College, Cambridge. His model of systematic expository preaching, pastoral visitation and interest in overseas mission powerfully influenced undergraduates, many of whom went into Anglican ministry.

By 1837 Congregational churches had 127,000 members, and there were around 100,000 in the main Baptist groupings. In 1791, the year of John Wesley's death, there were 56,600 Methodists, but this number had increased to 435,000 in 1840. Methodism was not without its divisions, as different groups sought more egalitarian structures with greater role for the laity. One such, Primitive Methodism, had over 62,000 members by 1836.

Religion in Victorian Britain was marked by the rise of voluntary religious societies. The Sunday school movement had the greatest impact. Its annual enrolment of around 200,000 children in 1800 reached 2 million in 1851 (around half of all children). By 1903 some 6 million children attended Sunday school, meaning almost every child had contact at some point. Although educational methods were limited, Sunday schools helped to raise literacy rates among working-class children who had little other access to education. By the 1830s some 60–75% of working-class children could read and 30% could write.

William Wilberforce

Evangelicals demonstrated a strong social conscience. The 'Clapham Sect', who gathered in Clapham, London, under the ministry of John Venn (1759–1813), included William Wilberforce (1759–1833) and Henry Thornton (1760–1815). A number were Members of Parliament or colonial administrators, and saw it as their duty to use their wealth and influence for the moral and social betterment of humanity. Their causes included promoting education for the poor. They also opposed the publication of obscene literature, Sabbath breaking, immoral amusements and cruelty to animals. Wilberforce experienced evangelical conversion in the mid-1780s, and he used his influence to challenge the formal, nominal Christianity of many elite members of society. He was persuaded by leading Evangelicals to take up the cause with which he became synonymous – the abolition of the slave trade.

Abolition of the slave trade

Between the fifteenth and late nineteenth centuries one of the most appalling and barbaric episodes in world history took place. The 'Rape of Africa' saw some 18 million Africans forcibly taken as slaves to the Americas and Asia. Ten million crossed the Atlantic, mainly in European ships, and around 7 million were taken to Asia and the Middle East by Arab slave traders. Possibly 4 million died in the process of transportation across Africa and then during the Atlantic crossing. A further 10 million were subjected to slavery at the hands of their fellow Africans. This trade was motivated by human greed, and conducted with violence and cruelty. The racist oppression of Europeans, Americans and Arabs who traded in the lives of black Africans was appalling. By 1810 there were around 1 million slaves in Brazil and 350,000 in Jamaica. The shipment of slaves into the USA was stopped in 1808, but by then there were 1.2 million slaves in the country. Through natural reproduction that number had reached 4 million in 1860.

Abolitionists exposed in graphic detail the cruelties inflicted on slaves, barbarically manacled or yoked as they were marched to the coast. Then they were packed together below decks on slave ships, allocated space the size of a coffin, which for many is what it literally became. Up to 30% of slaves died on the longest transatlantic crossings. Wilberforce picked up the anti-slavery gauntlet from Quakers and the Anglican Thomas Clarkson. They drew on Enlightenment sentiment as to the solidarity of the human race and the right of individuals to liberty and happiness. John Wesley's opposition was trenchant, declaring slavery an 'execrable villainy which is the scandal of religion'. The account by the former slave Olaudah Equiano of his enslavement, release and evangelical conversion, published in 1789, represented a powerful African voice.

Wilberforce's supporters were only a small group in the British Parliament and so were forced to use the tactics of 'holy worldliness' in the messy world of politics to win cross-party political and religious support. They made it a badge of evangelicalism to oppose slavery (something not achieved in the USA) through campaigning, petitioning, letter writing, fact gathering and public speaking. It took nearly twenty years of relentless effort before in 1807 slave trading in British ships was abolished. The Bible was used to promote abolitionism – stressing the universal brotherhood of humanity (Acts 17:26) and principles of spiritual equality (Gal. 3:28). The evangelical motif of spiritual redemption from the slavery of sin meshed closely with needs for physical redemption from the bondage of slavery. Other European powers slowly agreed to abolition after 1814, although the trade lingered on until the 1860s.

Alongside their campaigning in Parliament, Wilberforce and his friends invested heavily in practical measures to help freed slaves, establishing in 1791 the Sierra Leone Company. This was a part of Africa where all would be free and equal, with education for children and employment based on legitimate commerce. Sierra Leone was a brilliant dream, the morning star of Africa. The Americans followed suit in 1821 with the establishment of Liberia; and the French created Libreville in Gabon in 1848. By 1820 there were over 10,000 freed slaves in Sierra Leone, most of whom had been rescued from the holds of slave ships. Sierra Leone served as a base for Christian mission to West Africa. Africans from many different tribes, gathered in one location, proved a living language laboratory. The converted, educated slaves were culturally and linguistically equipped to take the gospel to their own tribes, and hundreds served as either ordained clergy, catechists, teachers or other mission workers.

Emancipation of slaves

The second phase of the abolition campaign was to deal with slave ownership. Wilberforce's mantle largely passed in Britain to Thomas Fowell Buxton (1786–1845), who led another long campaign of petitioning, information gathering and public speaking, highlighting the cruelties of the slave system, and the denials of civil and religious liberty attendant on it. In this the actions of especially Baptist, Congregationalist and Methodist missionaries in the West Indies were vital. They offered education, religious instruction and pastoral care to the slaves, not only befriending them but also proving advocates for the slaves, especially in cases of manifold injustice. John Smith of the London Missionary Society championed the cause of slave protests against excessive punishments. He was accused of encouraging a slave rebellion in Demerara in 1823 by various means, including reading aloud the book of Exodus to slaves. His death in prison gave the abolitionist cause a martyr.

The slaves also played a significant role in accelerating the emancipation process, including another rebellion, in Jamaica in 1831. A key figure in this rebellion was Sam Sharpe (1801–32), a slave who was a deacon in a local Baptist church. He argued that the Bible taught the natural equality of all men and that slaves were entitled to freedom. Although unsuccessful, and costing the lives of 50,000 slaves and fourteen white settlers, the revolt made West Indian slavery untenable. In 1833 Britain voted to progressively abolish slavery in its colonies. In 1838 the slaves were free, and flocked to mission churches, convinced that the Christian message had been vital in winning emancipation. Slaves had learned from the missionaries that they were made in the image of God and that they had individual rights – to learn the Christian truth freely and to self-expression.

Emancipation slowly spread: the French abolished slavery in their territories in 1848, Argentina, Peru and Bolivia in the 1850s, but Brazil not until 1888. Chile and Mexico abolished slavery when they gained independence in 1823 and 1829. Evangelicalism was a powerful, but not sole, factor in the success of the campaign. Economic growth in Europe made other trades more profitable; economists argued that a coerced workforce was not a productive one; Enlightenment humanitarianism awakened a wider social conscience; and middle-class votes changed the character of Parliament. But to find the source of the moral drive and resolute perseverance in the 'Great Cause', special attention needs to be given to the work and witness of evangelicals.

Social concern

Abolition was just one aspect of the evangelical social conscience in nineteenth-century Britain. In Glasgow Thomas Chalmers (1780–1847) reawakened the Reformation 'godly commonwealth' ideal in the early decades, with church and school operating together as redemptive units for society. His church also took on responsibility for raising and distributing poor relief in its parish. Most churches developed their own local visitation society, and David Nasmith (1799–1839) pioneered the city mission movement, starting with the Glasgow City Mission in 1826, created to take the Christian gospel to the darkest parts of the new urban areas.

In a society without state social welfare provision, a large range of philanthropic effort was undertaken by churches and Christian organizations. Children were a particular focus of concern. Education was largely in the hands of the churches until the State began its own efforts in the 1870s. Anglican and Catholic orphanages were widely established. The London Congregational minister Andrew Reed (1787–1862) started three orphanages, a hospital for children with severe learning difficulties and a home for people with incurable illness. George Müller's Ashley Down Orphanage supported some 2,000 children in Bristol in the 1880s. In the East End of London, Thomas Barnardo (1845–1905), who started a mission for young people, had by the time of his death rescued around 60,000 children. He pioneered approaches to fostering, operating a 'no destitute child refused admission' policy. In 1905 Barnardo's children's homes were caring for over 8,500 children, of whom 1,300 were disabled or suffering from serious illness.

One of Britain's most widely respected philanthropists and social reformers was Lord Shaftesbury (1801–85). He was strongly motivated by his evangelical social conscience, and steered legislation through Parliament to outlaw the employment of children in underground coal mines, to reduce the hours children worked in mills, and to improve housing conditions and the care offered to people with mental illness. Evangelical social reformers and philanthropists in Britain helped ameliorate some of the worst ills of the Industrial Revolution; indeed the nineteenth century has been called 'the Evangelical Century'. However, other issues remained unaddressed, and the biggest social reform provisions such as universal pensions and unemployment pay had to wait until government intervention at the start of the twentieth century.

Victorian Britain was an age of great preachers. Chalmers held over a thousand hearers spellbound each Sunday with sermons described by one hearer as 'thrilling, overwhelming. His whole soul seemed in every utterance'. His one-time assistant Edward Irving (1792–1834) had a similarly electrifying effect when he moved to London. Anglicanism produced its own great preachers, such as Henry Melvill (1798–1871), also in London. The undoubted Prince of Preachers was Charles Haddon Spurgeon (1834–92). During his ministry from 1854 to his death, he preached to London audiences of 12,000 on numerous occasions, and a weekly congregation of 6,000 people after the completion of the Metropolitan Tabernacle. His published sermons fill sixty-three volumes, rich with biblical quotation, anecdote and illustration, steeped in Calvinistic theology drawn from the Puritans, and enlivened by irrepressible humour. He started the Stockwell orphanage, and in 1856 founded a college that had trained 900 pastors by the time of his death.

Similar philanthropy and social concern was a strong feature of US evangelicalism, with efforts channelled through voluntary means. By 1830 the American Bible Society was distributing over 300,000 copies of the USA's 'Iconic Book', the Bible, or portions of scripture, each year. Education was another strong feature of the social concern agenda (by the 1820s there were 50,000 Sunday schools), together with Sabbath observance, and temperance: abstinence from the consumption of alcohol was promoted as the mark of the truly converted person. Campaigns for temperance increasingly focused on abolition of the sale of alcohol, and this was legislatively achieved through the Eighteenth Amendment which introduced Prohibition between 1920 and 1933.

The American Civil War

However, in the social conscience of the USA, commitment to abolish slavery never became the unequivocal hallmark of evangelicalism. This was a huge anomaly in a land that was built on the principles of liberty, and which had become the world's most actively Christian nation. In the end it took a horrific civil war to wipe away the stain of slavery. The economic self-interest of the planter-elite in the South drove the debate, although some slave holders appealed to Scripture to justify their practice. When delegates from Georgia and South Carolina refused to join a United States in which slavery was forbidden, the matter was left out of the Constitution. A slave was defined as three fifths of a person for census purposes. By 1860 the 500,000 free African Americans (half of them living in the South) were dwarfed by the 4 million living in slavery, with few rights and little education, facing constant exploitation and abuse. Most slaves attended churches, but often at the behest of their masters. Here preachers emphasized spiritual matters, submission and social control. Nonetheless, slaves drew patience and courage from their faith, and a hope for an eternal future where wrongs would be righted. The situation festered for a century, with slavery an intrinsic part of Southern states, but outlawed in the North. The work of the Quakers in the early abolition movement was boosted by the Second Great Awakening. Charles Finney was a strong abolitionist, combining moral indignation at slavery with revivalism. The American Anti-Slavery Society had 250,000 members by the end of the 1830s, producing huge amounts of literature and petitions to support the cause, with women playing an active role. The issue split the Baptist and the Methodist denominations in the North and South.

The balance of power between slave-holding and slave-free states became ever more precarious. The election in 1860 of Abraham Lincoln (1809–65) with a commitment to the 'ultimate extinction' of slavery led slave-holding states to secede from the Union. This plunged the country into a terrible civil war costing 600,000 lives. Both sides believed God was on their side, and both armies reported religious revivals in their midst, yet, as Lincoln sagely observed, 'God cannot be *for* and *against* the same thing at the same time.' Indeed, the Civil War has been called a conflict over biblical interpretation. Many in the South declared that an attack on slavery was an attack on the Bible. Campaigners in the North argued that the Old Testament merely regulated and ameliorated an ancient custom, and that the New Testament contained the principles that would inevitably lead to slavery's eradication. They pointed out the deep differences between Old Testament regulations and the barbaric practice in the slave plantations.

Abraham Lincoln

In 1863 Lincoln declared the slaves 'henceforth forever free', but their fate after the victory of the Northern anti-slave states remained precarious as deeply ingrained racist attitudes proved hard to eradicate. The poverty and racial discrimination suffered by many black people in Africa and North and South America in the twentieth century owed much to the legacy of slavery. With the new-found freedoms brought by emancipation, many African Americans rejected the racially mixed denominations they had been forced to attend, and chose instead autonomous black churches. Between 1860 and 1896 the African Methodist Episcopal Church grew from 20,000 members to 450,000.

Protestant missionary expansion

While Roman Catholicism remained the largest, and most geographically spread, Christian tradition, a significant upturn in Protestant engagement in mission in the nineteenth century was another legacy of the Evangelical Revival. Evangelicals were impelled by their conviction that those who did not hear and believe the gospel would be lost. The eighteenth-century revivals brought renewed confidence in the power of the Christian message to transform vast numbers of people. This was coupled with Enlightenment confidence in the capacity of education to awaken understanding and moral consciousness, leading to the belief that the extension of 'civilization' would create a seedbed in which the gospel could take root.

In 1792 the Baptist pastor William Carey (1761–1834) calculated that out of a global population of 731 million, Roman Catholics numbered 174 million, and just 44 million had access to Protestant teaching. A series of missionary societies was launched to address this need. The Particular (i.e. Calvinistic) Baptist Missionary Society was formed in 1792 by Carey, who transitioned from an early career as a shoemaker and village pastor to missionary statesman. From his base in Serampore near Calcutta, Carey, along with Joshua Marshman and William Ward, undertook a remarkable work of translating the Bible into six languages, running schools that educated several thousand children and creating a network of missionary churches through tireless preaching work. In 1795 the London Missionary Society (LMS) was founded, a society largely supported by Congregational churches, which focused its early efforts on the islands of the South Pacific but by 1830 was operating on every continent. An inspirational LMS pioneer was John Williams (1796–1839), who was martyred on the island of Erromanga.

What was to become the Church Missionary Society (CMS) was established by Anglicans, including Charles Simeon, in 1799. By 1830 it had sent out 166 missionaries, with West Africa being a focus of operations, despite the high mortality rate in the 'white man's grave'. The American Board of Commissioners for Foreign Missions was started in 1810. One of its most significant recruits was Adoniram Judson (1788–1850), who after 1813 did much to establish Christianity in Buddhist Burma (Myanmar), although he became a Baptist and his support was taken on by Baptists in the USA. Judson completed a Burmese translation of the Bible in 1834. Other missionaries joined him, and by 1851 there were some 30,000 Christians in Burma, many from the tribal peoples. Important European missionary societies followed, including the Basel Missionary Society (1815) in Switzerland and the Berlin Missionary Society (1824).

In 1783 Thomas Coke (1747–1814) drew up his plan for 'The Society for the Establishment of Missions Among the Heathens', with early Methodist efforts focused on the West Indies. A Methodist Missionary Society was formed in Britain in 1818, and a counterpart in North America in 1820. In 1830 Alexander Duff (1806–78), the first missionary sent out by the Church of Scotland, began a school in Calcutta with the support of the learned Indian Hindu reformer Ram Mohun Roy (1772–1833). His work was aimed at the higher castes, out of the belief that if conversions were won among them, Christianity would percolate down to the lower castes.

The British East India Company was required to employ chaplains, and in India these included the Anglican Henry Martyn (1781–1812), who had been Simeon's curate. Martyn undertook Bible translation work and evangelism among Hindus and Muslims. The first Anglican bishop of Calcutta was the moderate High Churchman Thomas Middleton (1769–1822). Tensions between British officials seeking political stability and British missionaries seeking to promote Christianity among the Indian population remained real throughout the nineteenth century, but within fifty years of Carey's death in 1834 there were half a million Protestants in India.

Anglican chaplains were also sent to the penal colonies in Australia, from where Samuel Marsden (1765–1838) promoted mission to the Maoris of New Zealand, conducting the first Christian service there in 1814. Johannes van der Kemp (1747–1811) arrived in what became South Africa under the auspices of the London Missionary Society in 1799, and built up a large Khoikhoi congregation. The legacy of his teaching was one of the influences on Ntiskana (1760–1820), the Xhosa prophet and hymn writer. Van der Kemp and the Scottish missionary John Philip (1775–1851), who arrived in 1819, faced criticism from colonial settlers for defending the interests of the black population.

These early Protestant mission societies remained small and survived with limited income, but by 1830 significant fruit was just beginning to be seen. The changing geopolitical scene was affording Protestants opportunities they had never before experienced. Africans, Asians and some Latin Americans were beginning to embrace their faith.

17. CHALLENGE AND CRISIS

Lifeline
1835 – Strauss's *Life of Jesus*
1845 – Newman converts to Catholicism
1848 – Marx's *Communist Manifesto*
1859 – Darwin's *Origin of Species*
1864 – *Syllabus of Errors*
1865 – China Inland Mission founded
1870 – First Vatican Council
1885 – Berlin Conference on Colonial Questions
1912 – death of Lottie Moon
1917 – Bolshevik Revolution in Russia

Midlife crisis can produce radical new courses of action and drastically changed circumstances. It can precipitate the end of established and familiar patterns, but may also be the start of new and fresh expressions. The aftershocks of the Enlightenment and French Revolution crises continued through the second half of the nineteenth century.

Developments in German philosophy and theology

A 'second Reformation' took place as a largely Lutheran German Empire emerged, although just over a third of its population remained Roman Catholic.

Growing German national self-identity was coupled with the belief that the nation stood in the vanguard of philosophical and intellectual developments. One response to Enlightenment rationalism was the emphasis on 'spirit' or *geist*, embracing the totality of a person's being. The poet and dramatist Johann Wolfgang von Goethe (1749–1832) rejected the Judaeo-Christian idea of God and spoke of a divine spirit which indwelt all creation and life. Romanticism emphasized intuition, emotion and imagination. It influenced art, music and philosophy. In his *Critique of Pure Reason* (1781) Immanuel Kant (1724–1804) argued that the knowledge of God comes not from the Bible or traditional Christian teaching, nor can it be grasped by the human mind which only deals with the outer essence of things. Instead, the heart, or feeling, is vital in perceiving 'Ideas' beyond reason's capacities.

Kant's influence on Friedrich Schleiermacher (1768–1834) was notable. In *On Religion* (1799) Schleiermacher gave primacy to the 'spirit', dismissing 'systems of theology' as external and 'cold argufying'. Instead religion was a personal sense of absolute dependence, 'of being and living in and through God'. In *The Christian Faith* (1821) Schleiermacher argued that doctrine springs from reflection on Christian feeling. This opened the door for a radical 'stripping away' of aspects of Christian teaching. He marginalized the traditional significance of miracles by suggesting they were expressions of felt faith, rather than the basis for faith. To Schleiermacher, making religious experience the root of authority, rather than the Bible or Christian tradition, appeared to be a solution to the Enlightenment critique that Christianity failed the test of reason. If Christian teaching was the fruit of religious feeling, it needed no scientific verification or rational proof. Yet Schleiermacher had driven a wedge between the intellect and feeling, between theological reflection and personal piety. He moved theology towards anthropology.

G. W. F. Hegel

Another German intellectual giant was G. W. F. Hegel (1770–1831), a practising Lutheran. He presented the human consciousness as being in progress towards knowledge of the Absolute, the Spirit, which he identified with the Christian God. He described a dialectic process by which the 'world spirit' works out the Absolute Idea through conflict – thesis being countered by antithesis, leading to synthesis, as the idea or process moves to a higher level. Hegel attempted to transform Christianity from religion, which represented the truth, into philosophy, which states the truth. He was more interested in the metaphysical truths behind Christian teaching than their historical basis.

In his *Life of Jesus Critically Examined* (1835) David Strauss (1808–74) made explicit what was implicit in Hegel, depicting the accounts of God's work in the Bible as vehicles by which universal truths were conveyed in the form of myths. He believed the true Jesus would be revealed by stripping away anything miraculous or irreconcilable with 'known and universal laws'. The depiction of Christ in the Gospels was therefore the product of the faith of the church, rather than an historical account. Strauss paved the way for the modern critical study of the New Testament. Old Testament study became dominated by literary theory and evolutionary views of religion. The 'Documentary Theory' of Julius Wellhausen (1844–1918) proposed that the Pentateuch was the fruit of various editors combining a series of originally independent narrative sources, and was the most recent part of the Old Testament. This approach dominated Protestant Old Testament studies into the twentieth century.

Radical Hegelians, such as Ludwig Feuerbach (1804–72), went further to propose that ideas of the Divine were a projection from the human consciousness of higher qualities, objectified into a divine Being who is then worshipped. Theology was therefore a form of anthropology, for religion is just human self-consciousness externalized. These themes recur in the writings of Friedrich Nietzsche (1844–1900) and were further developed by Sigmund Freud (1856–1939). Whereas the first Reformation was about deconstructing medieval Catholicism's understanding of the church and salvation, the second Reformation led to attempts to deconstruct the subject of theology, God himself.

Albrecht Ritschl (1822–89) shifted the theological focus from transcendence to the immanence of a relational God, emphasizing the kingdom of God founded by Christ. Salvation was to be understood in terms of the community into which the believer is brought. The proper response to salvation was devoted service in the kingdom of God. Ritschl did not see the miracles or resurrection as integral to understanding the historical Jesus. His approach paved the way for the early twentieth-century liberal 'Social Gospel'.

As an attempt to recast Christianity to make it acceptable in a modern rational age, the German second Reformation was not a success if judged by churchgoing. In 1891–5 average Sunday morning attendance at the Lutheran churches in Berlin was just 2% of the population, although regional variations were great. Theological liberalism had not provided answers to the key issues of life and death that people looked for, so much so that in 1882 Nietzsche declared 'God is dead.' Liberal and radical theology met resistance in Germany from evangelical theologians such as Friedrich Krummacher (1796–1868) and Friedrich Tholuck (1799–1877), who defended biblical orthodoxy against rationalism and called for a return to historic Lutheran orthodoxy.

Horace Bushnell (1802–76) shifted the locus of theological method from the head to the heart, and liberal theology into the American Protestant mainstream. He argued that theological words would always be inexact, unable to convey the precise truth intended. To Bushnell the Bible comprised 'inspirations and poetic forms of life', containing analogies and shadows of 'formless mysteries'. Doctrine needed to be held 'in a certain spirit of accommodation'. Creeds were to be read as poetical, not literal.

Responses to theological liberalism in North America and Britain

A sustained response to Bushnell and the German liberal theologians came especially from Princeton Seminary. One of its most influential theologians, Charles Hodge (1797–1878), had studied in Germany, and called for rigorous intellectual effort by evangelical theologians to counter critical theology and the experiential mysticism of Schleiermacher. Hodge's theological centre was the Bible, because its Author is God. He argued, 'Everything which the Bible affirms to be true is true.' Science, theology and ethics were to be held accountable to the Bible, rather than vice versa. Benjamin Breckinridge Warfield (1851–1921) strongly asserted biblical inerrancy, arguing that the original autographs of Scripture were without error. He took the battle to the modernists, asserting that seeking religious truth in a book filled with errors and inaccuracies was impossible: the means and the message had to be in conformity. The last in this great Princeton tradition was J. Gresham Machen (1881–1937), who taught at the seminary until 1929. When Princeton underwent a liberal realignment, he left to help found Westminster Theological Seminary.

Attempts to resist the advance of liberal theology led to heresy trials, including those of the Presbyterians David Swing (1830–94) and Charles Briggs (1841–1913). In the 'Downgrade Controversy' of the 1880s C. H. Spurgeon sought to check the encroachments of theological liberalism among English Baptists. Yet by 1920 theological liberalism claimed the status of academic orthodoxy, with a third of American Protestant ministers identifying with it, together with religious journals and publishing houses. Within Catholicism the weight of papal resistance to liberalism was strong. The 'errors' identified by Pope Pius X in 1907 included the promotion of biblical criticism and accommodation to modern science: modernism was the synthesis of all heresies.

In sharp contrast to theological liberalism stood the dispensational premillennial reading of Scripture popularized by John Nelson Darby (1800–82). Dispensationalism became rooted in emerging Bible institutes like the Moody Bible Institute (1886) and was propounded in the widely used Scofield Reference Bible (1909). In these circles, investment of time in high-level theological study to challenge theological liberalism, or promote active social concern, was not encouraged. The nineteenth-century Christian holiness movement was a particular focus for evangelical spirituality. Phoebe Palmer (1807–74) became a popular holiness speaker, emphasizing 'entire consecration'. Holiness fed into the revival of 1857–9 which grew out of prayer meetings in New York, spreading across North America and parts of Europe. The Keswick Convention, first held in 1875, promoted holiness but shifted its focus to empowerment for service. Iconic hymns included Joseph Scriven's 'What a Friend we have in Jesus' (1855) and Fanny J. Crosby's 'Blessed assurance, Jesus is mine' (1873), typifying the simple, deeply personal and Jesus-centred spirituality of most evangelicals.

Religion and scientific revolutions

Revolutionary change in the theological world was matched by that in natural philosophy, or science. Scientists began to present their findings as an all-encompassing explanation of cosmic reality, the authority of which could be challenged only on the basis of alternative scientific proof. In *Principles of Geology* (1831) Charles Lyell (1797–1875), building on the work of James Hutton (1726–97), argued that the geological history of the world should be dated in millions of years. The view that the six days of the Genesis creation account were figurative, not literal, gained ground. Even Hugh Miller (1802–56), an evangelical geological and fossil expert, suggested that they were 'great periods, not natural days'. Such 'old earth' approaches were supported by a number of other nineteenth-century Reformed thinkers. However, the eminent naturalist Philip Gosse (1810–88) of the Plymouth Brethren remained unshaken in his belief in a six-day creation. Although the world was only a few thousand years old, it had been created 'as though' it were much older. To conservatives the ultimate issue was final authority – did it lie with geology or the Bible? They sided with Scripture. As Moses Stuart (1780–1852), professor at Andover Seminary, argued, because Christ had affirmed the Pentateuch to be of divine origin, to question its teaching was to doubt Christ. In contrast, Baden Powell (1796–1860), professor at Oxford University, contended that in any conflict with the 'revelation' of science, the Word should give way.

Charles Darwin

In 1859 Charles Darwin (1809–82) published *On the Origin of Species*, effectively an alternative book of Genesis based on scientific theory. Darwin's portrait of natural selection through struggle drew on Hegel's dialectic of thesis and antithesis, and argued that descent with modification, of which natural selection was the most important means, could result in the appearance of new species over vast periods of time. This implied to his supporters that humans were just highly evolved animals rather than a work of special creation. Despite considering entering the Anglican ministry as a young man, Darwin had slowly lapsed into agnosticism and unbelief. But many in the liberal and Broad Church tradition simply assimilated the claims of evolution and geological dating into their theological system. As Frederick Temple, a future Archbishop of Canterbury, declared in 1884: 'He [God] did not make things . . . but He made them make themselves.' 'Darwin's Bulldog', T. H. Huxley, scornfully dismissed such reasoning in 1894: 'There must be some position from which the reconcilers of science and Genesis will not retreat', and declared himself a missionary apostle for science, seeking to 'convert the Christian Heathen . . . to the true faith'.

Others were sure that evolution could not be embraced without abandoning essential doctrines. Matthew Maury, founder of the science of oceanography, argued in 1855 that because the Author of nature is also the Author of revelation, 'it is impossible that they should contradict each other'. Charles Hodge similarly rejected the separation of science from theology: 'The denial of design in nature is virtually the denial of God.' He answered his own question, 'What is Darwinism?' simply: 'It is atheism.' Within the Catholic Church a Pontifical Biblical Commission established in 1902 instructed Catholic scholars to maintain 'Mosaic integrity'.

Responses to the pressures of social and political liberalism

Karl Marx (1818–83) claimed Darwin as an ally from the world of science in promoting his view of the evolutionary progress of society through conflict to

Pius IX

a classless society. Socialism decried the abuses of the capitalist system as the source of inequality, poverty and social disorder, and Marx shaped these ideas into a clearly defined philosophy and ideological system. Influenced by Feuerbach, he rejected religion as the man-made 'opium of the people' to be swept away, to free them for the revolutionary task. Marx's *Communist Manifesto* (1848) contained the elements that would make Marxism one of the great 'religions' of the twentieth century.

Social and political liberalism, with its emphasis on democratic rights, freedom of expression, free trade and an end to monopolies, left churches in uncharted territory. Catholicism adopted a policy of retrenchment. The *Syllabus of Errors* (1864) of Pope Pius IX condemned rationalism, socialism and communism as incompatible with the Catholic faith. Pius became an immensely attractive figure to Catholics: ultramontane devotion to the pope 'over the mountains' became almost mystical. The *ex cathedra* infallibility of the pope on matters of faith or morals was defined in 1870 at the First Vatican Council. Leo XIII's *Rerum novarum* (1891) reflected more nuanced responses to modern industrial society.

The pressures of social and political liberalism contributed to a series of church divisions, of which the Disruption in the Presbyterian Church of Scotland in 1843 was the most dramatic manifestation. Four hundred and seventy-four ministers and 30–50% of church members left to form the Free Church of Scotland, moved significantly by evangelical convictions to challenge the undemocratic system of patronage in the appointment of ministers, and the interference of the courts in ecclesiastical matters. Within Anglicanism the Oxford (or Tractarian) Movement attempted to defend Anglicanism against organizational reform at the hands of the British government, and to restore it to the practice of the medieval period and the doctrine of the patristic period. Its spiritual heart was John Keble (1792–1886), but John Henry Newman (1801–90) and Edward Bouverie Pusey (1800–82), Regius Professor of Hebrew, played significant roles. Eucharistic ritual and ornamented clerical vestments later became characteristic of Tractarian worship, mirrored in a return to the decorated and colourful medieval Gothic style of church architecture. Although Newman converted to Roman Catholicism in 1845 (becoming a cardinal in 1879), the resulting 'Anglo-Catholic' movement remained a highly influential tradition within Anglicanism. Others moved in the opposite ecclesiological direction, leaving Anglicanism in the 1820s to form the Plymouth Brethren, a conservative, Nonconformist, evangelical Christian movement. They sought to recreate the ideals of the New Testament church, seeing the Bible as the supreme authority for church doctrine and practice.

Within the 'Broad' Church, Charles Kingsley (1819–75) worked with Frederick Denison Maurice (1805–72) to develop Christian Socialism, out of fear that politically disenfranchised working people would embrace socialism. Maurice, an influential liberal theologian, emphasized the Fatherhood of God and the brotherhood of humanity, and rejected the substitutionary understanding of the atonement and eternal punishment. Among British Nonconformists, many working-class leaders engaged in society by taking important roles in trade unions and cooperatives. It has been said that the British Labour Party, formed in 1893, owed more to Methodism than to Marx.

In the light of the challenges posed by the modern liberal social and political agenda, the ongoing importance of religious forms in shaping the identities of many nations in the nineteenth century seems surprising. Canada went so far as to call itself the 'Dominion' of Canada when it was formed in 1867, the name drawn from Psalm 72:8 (KJV): 'He shall have dominion also from sea to sea'. The new nation balanced Protestant and Catholic religious and cultural interests. In Ireland, where some 80% of the population was Roman Catholic, Irish nationalism fused with Catholicism in the struggle for Home Rule. In the independent Ireland that emerged in 1921 the Catholic Church was granted a 'special position' in the constitution, but six counties in the north with strong Protestant majorities remained under British rule. In Lutheran Scandinavia, national churches provided a unifying cultural and social force, and sense of identity. It took until 1845 for religious dissenters to be given freedom to practise their faith in Norway, 1860 in Sweden and 1889 in Finland, although full religious freedom took longer. The Danish philosopher and theologian Søren Kierkegaard (1813–55) argued that authentic faith was less about institutional Christianity and more about individuality, subjectivity and authenticity.

Christianity and Latin American independence

The remarkable soldier-statesman Simón Bolívar (1783–1830) helped lead successful revolutionary campaigns in Venezuela (1817; independence was finally secured in 1821), Colombia (1819), Ecuador (1822) and Peru (1824). The independence of Upper Peru was proclaimed in 1825, and the country was named Bolivia in Bolívar's honour. The Roman Catholic hierarchy, which had strongly supported colonialism, was forced to recognize the legitimacy of the new Latin American republics in the 1830s. At first the new governments accepted church–state alliances to ensure stability and order in society, but these gradually gave way to separation between church and state, and the secular state became the model, with removal of discriminations based on religious profession. The disestablishment of religion took place in 1890 in Brazil, 1919 in Uruguay and 1925 in Chile, although implementation of the policy in Columbia (1853), Mexico (1859) and Guatemala (1879) occasioned great hostility. Yet the dominance of Spanish–Portuguese Catholic culture restricted the potential for Protestant advance in Latin America. By 1914 there were hardly more than 500,000 Protestants in Central and South America, many of them migrants.

Orthodoxy and national identity

Russia oscillated between liberal reform, with freer religious expression, and conservative reaction, through successive nineteenth-century regimes. During times of 'reaction' the connection between being Russian and belonging to the Russian Orthodox Church was strongly emphasized, which adversely affected Christian dissenters and Jews. The last tsar, Nicholas II (ruling 1894–1917), adopted reform too late to save the Romanov dynasty, and pent-up resentment was unleashed in the Bolshevik Revolution of 1917. For a while Christians outside the Orthodox Church were boosted by a decree that every citizen could profess any religion or none: by 1929 there were 500,000 baptized evangelicals, with some 4 million adherents. Then policies changed, and Russian Christians were left struggling under a totalitarian society in which Christianity played no part in conceptions of national identity, and atheism was officially promoted.

Elsewhere in the Orthodox world, the connection between church and national identity was more complex. In 1833 the Orthodox Church in Greece, which had supported the struggle for Greek independence between 1822 and 1831, was declared independent of that in Constantinople, but it was seventeen years before it was granted autocephaly by the Ecumenical Patriarch of Constantinople. Although the Ottoman Empire was forced to concede religious equality to all its subjects in the wake of the Crimean War, the position of Christians in the Balkans remained precarious. In an appalling genocide of 1914–15, somewhere between 1.1 and 1.8 million Armenian Christians were killed out of a total population of 2.5 million.

Arctic Ocean
ELLESMERE ISLAND
GREENLAND
SPITZBERGEN
BANKS ISLAND
ALASKA
BAFFIN ISLAND
ICELAND
NORWAY
NORTH
DOMINION OF CANADA
LABRADOR
BRITISH ISLES
DENMARK
NETH
BEL
GER
NEWFOUNDLAND
SWITZ
AMERICA
FRANCE
UNITED STATES
AZORE ISLANDS
PORTUGAL
SPAIN
ITALY
Atlantic Ocean
MOROCCO
ALGERIA
TRIPOLI
RIO DE ORO
MEXICO
WEST INDIES
AFRICA
PORTO RICO
SUDAN
BR HON
HON
CAPE VERDE ISLANDS
GUADALOUPE (FR)
GUATEMALA
NICARAGUA
SENEGAL
GAMBIA
TOGO
COSTA RICA
SIERRA LEONE
NIGERIA
VENEZUELA
DU
FR
CENTRAL AMERICA
PANAMA
COLOMBIA
BR
GUIANA
LIBERIA
IVORY COAST
DAHOMEY
KAMERUN
ECUADOR
BRAZIL
PERU
SOUTH
ANGOLA
BOLIVIA
PARAGUAY
GERMAN SW AFRICA
AMERICA
URUGUAY
CHILE
ARGENTINA
Pacific Ocean
GRAHAM LAND

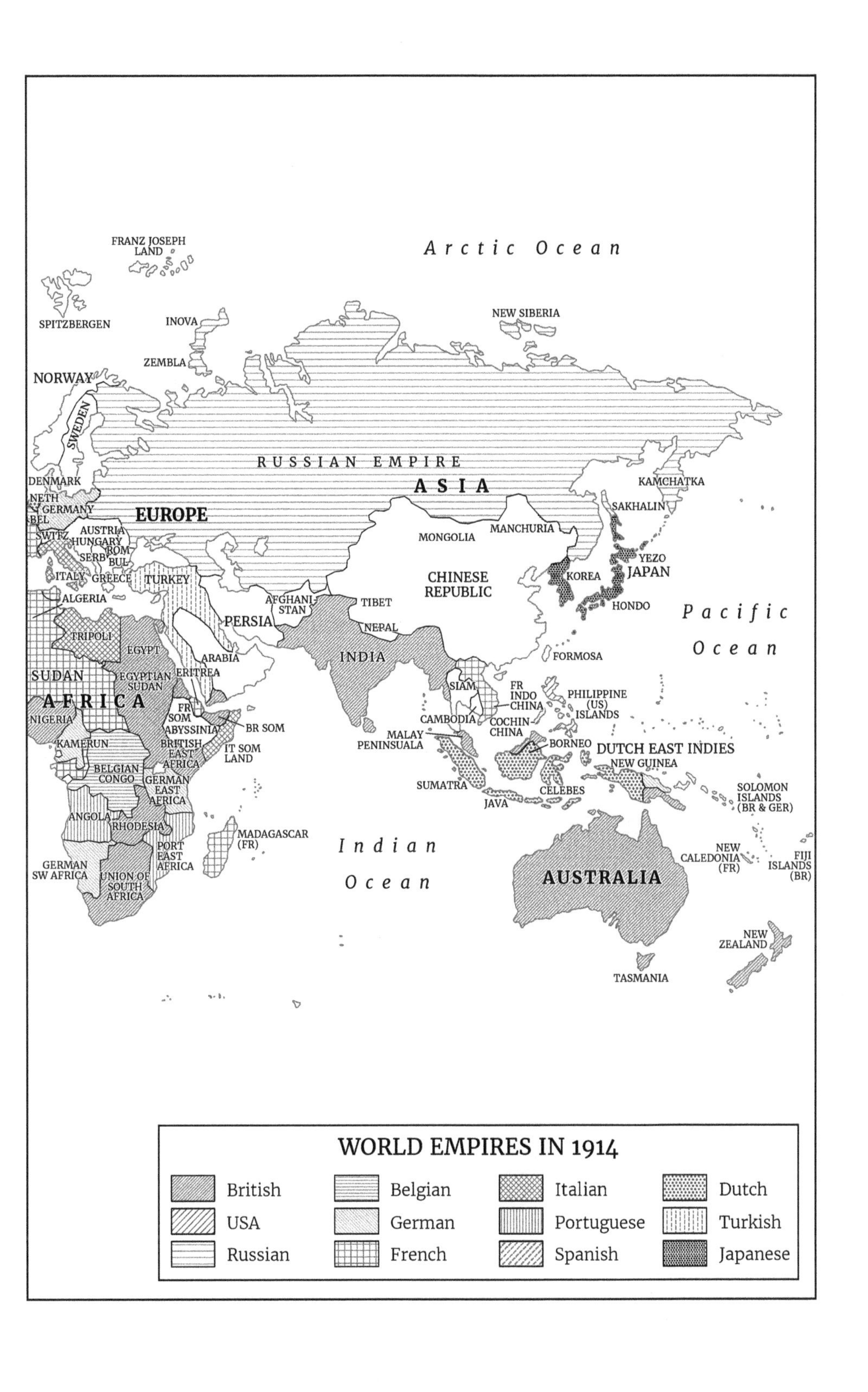
Arctic Ocean
FRANZ JOSEPH LAND
SPITZBERGEN
INOVA
ZEMBLA
NEW SIBERIA
NORWAY
SWEDEN
RUSSIAN EMPIRE
ASIA
DENMARK
NETH
GERMANY
BEL
EUROPE
SWITZ
AUSTRIA HUNGARY
SERB
ROM
BUL
ITALY
GREECE
TURKEY
KAMCHATKA
SAKHALIN
MONGOLIA
MANCHURIA
CHINESE REPUBLIC
KOREA
YEZO
JAPAN
HONDO
Pacific Ocean
ALGERIA
AFGHANISTAN
TIBET
PERSIA
NEPAL
TRIPOLI
EGYPT
INDIA
FORMOSA
ARABIA
SUDAN
EGYPTIAN SUDAN
ERITREA
SIAM
FR INDO CHINA
PHILIPPINE (US) ISLANDS
AFRICA
FR SOM
NIGERIA
ABYSSINIA
BR SOM
CAMBODIA
COCHIN-CHINA
MALAY PENINSUALA
KAMERUN
BRITISH EAST AFRICA
IT SOM LAND
BORNEO
DUTCH EAST INDIES
BELGIAN CONGO
NEW GUINEA
GERMAN EAST AFRICA
SUMATRA
CELEBES
SOLOMON ISLANDS (BR & GER)
JAVA
ANGOLA
RHODESIA
MADAGASCAR (FR)
Indian Ocean
PORT EAST AFRICA
NEW CALEDONIA (FR)
FIJI ISLANDS (BR)
GERMAN SW AFRICA
UNION OF SOUTH AFRICA
AUSTRALIA
NEW ZEALAND
TASMANIA
WORLD EMPIRES IN 1914
British
Belgian
Italian
Dutch
USA
German
Portuguese
Turkish
Russian
French
Spanish
Japanese

Late nineteenth-century mission

The internal challenges faced by European Christianity, and the growth of secular political models, makes the remarkable growth of missionary activity in the late nineteenth century particularly unusual, as if the decaying European parent plant was throwing out shoots into fresh soil to ensure its survival. The Conference on Colonial Questions held in Berlin in 1885 effectively 'carved up' large parts of Africa among the European powers. Although some missionaries were complicit in the imperialist subjugation of non-white peoples, the view that they went with Bible, flag and gun as handmaidens of colonialism has been significantly challenged. The country which by 1910 possessed the largest missionary force in the world, the United States, demonstrated no dash for empire. The work of missionaries brought educational gains: culture was enriched through studying indigenous languages (often with a view to Bible translation), which were preserved by being committed to writing. Missionaries offered skills training, economically empowering marginalized people; called colonial authorities to account over human rights abuses; and waged a steady campaign against the internal African slave trade. Nonetheless, ethnocentric (sometimes racist), paternalistic attitudes on the part of the missionaries often hindered the vision of self-governing, self-supporting, self-propagating churches. One beacon of hope was the appointment in 1864 of the converted former slave Samuel Ajayi Crowther (1807–91) as the first African Anglican bishop.

The profile of the global missionary contingent was changing. By 1900 there were over 4,000 American missionaries, of whom 1,200 were single women, reflecting another significant trend. The indomitable Southern Baptist missionary Charlotte Diggs 'Lottie' Moon (1840–1912) saw hundreds of converts in China before her untimely death of malnutrition during a famine in 1912. Mary Slessor (1848–1916), a former Scottish mill-girl, served with such distinction with the Calabar Mission that she was appointed a British vice-consul in 1898. Medical missionary work rose in importance: the American doctor Clara Swain began work in India in 1870, and by 1880 she was treating 7,000 patients a year.

Samuel Crowther

Interdenominational 'faith' missions, such as the Christian and Missionary Alliance, played an increasingly prominent role. James Hudson Taylor (1832–1905), founder of the China Inland Mission (CIM), was convinced that God's work, done in God's way, would not lack God's supplies. High-profile missionary recruits inspired others. The 'Cambridge Seven', who served with the CIM in 1885, included C. T. Studd (1860–1931), a gifted England cricketer; D. E. Hoste (1861–1946), who became Hudson Taylor's successor; and W. W. Cassels (1858–1925), who in 1895 became the first Anglican bishop in western China. In 1912 Studd also founded the 'Heart of Africa Mission', which later became the Worldwide Evangelization Crusade.

Mary Slessor

Those most likely to embrace Christianity were poor, socially marginalized, powerless, young and female. They usually learned the gospel through an indigenous convert, a catechist, teacher or evangelist, rather than from a European missionary. Among the Chuhras, in the Punjab, the evangelist Ditt saw most of his community brought to Christianity by 1914. Between 1800 and 1900 the number of Indian Christians increased more than threefold to 2,735,000. Greatest fruit was seen among the tribal groups: in the Telegu area alone, a million people joined the church in thirty years. Yet the emergence of senior indigenous leadership was slow. It was 1912 before Vedanayagam Samuel Azariah (1874–1945) was consecrated the first Indian bishop in the Anglican Communion. By 1880 the majority of the workers of the China Inland Mission were Chinese, which may account for much of its success: the best known was Xi Shengmo – Pastor Hsi (c. 1830–96).

The Welsh Baptist missionary Timothy Richard (1845–1919), who had adopted radical methods to express Christianity in ways Confucians and Buddhists could relate to, also engaged in widespread fundraising and distribution of relief during the terrible famine in northern China which cost nearly 10 million lives from 1876 to 1879. Richard helped make emergency relief an important feature of overseas mission concern. Missionary progress was not without cost. The Boxer Rising in China in 1899–1900 saw some

Xi Shengmo

20–30,000 Chinese Christians killed, together with over 200 European missionaries and their children. The establishment of the Chinese Republic in 1912 brought a heyday for missionary efforts, and by 1914 the Protestant community numbered over 252,000, with a similar number of adherents. The Chinese Catholic population of just over 1.4 million was still less than 1% of the population.

Missionaries continued to pay the ultimate price. James Chalmers (1841–1901) was killed by cannibals in Papua New Guinea after a remarkable pioneering ministry. Robert Thomas (1839–66), a Welsh missionary, was martyred on a Korean beach in 1865 where he had just landed, intending to distribute Bibles. Korea remained largely 'closed' until the 1880s. The cradle of Korean Protestantism was the home of Suh Sang-Yun (1848–1926), who gathered with a small group of believers in 1883, five years after his conversion. Methodist and Presbyterian missionaries arrived in 1885. *Methods of Mission Work* (1886) by the American Presbyterian John Nevius (1829–93) proved extremely influential, promoting a self-supporting church with strong indigenous leadership, free from missionary domination. In 1889 the tiny Protestant community numbered only 265, but it had grown to 167,352 by 1910, and there were 73,517 Roman Catholics. In Sumatra the indomitable work of Ludwig Ingwer Nommensen (1834–1918) after 1862 became a 'people's movement', creating a genuinely Batak Lutheran church, numbering 103,525 in 1911.

Siam (Thailand) opened itself up to foreign influence in the 1860s. Although in 1912 there were 36,000 Thai Christians, of whom 5,000 were Protestants, they were still less than 1% of the population. In Japan in 1888 there were 25,500 Protestant members, and by 1910 the Catholic community was around 63,000. Japanese Christian leaders included the Bible teacher Kanzo Uchimura (1861–1931), whose biblical lectures could attract a thousand hearers in Tokyo. A change in official attitudes was reflected in 1912 when Christian representatives were invited to join those of Shinto and Buddhism at the Three Religions Conference.

The missionary-explorer David Livingstone (1813–73) opened up awareness of, and routes into, the heart of Africa, producing significant missions response.

His focus on the Zambezi region inspired first an unsuccessful mission by High Anglicans, and then work by Scottish Presbyterians at Blantyre and Livingstonia in what is now Malawi. The annexation of Congo by Belgium in 1885 brought both ruthless imperialist exploitation and opportunities for Christian expansion. English Baptists planted mission stations along the Congo River, followed by American missionaries in the lower reaches of the river. Catholicism was far stronger – by 1910 there were some 50,000 baptized Catholics, although no Congolese priests.

David Livingstone

In the south of Africa the conversion of local chieftains proved significant. Khama III (c. 1837–1923) of the Bangwato in Bechuanaland (Botswana) furthered the interests of his own tribe as a Christian leader of considerable integrity. The Ugandan context was more complex. After the death in 1884 of King Mutesa, who had welcomed CMS missionaries to Kampala in 1877, his successors plunged the country into civil war, slaughtering missionaries and some 200 Ugandan Christians, and at one point attempting to create an Islamic state. Chaos was ended when a British protectorate was established in 1894, and Uganda was divided into Protestant and Catholic areas. By 1896 the Anglicans had 6,900 baptized members. There was something of a race for Africa with Islam, with missionaries attempting to occupy areas before Muslims arrived. Catholic missionaries also competed for territory. Cardinal Lavigerie (1825–92), appointed Archbishop of Carthage by the pope, and Primate of Africa, in 1868 founded the White Fathers for missions to Africa. He pressed Catholic expansion into Uganda, Kenya and Malawi, even though Protestant missionaries were already there, and built on Catholicism's legacy in Angola and Mozambique. A significant Catholic presence was also built up in Nigeria and Cameroon. However, even in 1923, there were just sixty-six African priests in sub-Saharan Africa.

The Middle East remained a difficult area for Christian witness, with very few converts reported even when mission was attempted. A small mission to Arabia between 1891 and 1941 reported just five converts. Protestant missionary work in North Africa had begun as early as 1829, and the North Africa Mission, formed in 1882, facilitated endeavours in Morocco, Tunis, Algeria and Libya.

Urban mission

The title of William Booth's *In Darkest England, and the Way Out* (1890) graphically highlighted the vast mission fields lying at the very heart of Christian empires. Although church membership grew by 6% in the USA between 1890 and 1906, attendance was falling in Europe, to just 15% in early twentieth-century Paris and 19% in London. Female attendees outnumbered male by two to one. The culture of social respectability ensured that religious weddings and funerals remained the norm. Although there was a small and growing body of 'agnostics', on the whole indifference was much more common than unbelief. Churches responded urgently to these missional challenges. By 1900 deaconesses were at work in every parish in Hanover, Germany, visiting, teaching nursery school children and caring for the sick, funded by the churches, the city and even local factory owners. Day schools, ragged schools and Sunday schools targeted needy children, together with schemes to redeem leisure hours with recreation and sporting activities. By 1911 the Young People's Society of Christian Endeavour, which had started in 1881, was an interdenominational movement with over 2.7 million US members, and others in overseas chapters. The YMCA, founded in 1844, had by 1910 a membership of a quarter of a million young people.

Attempts at Christian political and social engagement were seen in the nineteenth-century 'civic gospel' movements in Birmingham and Glasgow. In 1878 Adolf Stoecker (1835–1909) founded the Christian Social Party in Germany, mixing conservative theology with strong patriotism and 'Tory-radical' policies of improvements in living and working conditions. Samuel Barnett (1844–1913) attempted to break down the alienation between the classes through the Settlement Movement, started in east London. It was widely copied: by 1900 over a hundred 'Settlement Houses' had been started in the United States, and in Germany Walter Classen (1874–1954) established the Hamburg Volksheim.

Dwight Lyman Moody's (1837–99) crusading, Bible-only response to the secularizing challenges of late nineteenth-century society led to carefully choreographed revivalist meetings designed to create as few barriers to the gospel as possible. Moody delivered homely, practical sermons, deliberately low on theological content and liberally dosed with anecdotes, concluding with a direct, often emotional appeal for decision. His philosophy was simple: 'God has given me a lifeboat and said "Moody, save all you can."' His preaching was accompanied by simple gospel solos, sung with affecting pathos, by Ira D. Sankey (1840–1908). When he died in 1899, it was estimated Moody had addressed 100 million people. Moody inspired many to serve in overseas mission through the Student Volunteer Movement, launched in 1888. The watchword, 'the evangelization of the world in this generation', was widely used by pre-millennialists to connect missionary effort to belief that Christ's second coming would occur after every nation had heard the gospel, although some post-millennialists also used the motto.

William Booth (1829–1912) and his wife Catherine (1829–90) developed urban revivalism through the Salvation Army, with its brass bands, dramatic advertising, military-style uniforms and women preachers aimed especially at the 'submerged tenth', the poorest classes who appeared impervious to the outreach of churches. Evangelism was eventually coupled with social concern in the care and support of destitute and homeless people, prostitutes, alcoholics, discharged prisoners and deserted wives.

The nineteenth-century legacy was complex. In Europe working men found socialism an increasingly attractive alternative to religion. Liberal theology destabilized the simple certainties of the faith for many. Professional sport and popular entertainment offered an alternative emotional outlet to religion, and an accessible way of spending leisure hours. Church and charitable efforts to meet social needs were gradually superseded by local authority and government intervention. The future of Christianity as it entered the twentieth century was unclear: would it be determined rear-guard defence or glorious advance?

18. AN AGE OF TURMOIL

Lifeline
1904–5 – Welsh Revival
1906 – Pentecostal outbreak at Azusa Street, Los Angeles
1910 – start of publication of *The Fundamentals*
1913–14 – Wadé Harris's evangelistic mission across West Africa
1917 – Walter Rauschenbusch's *Theology for the Social Gospel* published
1929 – Church of Scotland reunion
1941–5 – the Holocaust
1943 – Dietrich Bonhoeffer arrested
1945 – atomic bombs dropped on Japan
1948 – foundation of World Council of Churches (WCC)

Late adulthood is supposedly when life is more settled, marked by the desire to spend time with children and grandchildren. It is time to retire, set one's house in order and begin to hand over responsibility. In the first half of the twentieth century European Christianity was losing ground under the looming shadows of war, racism and totalitarian ideology. Elsewhere Christianity was becoming flush with the vigour of youth, beginning to establish new forms free of parental constraints. Such was the diversity of twentieth-century Christian forms that some have spoken of various 'Christianities', each shaped by the contours of its context.

By 1900 Christians represented 34% of world population (although still 81% were white), but at least half of the people in the world remained 'unevangelized'. There were some 266 million Roman Catholics, 134 million Protestants and 115 million Orthodox Christians. Religious geography remained unbalanced, with 368 million Christians in Europe, around 60 million in North America, and the rest scattered across the globe. Yet the coming shift in the axis of world Christianity was now beginning. By the end of the twentieth century 60% of Christians would be living in Africa, Asia and South America.

The contexts in which Christianity existed were changing and often hostile. A state-sponsored attempt to deconstruct the Christian consensus of the West marked the Marxist–Leninist regime in Russia. Modern psychoanalysis, led by Sigmund Freud (1856–1939), sought to explain the human condition without resort to religion, explaining away the spiritual dimension of life. Analytical psychology reduced religion to a by-product of tensions between the subconscious and conscious parts of the human mind.

Sigmund Freud

Patriarchal understandings of the role and status of women were questioned, with increased recognition of their equal rights to education and equal legal, financial and social status. Although this challenged the stance of many churches, Emmeline Pankhurst (1858–1928) and her daughter Christabel (1880–1958), who led the campaign for female suffrage in Britain, held strong Christian convictions. Women were granted the vote in New Zealand in 1893, Britain and Germany in 1918, and in US presidential elections in 1920.

Liberalism and the Social Gospel

A distinctive feature of early twentieth-century Christianity was the advance of 'Social Gospel' teaching, especially in North America and Europe. The thinking of Walter Rauschenbusch (1861–1918), the foremost Social Gospel theologian, was shaped by his pastoral ministry on the edge of New York's notorious 'Hell's Kitchen' slum. He blamed the sufferings of the poor on the injustices of ruthless competition and monopolies, rather than on their personal sin. In *Christianizing the Social Order* (1912) and a *Theology for the Social Gospel* (1917) he combined aspects of liberal theology with a social concern agenda, to portray the 'Kingdom of God' as involving not only 'the immortal souls of men', but also church, family, home, state and society. All of these needed to be 'converted' and brought under the law of Christ.

Liberal theology, then ascendant in the West, questioned the value of the historic confessions of the church in the face of evolutionary theory, biblical higher criticism and social modernity. Sincerity was more important than doctrinal precision: humans were basically good, and evolutionary social progress would overcome evil and sin. In 1910 the Presbyterian Church in the USA attempted to halt the seemingly inevitable progress of theological liberalism by calling for candidates for ordained ministry to affirm the inerrancy of Scripture, the virgin birth of Christ, substitutionary atonement, the reality of the miracles of Christ, and his bodily resurrection. By 1927 the doctrinal tide had shifted and the denomination concluded that it could not mandate certain doctrines as 'essential and necessary'. In 1936 a number of leading evangelicals seceded to form the Presbyterian Church of America, renamed the Orthodox Presbyterian Church three years later.

Fundamentalism

To many the modernist modification of the Christian message was counterproductive. Lack of doctrinal clarity and certainty was alienating people from the church. Pope Pius X prompted a purge of modernists from Catholicism. *The Fundamentals: A Testimony to the Truth*, a series of pamphlets written between 1910 and 1915, was an evangelical response to modernism, tackling subjects like Scripture; the deity of Christ; the virgin birth; the Trinity; and sin. Coined in 1920, the term 'Fundamentalism' initially described the coalition of evangelical Protestants opposed to modernist theology and the secularization of culture. Over time, Fundamentalist subculture became more narrowly defined by revivalism, dispensational premillennialism, and opposition to Marxism, Catholicism, the sale of alcohol and the theatre. It heralded 'the Great Reversal' among many evangelicals, away from gospel preaching allied with active social concern into a defensive, inward-looking piety. It also brought a desire to separate from doctrinally mixed denominations. Fundamentalists came to dominate the Southern Baptist Convention. But conservative Christianity remained popular. After the baseball player Billy Sunday (1862–1935) became an evangelist, he drew huge crowds to hear his colloquial, frenetically delivered sermons.

Fundamentalism represented a move away from the Princeton-style conservative academic engagement with contemporary theological debates; indeed early twentieth-century evangelicalism produced few theologians of the stature of Hodge and Warfield. In Britain, Handley Moule (1841–1920), a convinced evangelical, was a professor of divinity in Cambridge before becoming bishop of Durham in 1901. P. T. Forsyth (1848–1921) was a Congregationalist theologian of considerable ability, as was the Presbyterian James Denney (1856–1917) in Scotland. More typical of Nonconformists in Britain were the Congregationalist preacher George Campbell Morgan (1863–1945), who despite lack of formal academic training produced many volumes of commentaries and sermons, and Graham Scroggie (1877–1958), a prolific Baptist writer.

The rise of Pentecostalism

One of the great historic revivals took place in Wales in 1904–5, where some 100,000 professed conversion. Related revivals were reported as far afield as Los Angeles, India and Korea. Evan Roberts (1878–1951), the leading figure, stressed a second-blessing experience for Christians, called 'baptism of the Holy Spirit', and brought a distinct holiness emphasis to the revival. The Welsh Revival created a context that aided the spread of Pentecostalism, one of the most notable religious movements of the twentieth century. Baptism in the Holy Spirit, holiness and physical healing were viewed as part of a restoration of the New Testament order preceding the return of Christ.

'Pentecostal' episodes had been reported in the nineteenth century, including those in London in 1831 under the ministry of Edward Irving (1792–1834) and in south India in the 1860s, but Charles Fox Parham (1873–1929) appears the main catalyst for modern Pentecostalism. He asserted that the definitive sign of being baptized in the Holy Spirit was speaking in 'tongues'. In 1901 Agnes Ozman (1870–1937) was the first of his students to report experiencing such glossolalia. William Seymour (1870–1922), an African American, had also heard Parham's teaching and started the Apostolic Faith Gospel Mission on Azusa Street, Los Angeles. Here a Pentecostal outbreak was reported in 1906, characterized by tongue speaking, prophesying, exuberant worship and people falling to the ground 'slain' by the Spirit. Seymour preached to a congregation of African Americans, white Americans, Hispanics and Asians a fourfold 'full gospel' message of personal conversion, baptism in the Holy Spirit accompanied by speaking in tongues, physical healing and an expectation of the imminent return of the Lord. The movement attained global significance, with many international visitors attending and then returning home determined to repeat events seen in Azusa Street.

By 1910 what would later become known as Pentecostalism was present in over twenty-five nations, including Chile, Brazil, Germany and Italy. The Pentecostal Revival churches were founded in Norway by Thomas B. Barratt (1862–1940) after a visit to the USA. Alexander Boddy (1854–1930), an Anglican vicar in Sunderland, visited Barratt and turned his church into a major Pentecostal centre in Britain. Boddy envisaged Pentecostalism as a movement within established churches, but Pentecostals tended to form their own networks. In 1915 George Jeffreys (1889–1962) founded the Elim Pentecostal Church, which became the largest Pentecostal denomination in the UK. Pentecostalism reached Portugal in 1913, Spain in 1923 (through Brazilian Pentecostals) and France in 1926. By the 1930s there were an estimated 80,000 Pentecostals in Russia, although they faced severe persecution and their founder Ivan Voronaev (1886–c. 1940) is believed to have died in a Soviet concentration camp.

Azusa Street missionaries reached Liberia and Angola as early as 1907. The following year, independent Pentecostal missionaries founded the Apostolic Faith Mission in South Africa. African leaders went on to form Apostolic Faith and Zion churches in Basutoland (Lesotho), Southern Rhodesia (Zimbabwe) and the Transvaal. The title 'Zion' (referring to a land without tears and alienation) included a sense of protest against the lack of political rights for black Christians. Pentecostal missions also quickly spread across India. A regional council for the Assemblies of God in south India was formed in 1929, and the Indian Pentecostal Church, which grew out of the work of K. E. Abraham (1899–1974), was registered in 1935. By the year 2000 these were the largest Indian Pentecostal denominations, each with 750,000 members. Pentecostal missionaries reached Java in 1922, and Filipino Pentecostal missionaries (converted in the USA) started churches in the Philippines in 1928. Pentecostalism had already reached China by 1907, and in 1932 Mary Rumsey, who had experienced baptism in the Spirit at Azusa Street, established the first Pentecostal church in Seoul, Korea, along with Heong Huh.

Nonetheless, this was a movement fraught with bitter opposition and division. More than twenty-five denominations trace their origins to Azusa Street. The largely African American Church of God in Christ was led by Charles Harrison Mason (1866–1961), the son of former slaves. The Assemblies of God, founded in 1914, became the largest white Pentecostal denomination, in time attracting some 60% of North American Pentecostals. Arguments in 1916 over the issue of whether baptism should be 'in the name of Jesus only' resulted in non-trinitarian Oneness Pentecostalism, the teaching adhered to by around 24 million Pentecostals in 2010. Aimee Semple McPherson (1890–1944) adapted Pentecostalism to Hollywood culture through her music, use of radio technology, speaking and writing. She founded what became the International Church of the Foursquare Gospel in 1927.

Ecumenism

Moves towards church unions were encouraged by declining confessionalism and signs of falling church attendance in the West. In 1900 much of the Free Church and the United Presbyterian Church in Scotland formed the United Free Church, paving the way for reunion of most Scottish Presbyterian churches into the Church of Scotland in 1929. The Methodist Church of Great Britain was formed in 1932 from most of the much-divided strands of Methodism. Other unions transcended ecclesiastical boundaries. The United Church of Canada, formed in 1925, included Congregationalists, Methodists and two thirds of Presbyterians. Even more notable was the creation of the Church of South India in 1947, including some Anglican churches alongside Congregational, Presbyterian, Methodist and Reformed. The Church of North India, formed in 1970, also included Baptists.

A significant impulse towards ecumenism was the Protestant overseas missionary movement. 'Comity' arrangements emerged to avoid missionary overlap and duplication. The 1910 Edinburgh World Missionary Conference emphasized the importance of cooperation between missions, although it remained wary of talk of united churches. Although styled a 'World' event, neither Roman Catholic nor Orthodox Christians were represented. One thousand out of 1,215 delegates came from Britain or North America, and only nineteen delegates from the non-Western world. Reports received at Edinburgh highlighted how Christianity had gained a footing in all parts of the world, although Tibet, Afghanistan and Nepal remained closed. Converts from every race and major world religion were reported, as was the growing maturity of the younger churches.

The ecumenical agenda was furthered by the pioneering Kikuyu Conference in Kenya in 1913, where missionaries including Scottish Presbyterians and Anglicans produced proposals for common baptismal procedures and inter-communion. Edinburgh also fed into the formation of the International Missionary Council in 1921, the Universal Conference on Life and Work in 1925, and the 1927 World Conference on Faith and Order. In 1938 a constitution for the World Council of Churches was drafted, although its formation was delayed until 1948 because of the onset of war. Its first assembly, in Amsterdam, included 351 delegates from 44 countries and 147 churches. Its simple basis of faith – 'The World Council of Churches is a fellowship of churches which accept our Lord Jesus Christ as God and Saviour' – allowed cooperation between many despite great differences. The more difficult task of structural reunion was avoided: there was to be no 'super-church'. To others, unity based on such doctrinally minimalist grounds was meaningless, and papered over major divisions. The Roman Catholic Church remained outside the ecumenical movement between the two world wars, the papacy asserting that schismatic churches should return to the 'mother' church.

Indigenous leaders and churches

More than a hundred years of Protestant mission had yielded just 1.5 million non-Western converts by 1900, although this number had almost doubled by 1910. In 1902 there were 558 US and European missionary societies, 18,682 missionaries and a further 79,396 local workers. Medical work had become an intrinsic part of mission activity. The translation of the Scriptures into local languages preserved vernacular languages and culture, and contributed to understandings of national identity. Missionaries sometimes served the colonialist agenda, but also demonstrated liberating capacities. The majority of baptisms were of women, who were given opportunities often denied them in traditional societies. Some missions offered refuge for escaped slaves.

Yet the process of recognizing indigenous leadership was painfully slow. In 1914 the Roman Catholic Church's only non-European bishops were the four in the ancient church of the Thomas Christians. Prescient missionaries realized that indigenous Christian evangelists, teachers and catechists accomplished in a few years what it took well-trained missionaries decades to achieve. Reluctance to entrust local leaders with responsibility, together with continuing racist attitudes, bred frustration and resentment. The formation of African Independent churches, many accommodating elements of traditional African religious belief into their Christian practice, became more noticeable after 1900. Here visions, charismatic gifts and a consciousness of the spirit world took a prominent place.

Notable among these emerging leaders was the Grebo preacher William Wadé Harris (c. 1865–1929). In 1913–14 he undertook a dynamic series of evangelistic journeys from Liberia into Côte d'Ivoire and Ghana. His was a largely orthodox Christian message, including the power of Christ over the spirits, and claims to perform many miracles. In seventeen months he preached to some 200,000 people, claiming around 100,000 converts whom he baptized. Most joined mainstream denominations, but a number of Harrist churches were formed, featuring African leadership, traditional music and dance, liturgical vestments and self-supporting preachers chosen by local congregations. His relationships with the women who accompanied him attracted adverse comment, and he died in poverty in Liberia in 1929. Yet the speed and scale of his success shocked missionaries who had seen little fruit over many years.

Other locally led indigenous African Christian movements, often led by untrained male and female preachers and prophets, include that of Garrick Sokari Braide (c. 1882–1918) between 1912 and 1916 in the Niger Delta. In South Africa, Engenas Barnabas Lekganyane (c. 1885–1948) founded the Zion Christian Church, mixing aspects of traditional Christianity with ecstatic dance, the role of the prophet-healer, and initiation and purification rites. When Lekganyane died the church had at least 50,000 members across southern Africa. In Uganda the Bamalaki broke away from missionary Christianity in 1914, combining elements of Christianity and Judaism, and a rejection of missionary medicine because they believed that sickness was caused by evil spirits or witchcraft. The prophetic (*ngunza*) movement in Congo, led by Simon Kimbangu (1887–1951) whose followers saw him as the special envoy of Jesus Christ, led to his arrest by colonial authorities fearing he was a revolutionary. The last thirty years of his life were spent in prison. The Balokole or 'saved ones' movement spread rapidly among Anglicans and others from Rwanda from the 1930s, alarming some missionary leaders due to its emphasis on public confession of sin. By the late 1940s the East African balokole revival had reached Kenya, Tanzania and Uganda, becoming a highly significant shaping force on African Christianity.

African Independent churches sought to be fully Christian and truly African. Mission churches generally considered them syncretistic, yet many Africans who attended a mission church on a Sunday continued to consult mediums and diviners through the week. There were connections between indigenous African Christianity and movements for political independence, such as that led by John Chilembwe (c. 1871–1915). After a missionary-sponsored Western education in the USA, he founded his own mission at Chiradzu, before in 1915 launching an armed revolt against British rule in Nyasaland (Malawi), mixing Christian teaching with elements of nationalism and calls for social justice. Six other revolts in Africa between 1906 and 1927 deepened white concerns about African Independent churches.

The paternalism, ethnocentrism and repressive behaviour of some colonial settlers in Africa, especially the Afrikaner nationalists in South Africa, coupled with the weaknesses of missions after the First World War, helped push Africans towards their own religious and political forms. Despite the efforts of enlightened leaders like the Anglican bishop Alfred Tucker (1849–1914) in East Africa, and the Church of Scotland missionary David Scott in Nyasaland (1853–1907), to assert the abilities of Africans to be equal to those of Europeans, 'Ethiopianism' offered an attractive appeal to return to the golden age of early African Christianity. One promoter was James Johnson (1836–1917) in what is now Nigeria. A fervent evangelical, loyal to Anglicanism, 'Holy' Johnson was committed to securing rights to education for Africans and the development of a self-sufficient church. Despite his evident abilities he only reached the rank of assistant bishop.

Although in 1939 Joseph Kiwanuka of Uganda became the first African Catholic diocesan bishop, by 1950 there were still no African Anglican diocesan bishops and few African mainstream denominational leaders. Churches were ill-equipped to meet the leadership opportunities and challenges afforded by independence.

African Protestants replicated the tendencies for division found in their parent European and American denominations, fuelled in part by the arrival of Pentecostalism after 1906 which furthered the trend to indigenous expression. Yet missionary Christianity was not devoid of life. Regular revivals of religion were reported in Africa between 1925 and 1935, including that which affected the Qua Iboe mission in Nigeria in 1927. The East African Revival continued to influence patterns of African Christian spirituality, leadership, culture and practice long after it was over, and far beyond the countries in which it had originated. By 1945 African Christianity had a marked tendency to charismatic spirituality, conservative and evangelical teaching, a vibrant liturgy, and interest in miracles, visions, dreams and healing.

Early twentieth-century mission

The collapse of the Ottoman Empire after the 1914–18 war brought a number of Muslim territories under Western control, but hopes that this would increase opportunities for the advance of Christian mission remained unfulfilled. With reduced resources, colonial authorities were aware of how sensitive an issue Christian missionary activity could be, and often ceded much authority to local Muslim rulers in return for peace. The Balfour Declaration of 1917, favouring the establishment of a national homeland for the Jewish people in Palestine, added a new level of instability into the Middle East, coupled with the advance of Zionism and increased Jewish settlement. In Indonesia the connection between Islam and the rise of nationalism made Dutch missionary engagement increasingly difficult in the 1920s.

By the 1930s the mission practice of the mainline denominations was moving away from direct evangelism. Shaped by the League of Nations concept of 'trusteeship', a broader concern for the welfare of colonized areas produced a focus on educational efforts to prepare local people for when they would rule themselves. African nationalism was cradled in the missionary schools. Kwame Nkrumah of Ghana and Julius Nyerere of Tanzania enjoyed Catholic schooling; Leopold Senghor, the first president of Senegal, trained for the priesthood;

Jomo Kenyatta of Kenya was educated by Presbyterian missionaries, and Kenneth Kaunda of Zambia had a Presbyterian upbringing.

In Asia the challenge to colonialism tended to come from those educated in Islam or Hinduism or Chinese religion, but C. F. Andrews (1871–1940), an Anglican priest, became a follower of Gandhi and supporter of Indian independence, although he left institutional forms of Christianity. Indian independence in 1947 was marked by appalling bloodshed. Initially two states emerged, India and Pakistan, from part of which Bangladesh was formed in 1971. Especially in the latter two countries, Christians were left as a small minority and under pressure.

Christianity in China suffered from the anti-Christian campaigns of the 1920s and the Japanese invasion of the 1930s. Chiang Kai-shek (Jiang Jieshi; 1888–1975), who led the Republic of China from 1928, offered hope to Western missionary leaders when he declared himself a Methodist in 1930, but the communist takeover of the Chinese mainland in 1949 saw the forcible expulsion of Western missionaries, deemed tools of imperialism. The Japanese occupation of much of East Asia and the Pacific led to the deportation, imprisonment or execution of many other missionaries. During this crisis the bishop of Hong Kong, R. O. Hall (1895–1975), ordained Florence Li Tim Oi, a Chinese woman, as the first female Anglican priest in 1942. The first Vietnamese Catholic bishop, Nguyen Ba Tong (1868–1949), was consecrated in 1933. After Japanese occupation, the national rising led by Ho Chi Minh and the communists saw Vietnam divided into a communist north and a French-backed south, where many Catholics fled after the ceasefire of 1954.

Faith missions, such as the China Inland Mission, the Africa Inland Mission and the Sudan Interior Mission, joined by the Pentecostal missions, maintained traditional patterns of mission through evangelism and church planting, distrustful of the liberal Protestantism that dominated the ecumenical movement. By 1910 some liberal theologians were proposing that major world religions such as Hinduism and Buddhism offered some form of saving knowledge of God. They still saw Christianity as the superior religion, but not an exclusive one. In contrast, evangelical missionaries upheld the uniqueness of Christ, making the eternal lost-ness of unbelievers a powerful motivation to mission, spurred by James Hudson Taylor's stark image in 1894 of: 'A great Niagara of souls passing into the dark . . . A million a month in China, they are dying without God.'

Racial ideology, totalitarianism and war

The early twentieth century saw a noticeable rise in racist thinking, including Aryan supremacist ideology in Germany. The English philosopher Herbert

Spencer (1820–1903) coined the phrase 'the survival of the fittest' to describe powerful societies overrunning less well-developed ones. Darwin's son Leonard, president of the Eugenics Society, took his father's thinking further to promote breeding a 'better' people. Social Darwinism and eugenics, used to justify the domination, or removal, of racial groups or those with disabilities deemed 'less pure', underpinned the rise of Nazism in twentieth-century Germany. In Africa racial segregation was enforced on the grounds of 'health' by French administrators after the 1890s. Despite the emancipation of the slaves, the USA's black population remained hugely disadvantaged in a white-dominated society. Some of the fiercest resistance to racism came from Christian missionaries who insisted that all humans were made in the image of God and stemmed from one special creative act; and that salvation through Jesus Christ was available to all humans, regardless of racial background.

Two appalling world wars bookended the first half of the twentieth century, shattering blithe liberal confidence in the inevitability of human progress. As Europe descended into war in 1914, Kaiser Wilhelm II called Germans to fight as a Christian nation: 'We trust in the Almighty to strengthen our defence and guide us to good issue.' Many clergy on both sides chose to enlist as soldiers rather than serve as chaplains, confident of the rightness of their particular cause. Pacifism was confined mainly to groups such as the Quakers, Mennonites, the Plymouth Brethren and the non-orthodox Jehovah's Witnesses. At the end of four years of madness, 8.5 million soldiers lay dead on the battlefields of Europe, with huge numbers of civilian casualties. European Christendom was over.

The French Catholic clergy viewed the war as divine judgment for the Third Republic's separation of state and church in 1905–7. The pope, with Catholics fighting on both sides, was reluctant to condemn the German invasions and subsequent atrocities. Yet the German deployment of submarines and zeppelins on civilian targets, and the use of poisoned gas, enabled the allies to condemn Germany as the axis of evil. Billy Sunday declared in 1918, 'If you turn Hell upside down, you will find "Made in Germany" stamped on the bottom.' That both armies believed they were fighting a holy war perhaps prolonged the bitter end. The religiosity of the troops facing likely death temporarily reversed the earlier decline in religious observance seen among men in the previous decades, but many also resorted to lucky charms and talismans. The war dead were celebrated as holy martyrs in the countless war memorials erected in every town and village, but this did not stop many families resorting to séances and spiritualism to try to contact their departed loved ones. Turkey's entry into the war in 1914 brought a declaration of jihad against the Allied powers. When Christians in Turkey supported the Allied forces it fuelled Turkish persecutions of Christians in Armenia, Syria and Lebanon.

Karl Barth (1886–1968), who worked in both Switzerland and Germany, was shocked at the ease with which the cause of war had been embraced by Christian leaders. He believed the atrocities had exposed the shallowness of liberal theology's gospel of the Fatherhood of God and the brotherhood of man. Barth's 'neo-orthodoxy', expressed in works like *Church Dogmatics*, made him the twentieth century's most prominent theologian, rejecting the Enlightenment construct that the divine was knowable through reason. Liberals deemed him too narrow, while some conservatives complained about the limitations of his natural theology, and that he was insufficiently clear about how the Bible was the Word of God, suggesting his theology was too speculative.

Karl Barth

The turbulence of the interwar years saw the Wall Street financial crash of 1929, followed by deep economic depression and the rise of extremist political movements of left and right. In Russia, atheist communism adopted a hostile attitude to the churches. Although Italian fascism and German Nazism claimed to draw on elements of the Christian tradition, they attempted to replace confessional institutions with new organizations tied to the single governing party. The treaties these regimes made with the papacy effectively removed the Catholic Church from political comment in return for its independence. The attempts by Adolf Hitler between 1933 and 1937 to win the churches in Germany to his policies led to church attendance being seen as an expression of support for his regime. Those opposed to this attempted Nazification of the church included Barth and Dietrich Bonhoeffer (1906–45). Bonhoeffer became a leader in the Confessing Church, which resisted aspects of Nazi ideology, before his arrest in 1943 and execution in 1945. However, Hitler's party proved adept at giving and removing favours from churches, undercutting any concerted Christian response to his policies. The German invasion of Russia in June 1941 was portrayed as a Christian crusade against the Soviet antichrist.

The most notorious of Hitler's abhorrent ideologies was anti-Semitism. It led to state-sponsored genocide on an industrial scale of some 6 million Jews by the Nazi regime, herded like cattle, starved, tortured and brutalized for months before their murder. The policy of exterminating 'undesirables' led to the killing of a further 5 million gypsies, Poles, communists, homosexuals, people with physical and mental disabilities, some Christian pastors and some prisoners of war. This appalling period also saw somewhere between 6 and 9 million people die in Stalin's Russian gulags (forced labour camps) or through his other repressive policies.

When accounts of the Holocaust emerged they were so hard to comprehend they were scarcely believed, and the Vatican's response was slow. It was 1943 before protests at the 'extermination measures' were heard. The Prussian synod of the Confessing Church deplored the murder of people 'solely because they are members of a foreign race, or because they are old, or mentally ill'. The persecution of Jews prompted many acts of heroic courage by Christians. The French Capuchin friar Pierre Marie-Benoît assisted the safe passage of thousands of Jews from southern France. The small French Protestant community of Le Chambon, numbering just 3,000 people, had by the end of the war hidden 5,000 Jews. The family of Corrie Ten Boom (1892–1983) were arrested and imprisoned for hiding Jews from the German authorities in their Dutch home: her father Casper died in prison, and her sister Betsie in a concentration camp. The Holocaust posed profound questions of theodicy – where was God in all this horror? It increased the determination to create a homeland for the Jews as a safe haven, resulting in the foundation of the state of Israel in 1948.

In Britain churches were unclear over how to respond to totalitarianism. Most recognized the failure of appeasement, and the need for a 'just war' against the tyranny of Nazism, rather than simply the German people. When conflict broke out in 1939, Catholics were living in all the participant nations, and a papal policy of neutrality was again adopted, later criticized for being lacking in moral leadership. Catholics suffered severely in Poland: many priests were shot or sent to concentration camps. In France the collaborating Vichy government offered favours to the Catholic Church, including the restoration of religious education to state schools, but local clergy remained willing to assist escaped Allied prisoners and resistance fighters.

Hitler's regime was defeated by Allied forces in 1945. In Asia the defeat of the German allies, the Japanese, came after atomic bombs were dropped on Hiroshima and Nagasaki. These cities, and those across Europe from Stalingrad to Coventry, from London to Dresden, lay in ruins, levelled by merciless shelling from land or bombing from the air. Church buildings were devastated in the indiscriminate bombardments. Although their physical structures were often quickly rebuilt or repaired, it was by no means certain whether they, and the Christian church itself, would ever be restored to their position at the heart of belief and practice in Western church and society in the second half of the century.

19. CREEPING INTO OLD AGE OR ADVANCING INTO YOUNG ADULTHOOD?

Lifeline

1949 – start of expulsion of Christian missionaries from mainland China
1962 – Vatican II starts
1963 – Martin Luther King Jr marches on Washington
1968 – assassination of Martin Luther King Jr
1968 – *Humanae Vitae* issued
1974 – Lausanne Congress on World Evangelization
1978 – election of Pope John Paul II
1990 – Dutch Reformed Church declares apartheid a sin
1991 – dissolution of the Soviet Union

As one generation reaches old age, its hope is that a younger generation will take on the legacy it has left, build on it and perpetuate the family name. As European Christianity passed into what appeared senior citizenship, younger vibrant churches were growing at enormous speed in the non-Western world. Christianity had a future, but it looked very different geographically from its shape in the immediately preceding centuries. Indeed Christianity was returning with even greater vigour to lands it had reached in its early centuries and becoming strong in others which had previously seen only limited Christian presence.

A pronounced feature of the second half of the twentieth century was globalization. Internal combustion engines, and then jet engines, revolutionized travel. The resultant boom in oil production brought wealth to nations committed to expanding Islam, including by military force. A communications revolution brought the telephone into homes and eventually most pockets. Radio, television, and then the internet, spread news and information globally within minutes. Pacific Rim countries advanced to rival Western counterparts, but vast disparities of wealth opened up between the Developed and the Majority World. In 2005 around 80% of the world's population survived on under ten US dollars a day.

Christianity and communism

For much of the period the world shivered in the icy blast of the Cold War. The superpowers of the Soviet Union and the USA squared off against each other, assured of 'mutually assured destruction' should nuclear war happen. Conventional wars continued unabated with appalling brutality.

Western fears of expansionist Soviet and Chinese communism were palpable in the 1950s. In the USA the National Council of Churches of Christ was founded in 1950 to confront communism, materialism and secularism, and bolster Christianity as the core of national identity. In 1954 'In God we trust' was placed on US currency. During the Second World War state repression of the Russian Orthodox Church gave way to cooperation, and after the war it was granted legal status. Anti-religious propaganda intensified after Stalin's death, with half of Russia's churches closed between 1959 and 1964. Communism sought to create an alternative, atheistic and totalitarian form of faith, and Christians faced active discrimination in education and employment. Persecution increased in the 1980s in an attempt to halt the growth of the 'underground' church, which included many evangelical and Pentecostal groups. In 1967 Enver Hoxha's Albania declared itself the world's first 'atheist state', with profession of religious faith made illegal.

Generally, however, across communist Eastern Europe a form of coexistence developed between the State and the mainline churches. Catholicism remained strong in Poland, Lithuania and in what later became the nations of Slovakia, Slovenia and Croatia. Protestantism was active in East Germany, and in Romania a mixture of denominations remained strong. Churches were one of the few social spaces that communist states found hard to control: church attendance provided a sense of national identity against Sovietization, and a form of passive resistance. The Vatican's anti-communist alliance with the USA also allowed it to challenge Russian Orthodox ascendancy in Eastern Europe. The World Council of Churches called for a 'third way', refusing to identify the Christian cause with that of the West, boosted by the Russian Orthodox Church joining its ranks in 1961.

The 'glasnost' and 'perestroika' policies of Soviet leader Mikhail Gorbachev from 1985 to 1991 opened the door to change, but Christianity was also a powerful countercultural force. The election of the Polish Karol Wojtyła as Pope John Paul II in 1978 proved highly significant. Elections in 1989 produced a non-Communist Polish government; the Berlin Wall fell that November; and the following month the brutal Ceausescu regime in Romania was toppled after protests over the attempted arrest of the Hungarian Reformed pastor László Tőkés.

John Paul II

In the years after 1989 the experiences of the churches in Eastern Europe were mixed. Lech Wałęsa's efforts to recreate Poland as a Catholic nation ended with his electoral defeat in 1995, reflecting the feeling that the Catholic Church had become too powerful. Where the Catholic or Orthodox churches assumed a dominant position in post-communist societies, they struggled to concede that all religious groups should enjoy religious freedoms. While many embraced new-found liberties for worship and Christian proclamation, and churches in Ukraine and Romania remained particularly strong, elsewhere a legacy of anti-clericalism and religious scepticism persisted from the communist years. Low levels of church attendance were reported in Estonia and the Czech Republic: by 2003, 70% of the former East Germany's population claimed to be 'without religion'. The burst of missionary enthusiasm from the West after 1989 was short-lived. Former-communist Yugoslavia disintegrated into a series of bitterly fighting national groups, fuelled by religious tensions between the Orthodox, Catholics and Muslims.

In communist China the advance of Christianity after the expulsion of Western missionaries and Christian agencies began in 1949, was astonishing. The several million Chinese Christians they left behind were estimated fifty years later to number between 30 and 90 million. Although dismissed as an imperialist religion by the communist regime, Christianity's message of salvation and eternal hope, and its strong personal and moral ethic, appealed to many disillusioned with Marxism.

Some Protestants cooperated with the communist government through the Three-Self Patriotic Movement (TSPM) controlled by the Religious Affairs Bureau. In 1950 Y. T. Wu (1893–1979) produced a 'Christian Manifesto' seeking to align Chinese Christianity with the Chinese Communist Party, which was approved by the premier Zhou Enlai. During the Cultural Revolution and its aftermath (1966–76), the TSPM's role was minimal, but it was revitalized in the 1980s by K. H. Ting (1915–2012). By 2002 it claimed 15 million members. Historically it proved open to theological liberalism, although in some regions it was more evangelical.

Millions of Chinese, including Christians, who refused to conform, especially during the Cultural Revolution, were executed or sent to labour colonies. Wang Mingdao (1900–91), who became a significant unregistered church leader, was imprisoned between 1959 and 1979. In the 1980s evidence emerged of an unofficial, Chinese-initiated Christianity surviving by meeting as 'house churches'. These tended to be strongly evangelical in theology and practice, ranging from the Pentecostal to the Reformed. The Little Flock, founded by Watchman Nee (1903–72), brought a holiness emphasis on the Holy Spirit. Not all interpreted the Bible in an orthodox way: estimates in 2000 suggested that 10% of Chinese Protestants belonged to the unitarian True Jesus Church.

The size of the unregistered churches was impossible to assess: some suggested up to 50 million adherents by 2010. They viewed the TSPM as too close to the State, leaving relationships strained. The post-1978 easing of policy towards Christians was reversed after the suppression of pro-democracy demonstrations in Tiananmen Square in 1989. By the year 2000 there were some 12 million Catholics in China, with two thirds of them in 'underground' churches.

Although the Cold War was portrayed as being between the free Christian West and repressive Marxist atheism, by the end of the twentieth century streams of radical secularist doubt, such as existentialism, were having a strong influence in Western Europe. The intellectual approach of deconstructionism challenged all presuppositions with radical questioning in a search for meaning, although it was doubted if 'meaning' could be discovered. Such influences, coupled with religious indifference, probably proved more harmful to Christianity than atheistic communism. Political discourse in the 1960s reflected this radicalism, with anti-Vietnam War protests, and student demonstrations.

In 1971 the Peruvian Catholic priest Gustavo Gutiérrez set out his radical response to poverty and oppression in *A Theology of Liberation: History, Politics and Salvation*, although liberation theology was dismissed by some as Christianized Marxism. Also radical were the World Council of Churches' grants to oppressed peoples after 1970, including funds for African liberation movements engaged in guerrilla warfare. The radical doubt of Bishop John Robinson's *Honest to God* (1963) caught the attention of the media, but theological modernism lacked widespread popular appeal. Some radical theology of the 1960s–1970s was little different from secular humanism, and in the late twentieth century European denominations dominated by theological liberalism were sharply declining. After 1990 less than 10% of the British population attended church, and in Denmark in 2004 just 3%.

The USA, the world's most economically advanced nation, also boasted the highest levels of Christian profession and adherence: in 1954 the Pledge of Allegiance was extended to include the words 'under God'. Yet this Christian predominance was under threat. The number of Americans who self-identified as Christians fell from over 85% to under 70% between 1990 and 2014, when weekly church attendance dropped significantly to under 50%.

The Moral Majority movement in the USA was most notably active during Ronald Reagan's presidency (1981–9), challenging issues such as the legalization of abortion by the Supreme Court in 1973 and the banning of school prayers. With educational and scientific circles dominated by a Darwinian materialist worldview, some evangelicals sought to develop a scientifically credible and biblically faithful 'creation science'. In the 1950s a number of US states legislated that 'creation science' be taught equally with Darwinism. The 1980s saw more focus on 'Intelligent Design'. Other theologians with scientific backgrounds attempted to develop a new natural theology, arguing that behind the Big Bang lay a Creator who directed subsequent evolution. The Catholic Pontifical Biblical Commission had already, in 1909, proclaimed that the Creation story in Genesis need not be taken literally.

Human sexuality

The sexual revolution after 1960 was fuelled by advances in contraception, although in 2008 around 44 million pregnancies were still terminated by induced abortions. This, together with changes in divorce laws and attitudes to sex outside marriage, raised numerous theological and ethical challenges. Although in 1968 the Anglican Church had declared artificial contraception part of the 'order established by God', Pope Paul VI's *Humanae Vitae* strongly condemned it. This attempt to reassert papal authority over personal moral questions left many Catholics choosing to ignore the official teachings of their church. It created serious issues in parts of the world where the spread of sexually transmitted diseases, including AIDS, might have been reduced by the use of condoms.

Probably the most dramatic change in public morality in the West was over attitudes to homosexuality. An influential gay liberation media campaign prompted a wholesale shift in public opinion. From being a crime punishable by law, homosexuality became an openly expressed sexual orientation with defined equality rights under law, including the legalization of gay and lesbian marriages. Liberal theologians rejected the biblical condemnation of homosexuality as stemming from an outdated context, and proposed an ethic of 'love' as a basis for morality. The Metropolitan Community Church, 'inclusive' of homosexuals, was founded in Los Angeles in 1968 by Troy Perry, a former Pentecostal pastor, and quickly became an international fellowship of churches.

For many conservative evangelicals and Catholics the ordination of homosexual clergy was a line in the sand, raising profound questions over the authority of Scripture. In 1998 the Anglican Lambeth Conference, under strong pressure from bishops from Global South countries such as Uganda, Nigeria and Kenya, resisted the ordination of practising homosexuals to the Anglican priesthood and episcopate. However, the election of Gene Robinson as an openly gay bishop in New Hampshire in 2004 pushed global Anglicanism to the edge of fracture.

Women's rights

Attitudes towards women were also radically changing. Feminist theologians rejected much theology as 'heterosexist', and church leadership as patriarchal and oppressive. English Baptist and Congregational churches had begun to ordain small numbers of women after 1918, and US Presbyterians and Methodists began to ordain women in the 1950s. In 1992 the Church of England accepted the ordination of women as priests. By 2004 there were 2,654 female priests in the Church of England, compared to 8,852 male priests. More than 10,000 United Methodist clergy were women, and sixteen bishops. In African Pentecostalism women played a prominent role. Evangelicals divided between egalitarian and complementarian positions, while the Orthodox and Catholic churches continued their policies of not ordaining women. In 1977 the Vatican declared, 'Christ established a bond between maleness and the priesthood which cannot be altered.'

Nonetheless, the typical Christian was by 2010 female and from the Global South. Christians were also likely to be poor and with limited educational opportunities, finding in Christianity the spiritual, social and personal liberty that transcended the limitations of circumstance and culture. Women were the most active in church-based social concern and Sunday schools. In 2005 they made up just under half of full-time foreign mission personnel.

Human rights and anti-apartheid

The church in the late twentieth century belatedly faced up to some of the most grievous issues it had been involved in or remained silent over. In the Civil Rights campaign in the USA, African American Christianity provided the moral impetus and organizational structure. To a nation globally championing freedoms and democratic rights, the racial inequalities of the 'separate but equal' policies of some states were an ugly stain from the days of slavery. When, in 1955, Rosa Parks was ordered by the driver to give up her seat on a bus to a white person and refused, she precipitated a campaign founded on the Christian principles of love for enemies, and the passive resistance tactics of Gandhi. Its leaders were the black Baptist pastor Martin Luther King Jr (1929–68) and the Southern Christian Leadership Conference (SCLC), formed in February 1957. Using biblical images, hymns and community solidarity, the campaign withstood outrages such as the bombing of a church in 1963 which killed four young black girls. It led to the passing of the Civil Rights Act in 1964 and the Voting Rights Act in 1965. Many white Christian leaders lost much credibility with their silence on Civil Rights. James Cone expressed the radical critique of Black Theology, portraying white theology as so deficient that it could not be called Christian.

After 1948 the South African government enshrined the racist ideology of apartheid (separateness) in legislation. The policy was backed by the Dutch Reformed Church (DRC), which had since 1857 allowed the formation of white, 'coloured', black and Indian sections. By disastrously equating theological conservatism and political conservatism the DRC condemned Africans (including fellow church members) to second- or third-class status because of their skin colour. After the African National Congress was banned in 1960, the churches offered one of the few means to express opposition to apartheid. At the WCC's 1960 Cottesloe consultation even the Dutch Reformed Church delegates accepted mild resolutions criticizing apartheid, although the DRC leadership promptly withdrew from the WCC. One delegate, Beyers Naudé (1915–2004), was expelled from the church for refusing to recant after signing the resolutions, becoming the leading Christian Afrikaner in the anti-apartheid protest. The South African Council of Churches also declared apartheid anti-Christian and a 'false gospel'. The Anglican bishop Desmond Tutu (1931–) led anti-apartheid campaigns both at home and abroad, calling for non-violent approaches and reconciliation. In 1990 the Dutch Reformed Church finally declared apartheid a sin. That year Nelson Mandela was released after twenty-seven years' detention, and the churches played an important role in the successful 1994 transfer of power to a non-racial democratic government.

From the 1990s onward, churches also needed to address deeply disturbing revelations of sexual abuse, sometimes against children, perpetrated by their clergy. Pope John Paul II began a series of apologies for the wrongs committed by the Catholic Church. Such profound failures deeply undermined trust in the church's moral authority at a time of ageing membership, deteriorating buildings and reductions in the numbers of clergy recruits.

Late twentieth-century Catholicism

It had seemed that the traditionalist approach of Catholicism would continue through the second half of the twentieth century when the elderly conservative Pope John XXIII was elected pontiff in 1958. Surprisingly he summoned the Second Vatican Council, which met between 1962 and 1965, designed as an *aggiornamento* of Catholicism, to 'throw open the windows of the church'. Four hundred years after being rejected at the Council of Trent, permission was granted for the celebration of the mass in vernacular languages. Bible versions in the 'mother tongues' of the faithful were encouraged. The Roman Catholic Church began dialogue with the Orthodox and the Anglican churches, and with the World Council of Churches, although it did not formally join. In 1965 the pope and the Ecumenical Patriarch cancelled the mutual excommunications of 1054. However, the Roman Catholic Church continued to assert in its catechism that 'The sole Church of Christ . . . constituted and organized as a society in the present world, subsists in the Catholic Church, which is governed by the successor of Peter and by the bishops in communion with him.'

Mother Teresa

In a number of ways the windows that Vatican II had sought to open were shut by succeeding popes. The pontificate of John Paul II (1978–2005) brought a change in image, while promoting a very conservative theology. Visiting 129 countries, he took the papacy to the masses and to the world. One of the best-known Catholic figures of the late twentieth century was Anjezë Bojaxhiu (1910–97), born in Skopje, Macedonia. She became renowned as Mother Teresa, working among the sick and poor in the slums of Kolkata (Calcutta). In 2013 Jorge Mario Bergoglio was elected as Pope Francis, the first Latin American, and the first Jesuit, pope. He assumed the leadership of a church which had lost its dominant social and political influence over many European Catholic majority countries and which was losing ground to Pentecostalism in Latin America.

Evangelicalism

The term 'evangelical' became the preferred self-designation of post-war theological conservatives such as Carl Henry (1913–2003), in careful differentiation from fundamentalism, the neo-orthodoxy of Barth, and liberalism. The global figurehead for evangelicalism became Billy Graham (1918–), an international religious celebrity, and friend and *confident* of US presidents. His hugely successful evangelistic preaching campaigns around the world from the 1950s to the 1990s included a crowd estimated at 1.1 million in Seoul, South Korea, in June 1973. His pragmatic strategy of cooperation with a wide range of denominations, including non-evangelicals, to secure the largest possible audiences, produced criticism. So did the decision to preach in Soviet Russia in the 1980s, especially when Graham refused to publicly condemn communism.

Billy Graham

Evangelicals became increasingly interested in academic theology, seeking to challenge the prevailing liberal agenda. The evangelical presence in theological departments of universities was led in the UK by F. F. Bruce (1910–90). The fruit was seen in the 1950s onwards by the increased output of evangelical biblical commentaries and theological writings. The Bible remained for evangelicals the basis of preaching, personal devotion, morality and lifestyle. In the Global South many Christians saw a close correspondence between the world of the Bible and that in which they daily lived. In the West, debates over the Bible focused on matters of inspiration, authority and interpretation. The issue of biblical 'inerrancy' became a significant feature of the North American scene after the late 1970s.

Significant stresses were created within evangelicalism as theological conservatism began to decouple itself from political conservatism. At the 1974 Lausanne Congress on World Evangelization evangelical leaders from the Global South, such as René Padilla and Samuel Escobar, demanded a more conscious connection between the evangelical gospel, and social concern and political consciousness. Although this was something of a return to patterns of early nineteenth-century evangelical thinking, it shocked late twentieth-century evangelicals, especially in North America. Growing evangelical interest in social concern was reflected in the foundation of World Vision by Bob Pierce. The Evangelical Alliance Relief (TEAR) Fund was formed in the UK in 1968. After 1974 it was clear that issues of social justice and concern for the poor were no longer the exclusive purview of theological liberals.

The chief British architect of late twentieth-century evangelicalism was the Anglican John Stott (1921–2011), a fine expository preacher, biblical commentator and theologian. He influenced many global evangelical leaders through his extensive international ministry. Stott promoted a thoroughgoing evangelicalism alongside a loyal commitment to the theologically plural Anglican Church. Among conservative evangelicals in the Free Churches, Martyn Lloyd-Jones (1899–1981) was particularly influential, especially his Reformed model of detailed exposition of the biblical text. Lloyd-Jones also emphasized classic revival teaching and the experiential dimension of evangelicalism, including a measure of interest in the spiritual gifts. Growing interest in Reformed and Puritan literature prompted the foundation of the Banner of Truth Trust in 1957. One of the most influential figures on evangelicals was C. S. Lewis (1898–1963), although his views of the Bible were not always conservative. His Christian apologetic works, such as *Mere Christianity*, and the seven volumes of the *Chronicles of Narnia* were widely read.

John Stott

Between 1945 and 2000 evangelicalism became a truly global movement, strengthened through a series of networks which, though informal, brought the sort of international unity that the WCC was attempting to achieve organizationally. In 1947 the International Fellowship of Evangelical Students, a global family of student bodies, was formed. After 1947 Scripture Union added an international emphasis to its work: by 1982 it had staff working in twenty-five African nations alone. Flexible and more informal agencies such as Youth With a Mission, founded in 1960, and Operation Mobilization, founded in 1961, encouraged hundreds of young evangelicals into short-term mission, often bypassing older Western denominational missionary societies. By 2010 the global international missionary force stood at 400,000. The USA led the way in sending 127,000 missionaries, followed by 34,000 from Brazil.

Pentecostalism and the charismatic movement

Christianity at the end of its second millennium was far more global than ever before, and increasingly non-white and non-Western. The impact of evangelicalism was notable in the Hispanic, Francophone, Lusophone and Chinese-speaking world. In this process Pentecostal and neo-Pentecostal (charismatic) movements were important. Estimates in 2000 suggested that globally there were some 520 million Pentecostal and charismatic Christians. They combined the key tenets of evangelicalism with elements of black spirituality and a belief that the New Testament gifts of the Holy Spirit were repeatable in the contemporary church. Pentecostalism reached literate and preliterate cultures, appealing to the unchurched and those disillusioned with traditional Christian expressions. It had a personal impact on the poor and marginalized in the vast slums of the cities of the Majority World, and those on the ethnic margins, more than liberation theology ever had.

By 2000 over 10% of Africa's population were Pentecostals: Nigeria had some of the largest Pentecostal churches in the world. In Chile some 80% of Protestants were Pentecostals. Ten per cent of Filipinos were Pentecostals and charismatics, and China had possibly the largest number of charismatic Christians in Asia. While prayer for healing was an important part of Pentecostal expression, some went further to promote 'prosperity gospel' teaching that spiritual wholeness should also be accompanied by material blessing. Often delivered by flamboyant preachers, and promoted by satellite TV channels, the health-and-wealth prosperity teaching of US televangelists was severely damaged by a series of financial and sexual scandals in the 1980s and 1990s.

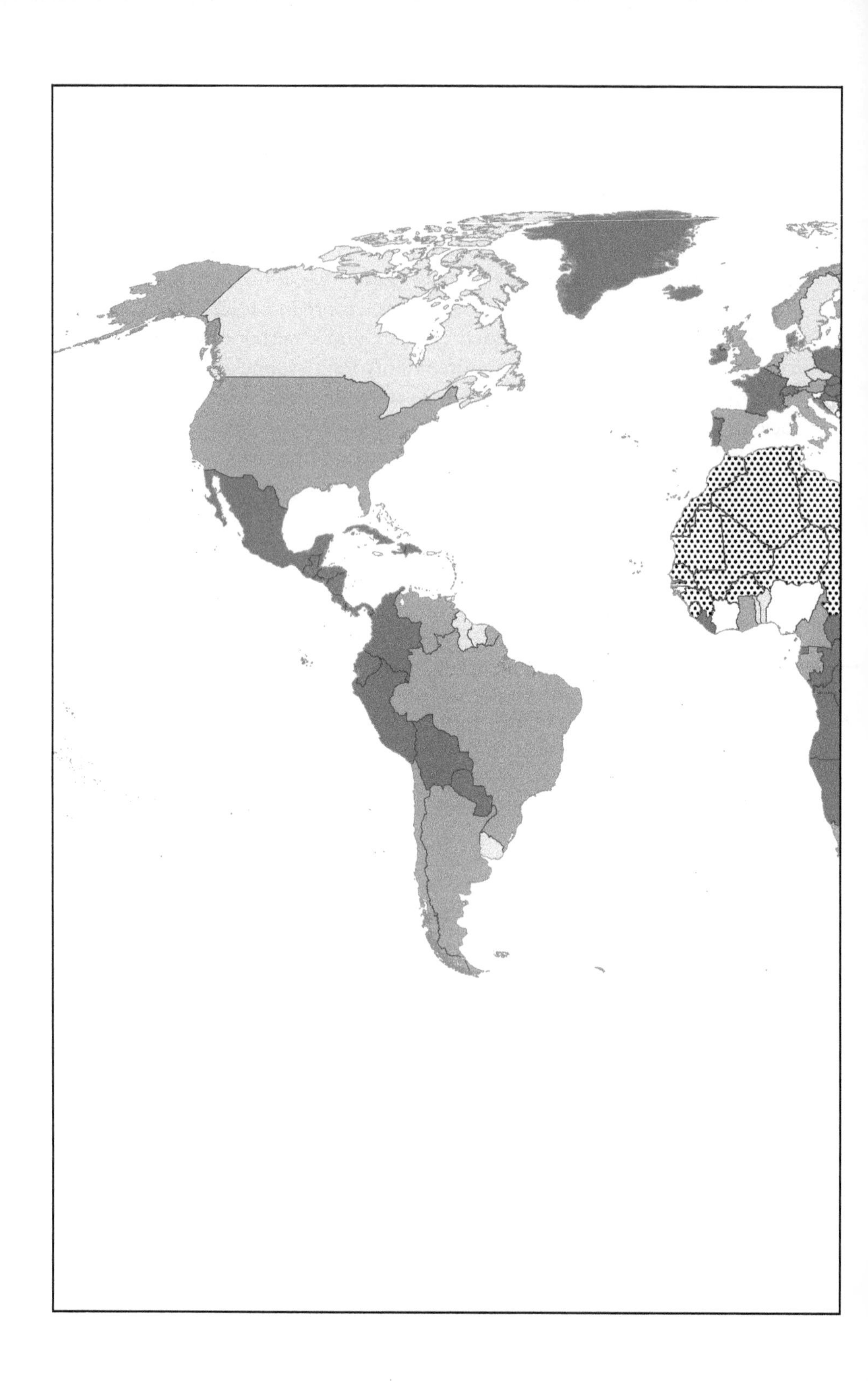

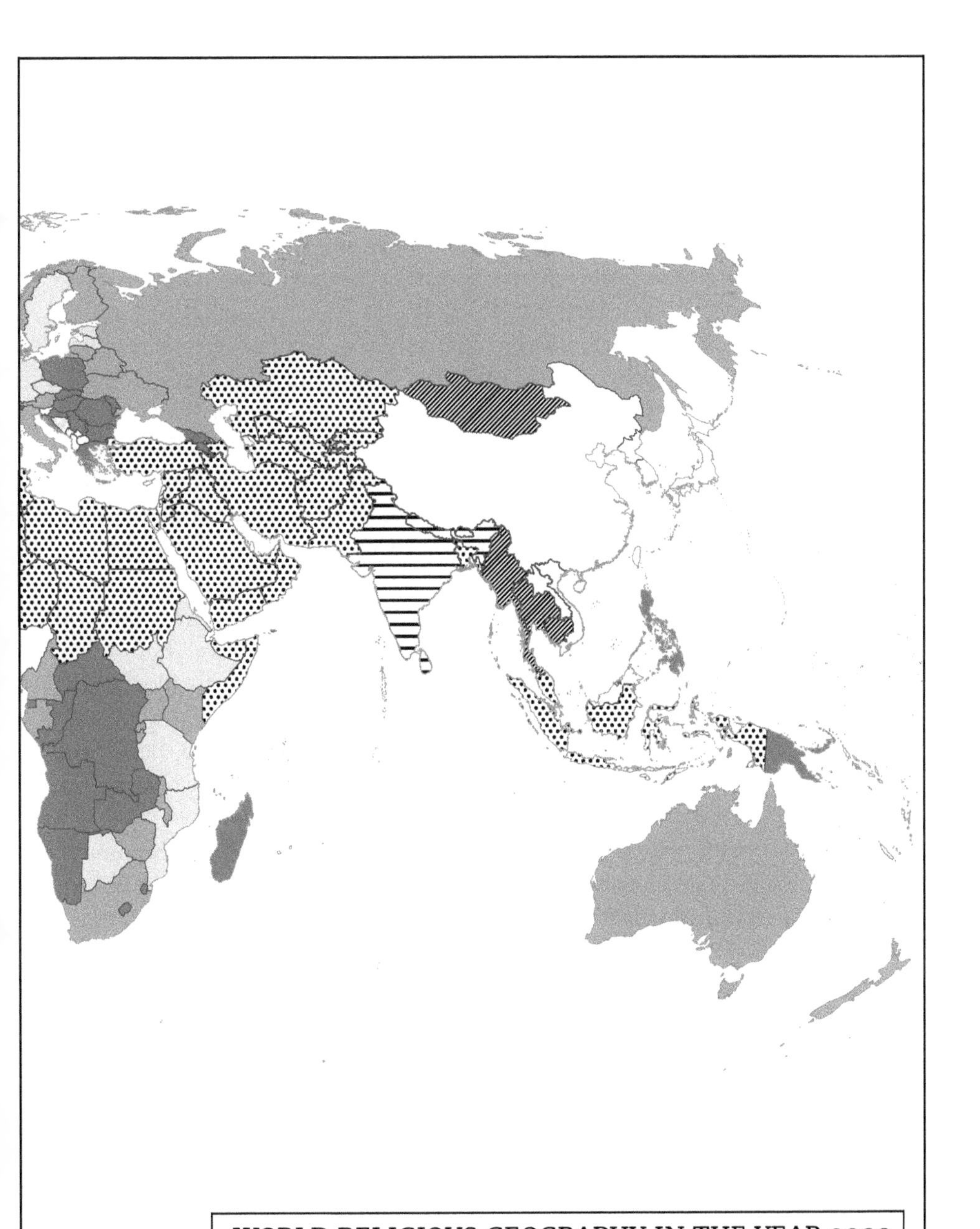

WORLD RELIGIOUS GEOGRAPHY IN THE YEAR 2000

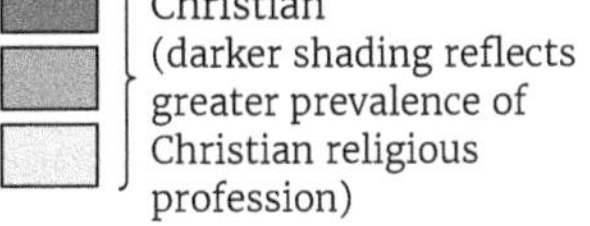

Christian (darker shading reflects greater prevalence of Christian religious profession)

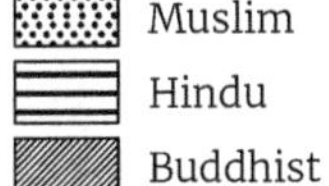

Muslim

Hindu

Buddhist

No clear majority religion, other religion or no religion

The charismatic (neo-Pentecostal) movement emerged during the radical 1960s in the USA and Europe. New approaches were coupled with a traditionalist desire to recreate first-century Christianity. Through the encouragement of Dennis Bennett (1917–91), an American Episcopalian minister, many were drawn into the charismatic movement. Unlike in classical Pentecostalism, charismatics predominantly remained within denominations, although some left to form independent churches. From the late 1960s a significant Catholic charismatic movement also emerged, which by the end of the century was thought to include around 11% of Catholics, numbering some 120 million.

The charismatic movement was characterized by a succession of new waves – the 'restoration' movement of the late 1970s, the 'shepherding' or 'discipleship' movement from 1970 to 1986, and the 'Third Wave' movement in the 1980s associated with John Wimber (1934–97) and his Vineyard churches. His 'power evangelism' was built on the theories of C. Peter Wagner (1930–) that the accompaniment of preaching with signs and wonders was key to rapid church growth. In 1994 the 'Toronto Blessing' at the Toronto Airport Vineyard Church featured unusual manifestations, including 'holy laughter'. The 'Pensacola Outpouring' or 'Brownsville Revival', which began among Pentecostals in Florida the following year, claimed 1.5 million visitors and 100,000 converts, reporting manifestations such as twitching and jerking. The Pentecostal and charismatic focus on evangelism was typified in contrasting ways by the preaching to vast crowds across Africa of the German evangelist Reinhard Bonnke (1940–), and the Alpha course for small groups, pioneered by Holy Trinity Church, Brompton, London; by 2015 it was claimed that over 27 million people had taken the course.

Charismatic distinctives – including 'every member ministry'; small groups for Bible study, discipleship and prayer; and modern worship songs and instrumentation – were adopted by many non-charismatics, contributing to evangelical internationalization. Yet Pentecostalism and the charismatic movement had a marked propensity to fragmentation, producing probably more variant groupings between 1900 and 2000 than had been seen in Christianity over the previous 2,000 years. Some conservative evangelicals feared that experience was being elevated above the Bible and doctrine.

Christianity and African independence

As most of sub-Saharan Africa gained political independence between the 1950s and 1960s, nationalist leaders freely deployed Christian concepts such as salvation and regeneration. Initial ideals of multiparty democracy were often quickly given up for ethnically based one-party states and autocratic regimes. Bodies capable of challenging them were restricted, including trade unions, foreign companies, and churches. In 1970s' Uganda, Idi Amin ruthlessly disposed of critics, including many clergy. Fifteen out of forty-four newly created sub-Saharan nations leaned towards Marxism. Menghistu Haile Mariam's communist military junta in Ethiopia (1974–87) seized the property of churches and repressed the Orthodox Church, although a large and vibrant underground church continued. In contrast, in 1991 President Chiluba declared Zambia a 'Christian state'.

Despite its association with the colonial past, Christianity was not rejected as the religion of the oppressors in the post-independence years. Instead the growth in Christian adherence was extraordinary. There were already some 75 million African Christians in 1965, but by 2000 they numbered around 350 million. Yet there was a growing recognition that missionary Christianity, with its associated 'cultural baggage', was no longer a 'good fit'. In the early 1970s some African Christian leaders called for a missionary moratorium, pushing missions to develop a new paradigm of serving local churches, often through healthcare, the provision of water, and theological training.

Although mainline denominations saw significant growth, it was the African Independent churches (AICs), and Pentecostal and charismatic churches, that proliferated after 1950, part of an 'African reformation' that took place away from the missionary-founded churches. In the year 2000, one in ten African Christians belonged to AICs. Some of the early independent 'Spiritual' churches became major religious traditions, with structures mirroring the mission churches they previously challenged. Around 6 million people attended Kimbanguist churches in the Congo in 2000; the denomination had been admitted to the WCC in 1969.

After the 1980s, African church leaders became increasingly willing to condemn the failings of African administrations. Yet the inability of Christian leaders to avert the horrific genocide in Catholic-dominated Rwanda, where in 1994 2 million Tutsi and moderate Hutu were slaughtered, raised profound questions about the depth of the Christian profession of many. One Seventh-Day Adventist church leader was eventually taken to the International Criminal Tribunal for his role in the genocide. Nonetheless, over a hundred other church leaders died trying to stop the violence, and others took a prominent role in subsequent peacemaking. Postcolonial Africa also saw repeated conflict between Muslims and Christians, especially in northern Nigeria and southern Sudan.

Asian Christianity

When Mohandas K. Gandhi (1869–1948) led his highly effective Indian nationalist campaign of non-violent civil disobedience, his doctrine of *swadeshi*, resistance to foreign imports, included Christianity, deeming it averse to Indian culture. This made efforts to 'Indianize' Christianity vital. After independence, India embraced a 'secular' model, encouraging the coexistence of many religions, although the rise of Hindu nationalism in the 1980s and 1990s placed severe pressures on the Christian community. Nonetheless, Christianity grew significantly, with the greatest response coming from the socially and economically marginalized Dalits ('untouchables'). By 2011, although India's Christian population was officially under 3%, it still numbered around 30 million people.

Gandhi

Between 1900 and 1990 the proportion of Christians in South-East Asia rose from 10% to around 20%, as Christianity established itself there as a non-Western religion. The only predominantly Christian country in the region remained the Philippines, with around 68 million Christians. Muslim-majority Indonesia included 28 million Christians, and about a third of east Malaysia's population professed Christianity. It made most progress among those from tribal and Chinese folk-religion backgrounds, with adherents of Islam and Buddhism less likely to convert. In Japan, by the year 2000, Christians were still under 2% of the population. Non-orthodox churches also advanced: by 1990 the non-trinitarian Iglesia ni Cristo churches in the Philippines had over 1.4 million members.

Communist advances in South-East Asia provoked wars in Korea and Vietnam, and major displacement of Christians, contributing to great regional variations. After the Korean War from 1950 to 1953 only a tiny underground church was left in the North, whereas in South Korea, between 1900 and 2000 Christianity grew from 0.5% to 40% of the population. Yoido Full Gospel Church, started by David (formerly Paul) Yonggi Cho (1936–), claimed to have 830,000 members in 2007.

Latin America and the Middle East

The Marxist–communist threat was also significant in Central America. When in 1959 Cuba fell to communist rule, most priests and nuns were expelled. Under authoritarian regimes, such as those in Brazil (1964–85) and Chile (1973–90), Catholic and Protestant churches were sometimes the only major social organizations not under government control, and played an important role in advocating human rights. Thousands of clergy and laity who opposed oppression were tortured, imprisoned or killed, including Archbishop Oscar Romero of San Salvador (1917–80).

In 1950 the Protestant presence in Latin America, at around 5% of total population, was dwarfed by that of Roman Catholicism. However, between 1990 and 2000 the number of Protestants in Brazil doubled from 13 to 26 million, led by the spectacular growth of Pentecostalism. There was also a significant growth in the percentage of Latin Americans considering themselves to have 'no religion': by 2000 this was 12% in Guatemala and 17% in Uruguay.

Arab-world Christians continued to face hostility and endure the status of second-class citizens. In the aftermath of the Iranian Islamic Revolution in 1979, they were increasingly treated as scapegoats for the sins and failures of the 'Christian' West. The historic Christian communities in Egypt, Syria, Iran and Iraq came under particular pressure, and many emigrated to the West.

In the years after 1945 a 'second age' of world Christianity dawned, creating an impact on parts of Africa and Asia touched in the first age, and flourishing in parts it had never reached before. Once decried as a Western, imperial import, Christianity showed itself a truly global religion, with leaders such as Kwame Bediako and René Padilla highlighting the growing theological maturity of the Global South, in which an evangelical voice was clearly discernible.

20. TOWARDS THE NEXT CHAPTER IN LIFE

What does the future of Christianity look like – will it be like the past?

At the heart of Sherwood Forest in England stands an ancient tree, the Major Oak. It is about a thousand years old and still spreads its branches skywards, but its core is hollow and it is slowly dying. By contrast the Great Banyan tree near Kolkata, India, is thought to be about 1,250 years old. Although its centre is also dying, it has survived by becoming a clonal colony of trees, throwing out multiple shoots to expand into the area around. The two trees reflect something of global Christianity. Although Christianity spread quickly into the non-Western world its early expressions struggled, but fresh growth there since the nineteenth century has left it vigorous and strong. In the West, after a slow start and then vigorous growth, in many parts decline has been a feature for much of the last century. If the Western church has reached the stage of old age, the non-Western church still demonstrates the characteristics of youth and full vigour.

Christianity has certainly played a huge role in the history of Western civilization. This is not to discount the importance of other civilizations, such as those of the Incas in Peru, or Great Zimbabwe, or the Mughals in India, or the great Chinese civilizations of the past. That this book has not given detailed attention to them is simply because Christianity did not play a prominent role in their history. Indeed, to tell the history of the past twenty centuries without giving significant attention to the influence of Christianity, as some do, would exclude a very major feature of social and cultural life, and this book has concentrated upon that. Reporting the religious dimension of history is an important part of the task of historians.

Perspectives are all-important in telling the history of a movement. Written from a European, or even a North American, perspective at the start of the twenty-first century, as most accounts of the history of Christianity are, the next chapter in the biography would not appear to look promising. In North America, debate about the role of religion in public life continued, but became less prominent than in much of the second half of the twentieth century. In Europe, a region with thinking moulded by Christianity, and laws inspired by the Christian ethical code, it was significant that the European Union's draft constitution in 2005 made no reference to Christianity as part of European identity: Europe was officially post-Christian. Yet Christianity certainly did advance in the twentieth century, if not in its previous heartlands. By that century's last quarter, the axis of global Christianity had moved to the southern hemisphere, with over 1 billion Christians in the non-Western World, compared to 750 million in the West. The next stages of Christianity's biography would be significantly determined in Africa, Latin America, parts of Asia and the Pacific.

Christianity changed more rapidly in the twentieth century than in any century since the first. In 1900 there were just under 9 million Christians in Africa, but by 2000 this was 335 million. In Asia numbers had increased from 20 million to just over 300 million; in Latin America from 60 million to 475 million. Christians had also grown in Oceania from 4 million to 21 million, and in North America from 60 to 212 million, although migration played a significant role in that. In Europe those with some form of connection with a church had increased from 368 million to 536 million, but often with limited levels of adherence: the phrase 'believing without belonging' became particularly apposite. Indeed the decline in religious attendance and formal Christian expression in Western Europe in the twentieth century was faster than that experienced in the face of the rapid spread of Islam in the Middle East and North Africa after the seventh century. By the end of the twentieth century a paradigm shift in Christian geography was completed – making it a predominantly non-Western religion.

Roman Catholicism continued to grow through the twentieth century, its adherents increasing from 266 million to 1 billion. Protestantism (including Anglicans) also grew, from 134 to 423 million, and the Orthodox from 116 to 215 million. Indigenous expressions of Christianity also multiplied, from around 7 million adherents to 380 million, most being non-white. By 2011 the global Christian population included just over 584 million Pentecostals and charismatic Christians, and a further 285 million evangelicals – when combined totalling just under 40% of all Christians and over 12% of world population. Pentecostalism had become the fastest-growing Christian tradition.

Despite the numerical growth of Christianity throughout the twentieth century, from around 558 million to over 2 billion, this took place when world population was also growing, and the percentage of Christians actually fell slightly, from just over 35% to 32%. Estimates suggested that in 2000 still 25% of the world remained 'unevangelized', although this was significantly down from 50% in 1900. Other religions were also seeing significant growth: the number of Muslims increased from 200 million in 1900 to almost 1.2 billion in 2000, Hindus from 203 million to 811 million, and Buddhists from 127 to 360 million. There was also a remarkable increase in professed atheists, from around 225,000 at the start of the century to 150 million in 2000.

As the statistical centre of gravity of global Christianity has progressively shifted south – from north Italy in 1800, to Spain in 1900, to Morocco in 1970, to Timbuktu in 2010 – other changes have followed. By the end of the twentieth century Spanish was the first language spoken by more Christians than any other – with Chinese, Hindi and Swahili growing in importance alongside English and French. In 2000 more people actively attended Anglican churches in Nigeria than in England, and there were more Presbyterians in South Korea than in Scotland.

In the Majority World the theological core remained the Bible; indeed it spoke with relevance and clarity to readers in Africa, Asia and Latin America about issues such as ritual and sacrifice, spiritual forces of good and evil, poverty and injustice, hope and peace. Social concern and social justice were prominent topics in contexts where poverty, polluted water, corruption and AIDS were prevalent. In the West, with populations surrounded by good healthcare, secure pensions and unemployment benefits, such issues had less immediacy.

The 18,682 foreign missionaries of 1900 had grown to 420,000 by 2000, their source of recruitment beginning to mirror the shifting axis of global Christianity to the south. Foreign missionaries from Asia, Africa and Latin America totalled 126,000, compared to 135,000 from North America and just under 133,000 from Europe. South Korea, India, the Philippines, Nigeria and Brazil became strong missionary-sending countries. In the Global South much missionary work in terms of gospel proclamation by those from the West became less significant; local agency was far more numerous and effective, with a focus instead on consolidation and strengthening.

Important questions arose as to whether the remarkable economic growth in China and the Pacific Rim, where Christianity has tended to appeal to educated, upwardly mobile professionals, would eventually be accompanied by the decline in Christian observance and personal faith found in the West. At the same time, the appeal of Christianity to the poor of the slums of African and Latin American cities has been immense. Such patterns defy simple categorization.

Global population movements contributed to the reshaping of the geography of world Christianity. By the year 2000, 35 million Americans were of Hispanic origin, of whom some 20% were evangelical Protestants. A further 12 million Americans were of Asian descent, with Christians outnumbering Buddhists by ten to one in the American Korean community. The historic Christian communities of the Middle East remained increasingly under pressure, and displaced, in the aftermath of wars in Iraq and Syria.

Evangelicalism also changed. In 2010 the typical evangelical was not white, male and middle class, but poor, female, non-white and living in a Global South megacity. As with Christianity as a whole, evangelicalism was likely to find its future shaped by Africa, Latin America, parts of Asia and the Pacific. Key answers to issues of approaches to gospel proclamation, and dialogue with other world religions, were beginning to come from evangelicals living in pluralist contexts like India or China. Despite the Western challenges of postmodernism and postcolonialism, in 2010 it looked like the future of Christianity was in the hands of people who believed in the Bible, and in a God who intervenes in the world and answers prayer. After 1960 Africa witnessed probably the greatest movement of conversion to Christianity from people of a primal religious background in the history of Christianity, although by the early twenty-first century a number were reverting to their original beliefs and practices.

By 2000 liberal Protestantism was in major decline. Yet evangelicalism also reflected a lack of clear theological and cultural cohesion. Evangelicals remained a very broad grouping. 'Open' evangelicals sought to accommodate evangelicalism to postmodernism, rejecting precise and propositional statements of truth and absolute moral certainties, replacing them with symbols, and judgments adapted to changed cultural contexts. The results might in the nineteenth century have been considered liberal, although the term 'post-evangelical' has been used. Reformed evangelicals have emphasized biblical authority and continuity with past evangelical tradition. Pentecostalism continued to work within accepted definitions of evangelicalism, but if its focus on the Word and Spirit was replaced by a Spirit-only focus, that would fall open to question. A number of charismatic pioneers moved in the direction of the Orthodox Church, and others into Anglo-Catholicism, seeking the certainties of tradition. Within significant parts of the Majority World, 'prosperity teaching' proved increasingly popular, moving the gospel from a Bible-based, soteriological message with an active social concern, to a theology of divine blessing, with a promise of health and wealth to its adherents. Evangelicalism was faced with the need to produce clear responses to the challenges of poverty, hunger, injustice, corruption and diseases, to make its 'now but not yet' eschatology attractive in the face of those who proclaimed the immediate blessings of the kingdom.

The late twentieth century also saw foundations laid for a major theological revolution in the twenty-first century. This migration of Christianity to the southern hemisphere began to move the focus in theological discourse away from the dominance of Western questions and approaches raised by the Enlightenment. The numerical strength of the churches in the Global South was beginning to be matched by growth in Christian training. Evangelical leaders from the Global South were finding their voices and taking on the responsibility of articulating a faith and witness that was faithful to the Bible but also at home in a variety of cultures. As Christianity engaged with African, Asian and Latin American contexts, theological reflection increased, with a particular interest in multidimensional and interdisciplinary approaches. Genuine indigenous theology began to emerge, with signs of growing interest in the West in the vibrant theological thought of the Majority World.

By early in the twenty-first century, Christianity had returned to what it originally was – a global faith. It had been present in parts of Asia for 1,500 years before the Western missionaries 'reached' there. Parts of Africa have a longer and richer continuous Christian history than much of Europe. Yet persecution and repression continued to be part of the Christian experience. It has been claimed that more Christians suffered martyrdom in the twentieth century than in any other century. By 2010 Christianity was again a faith of people from many cultural and linguistic backgrounds, with no common centre or single theological language. Christianity has always needed to be translated but has always proved translatable. If Revelation 7:9 and 20:12 present the culmination of the biography of Christianity, with the image of people from every tribe and tongue gathered round the throne of God, then by the start of the twenty-first century the reality of global Christianity more closely resembled that picture than ever before.

COPYRIGHT ACKNOWLEDGMENTS

The publisher and author acknowledge with thanks permission to reproduce the following. Every effort has been made to seek permission to use copyright material reproduced in this book. The publisher apologizes for those cases where permission might not have been sought and, if notified, will formally seek permission at the earliest opportunity.

Figures

Tertullian: Image © Classic Image / Alamy Stock Photo
Samuel Crowther: Image © Chronicle / Alamy Stock Photo
Mary Slessor: Image © CH Collection / Alamy Stock Photo
Xi Shengmo: Used with permission of OMF International
Karl Barth: Image © Everett Collection Historical / Alamy Stock Photo
John Stott: Used with permission of Corey Widmer, Langham Partnership
All other images © Shutterstock.com.

Maps

Maps produced by <www.themappingcompany.co.uk>.

FURTHER READING

The following books are suggestions for reading that build on the introduction to the history of Christianity provided by *Christianity: The Biography*. The focus in the list below is on global and regional studies, some comprehensively covering the whole 2,000 years, and others more specifically focused. These resources should then lead the reader to further studies of individual countries, strategic events and key individuals, which are too numerous to mention here.

History of Christianity overviews

Global

Irvin, D., and S. Sunquist, *History of the World Christian Movement*, vols. 1 and 2 (Maryknoll: Orbis, 2001, 2012).
MacCulloch, D., *A History of Christianity* (London: Allen Lane, 2009).
Neill, S., *History of Christian Missions* (Harmondsworth: Penguin, 1986).

Regional

González, O. E., and J. L. González, *Christianity in Latin America: A History* (Cambridge: Cambridge University Press, 2008).
Moffett, S., *A History of Christianity in Asia*, vols. 1 and 2 (Maryknoll: Orbis, 1998, 2005).

Sundkler, B., and C. Steed, *A History of the Church in Africa* (Cambridge: Cambridge University Press, 2000).

Early church period

Casiday, A., and F. W. Norris (eds.), *The Cambridge History of Christianity, vol. 2: Constantine to c. 600* (Cambridge: Cambridge University Press, 2007).
Davidson, I. J., *The Birth of the Church* (Oxford: Monarch, 2005).
Esler, P. F. (ed.), *The Early Christian World*, 2 vols. (Oxford: Routledge, 2000).
Frend, W. H. C., *The Rise of Christianity* (London: Darton, Longman and Todd, 1984).
Mitchell, M. M., and F. M. Young (eds.), *The Cambridge History of Christianity, vol. 1: Origins to Constantine* (Cambridge: Cambridge University Press, 2006).
Needham, N., *2000 Years of Christ's Power, Part 1: The Age of the Early Church Fathers* (Darlington: Grace, 1998).
Neill, S., *A History of Christianity in India: The Beginnings to AD 1707* (Cambridge: Cambridge University Press, 1984).
Reeves, M., *The Breeze of the Centuries: Great Theologians from the Apostolic Fathers to Aquinas* (Leicester: IVP, 2010).

Medieval period and Reformation

Angold, M. (ed.), *The Cambridge History of Christianity, vol. 5: Eastern Christianity* (Cambridge: Cambridge University Press, 2006).
Bagchi, D., and D. C. Steinmetz (eds.), *The Cambridge Companion to Reformation Theology* (Cambridge: Cambridge University Press, 2004).
Cameron, E., *The European Reformation* (Oxford: Clarendon, 1991).
Hsia, R. P. (ed.), *The Cambridge History of Christianity, vol. 6: Reform and Expansion, 1500–1660* (Cambridge: Cambridge University Press, 2007).
Koschorke, K., L. Frieder and M. Delgado, *History of Christianity in Asia, Africa and Latin America, 1450–1990* (Grand Rapids: Eerdmans, 2007).
Needham, N., *2000 Years of Christ's Power, Part 2: The Middle Ages* (Darlington: Grace, 2000).
Needham, N., *2000 Years of Christ's Power, Part 3: Renaissance and Reformation* (Darlington: Grace, 2003).
Noble, T. F. X., and J. M. H. Smith (eds.), *The Cambridge History of Christianity, vol. 3: Early Medieval Christianities, c. 600–c. 1100* (Cambridge: Cambridge University Press, 2008).

Reeves, M., *The Unquenchable Flame: Discovering the Heart of the Reformation* (Leicester: IVP, 2010).
Rubin, M., and W. Simons (eds.), *The Cambridge History of Christianity, vol. 4: Christianity in Western Europe, c. 1100–c. 1500* (Cambridge: Cambridge University Press, 2009).

Modern period

Bays, D. (ed.), *Christianity in China from the Eighteenth Century to the Present* (Oxford: Wiley-Blackwell, 2011).
Brown, S. J., and T. Tackett (eds.), *The Cambridge History of Christianity, vol. 7: Enlightenment, Reawakening and Revolution, 1668–1815* (Cambridge: Cambridge University Press, 2006).
Gilley, S., and B. Stanley (eds.), *The Cambridge History of Christianity, vol. 8: World Christianities, c. 1815–c. 1914* (Cambridge: Cambridge University Press, 2006).
McLeod, H. (ed.), *The Cambridge History of Christianity, vol. 9: World Christianities, c. 1914–c. 2000* (Cambridge: Cambridge University Press, 2006).
Jenkins, P., *The Next Christendom: The Coming of Global Christianity* (Oxford: Oxford University Press, 2002).
Neill, S., *A History of Christianity in India: 1707–1858* (Cambridge: Cambridge University Press, 1985).
Reeves, M., *On Giants' Shoulders: Great Theologians from Luther to Barth* (Leicester: IVP, 2011).
Shaw, I. J., *Churches, Revolutions and Empires, 1789–1914* (Fearn: Christian Focus, 2012).
Sunquist, S. W., *The Unexpected Christian Century: The Reversal and Transformation of Global Christianity, 1900–2000* (Grand Rapids: Baker Academic, 2015).

General study skills for church history

Bradley, J. E., and R. A. Muller, *Church History: An Introduction to Research, Reference Works, and Methods* (Grand Rapids: Eerdmans, 1995).

INDEX

Lightning Source UK Ltd.
Milton Keynes UK
UKHW021239160822
407378UK00007B/1235